LEADING INITIATIVES

For Peter, may he learn from the experience
of 'the gallant gentlemen'

LEADING INITIATIVES

Leadership, Teamwork and the Bottom Line

*Leadership is of the spirit, compounded of
personality; its study a science and its practice
an art*

Jeremy Tozer

BUTTERWORTH
HEINEMANN
AUSTRALIA

Australia
  Butterworth-Heinemann, 18 Salmon Street, Port Melbourne, Vic. 3207

Singapore
  Butterworth-Heinemann Asia

United Kingdom
  Butterworth-Heinemann Ltd, Oxford

USA
  Butterworth-Heinemann, Newton

National Library of Australia Cataloguing-in-Publication entry

Tozer, Jeremy, 1961– .
  Leading initiatives: leadership, teamwork and the bottom line.

  Includes index.
  ISBN 0 7506 8948 X.

  1. Leadership. 2. Teams in the workplace. I. Title.

658.4092

Enquiries should be addressed to the publisher.
Typeset by DOCUPRO, Sydney
Printed by Kin Keong Printing Co. Pte. Ltd.

CONTENTS

Preface   ix

About the Author   xi

Acknowledgements   xii

Glossary   xv

Introduction   1

CHAPTER 1 INTRODUCTION TO LEADERSHIP   8

The relationship between leadership and management—
leadership defined—a template for leadership
development—fundamental themes of leadership—the role of
leadership in business success and organisational development

CHAPTER 2 PERSONALITY, SELF-CONCEPT
AND SELF-PERCEPTION   26

The factors influencing personality development—leaders'
personalities and why leaders must know themselves—genetic
inheritance—environmental influences—learned
experiences—personal characteristics

CHAPTER 3 PERCEPTION   36

The influences of perception—why 'followers' perceive
differently from 'leaders'—perception and the needs of
leadership—the unique nature of perception—how perception
works—what leaders can control—simplification of perceptual
clues—the effects of perception

v

CHAPTER 4 TEAMS AND GROUPS: THEIR CHARACTERISTICS AND DYNAMICS — 44

Group dynamics—the strengths, characteristics and weaknesses of teams—discipline and the team—competition versus cooperation—the stages of team development—leaderless teams

CHAPTER 5 THE FUNCTIONAL APPROACH TO LEADERSHIP — 58

John Adair's three circles model of functional leadership—key functions of a leader—'The Functional Leadership Check-list'—balancing conflicting needs

CHAPTER 6—PERSONAL QUALITIES OF LEADERSHIP: INSPIRATION, CHARISMA AND TRUST — 66

The importance of personal qualities of leadership—the key personal qualities defined—the elements of inspiration—the nature of charisma—why charismatic leaders fail

CHAPTER 7 MISSION ANALYSIS AND THE APPRECIATION: PROBLEM SOLVING AND DECISION MAKING — 94

Perception and types of problems—perceptual clues and types of thinking—clarity of thought and purpose—a universal logical problem-solving and decision-making process—developing strategic thinking and vision for later life—concept of operations—removing vested interests

CHAPTER 8 PLANNING AND BRIEFING — 112

Adding detail to the outline plan—briefing a team on a plan—preventing ambiguity and building commitment

CHAPTER 9 THE ROLE OF ORGANISATION IN LEADERSHIP — 123

Principles of team deployment and resource management—unity of leadership—span of control—grouping of similar assignments—delegation of tasks—defined duties and accountabilities—standardisation—'requisite' structure—type of structure

CHAPTER 10 BUILDING AND MAINTAINING THE TEAM — 146

Building a high performing team—the stages of team development—the maintenance of team spirit—characteristics of norms—the factors affecting team performance—advice on leader–follower relations—coaching—mentoring—performance appraisal

CHAPTER 11 DIRECTION, COORDINATION, CONTROL AND EVALUATION 170

Clear objectives and procedures—controlling and measuring the progress of a task—evaluating success—objective setting—ways and means of gathering information—the concept of 'positive' control—means of control and influence—the importance of timing

CHAPTER 12 MOTIVATING THE INDIVIDUAL 177

What motivation can achieve—Maslow's hierarchy of needs—Herzberg's two-factor theory—practical application of theory —the importance of delegation

CHAPTER 13 MORALE 188

The nature of morale—the importance of morale in team effectiveness—the essentials of morale (spiritual/intellectual/material)—factors that affect morale—signs that morale is deteriorating

CHAPTER 14 STYLES OF LEADERSHIP, LEVELS OF LEADERSHIP 204

The manner in which leadership is exercised—environmental influences—the concept of organisational, ambient and episodic leadership—the X–Y theory—situational leadership—relationships with subordinates—signs of strong or poor relationships

CHAPTER 15 LEADERSHIP ACROSS CULTURES 222

The meaning of culture—cultural 'perceptual filters'—the need for sensitivity—appreciation of different cultural values—cross-cultural misinterpretation—productivity loss and gain—differences in cross-cultural motivation, decision making and planning—conditions for team effectiveness

CHAPTER 16 DISCIPLINE 233

Discipline as a constructive force—leadership and discipline—self-discipline and sense of duty

CHAPTER 17 LOYALTY 241

How leadership develops loyalty within the organisation—loyalty in shareholders and customers—the commercial implications of 'the loyalty effect'

CHAPTER 18 ORGANISATIONAL LEADERSHIP: VISION, MISSION AND THE LINK TO VALUES   248

The CEO's vision linked to the mission and values of an organisation—the role of vision, mission and values in transferring the ownership of tasks to employees—links to strategy—values and decision making—effective vision, mission and values statements

CHAPTER 19 LEADING CHANGE AND INNOVATION   259

Values and the behaviour they guide during change—people's reaction to change—the stages of, and the barriers to, change—principles of implementing change—the role of leadership in change—leadership and innovation

CHAPTER 20 STRATEGIC DIRECTION AND PLANNING   274

Strategic planning—the link between strategic business planning and leadership—the driving principles of business—strategic success model—customer value model—business logic—strategy and tactics—implementing strategy

CHAPTER 21 TRAINING FOR AND DEVELOPING LEADERSHIP   301

Aims and objectives of training—principles of training—approaches to leadership training—the composite approach—transfer of training

CHAPTER 22 CONCLUSION   333

PREFACE

In mid-1995, I had a meeting to discuss leadership with the then Human Resources Director of United Distillers Australia, Chris Matchan (who has subsequently taken on a regional human resources Director role in London). We knew each other well and his opening question for me was 'You've been in an army that is constantly doing things for real in very different environments; what makes the British Army so successful and how can I reproduce that culture of leadership and teamwork here?' My initial answer was relatively short, but soon expanded into a two-hour discussion.

These were the initial thoughts that I shared with Chris: in no field of human endeavour are the consequences of failure so awful. A businessman may lose money, an officer loses his soldiers' lives. The British Army has learnt the hard way the necessity for developing leadership at every level; it has arguably the most thorough assessment centre in the world to select potential officers and it does not compromise on their leadership training or that of the non-commissioned officers. While efficient and flexible 'standard operating procedures' are universal, decision making is pushed to the lowest possible level: that builds trust and organisational agility. It has (unwritten) values that are inviolate and universally shared that do offer security and stability in a turbulent environment and underpin the way people behave and make decisions. It has evolved a structure, systems and procedures that allow leadership to grow and flourish and are flexible enough to rapidly assemble new groupings of 'strangers' and operate with little unnecessary angst from the Falklands to the Gulf. It truly understands the value of morale and what it can achieve and is careful not to allow it to deteriorate. Its culture of leadership and teamwork is so deeply embedded it has become self-perpetuating.

This book introduces you to a concept of leadership and the knowledge, skills, 'tools', processes, and principles that allow you to develop your own self-perpetuating culture of leadership, teamwork, continuous learning and improvement.

Jeremy Tozer
August 1997

ABOUT THE AUTHOR:
A PROFILE OF JEREMY TOZER

Jeremy was born in England, educated in the UK at Welbeck College, The Royal Military Academy Sandhurst, the University of Warwick (where he gained a BSc (Hons) in electronic engineering) and Junior Division, The Staff College. He was commissioned into the Intelligence Corps and subsequently re-badged to The Duke of Edinburgh's Royal Regiment (Berkshire and Wiltshire).

During ten years in the Army, Jeremy served three one-year tours on operations in Northern Ireland where he developed his own personal leadership ability and came to understand 'people'. He has lived and soldiered in Cyprus, Turkey, Norway, Denmark and Italy, Berline, Brunei, and Hong Kong. He is a qualified instructor in Jungle and Arctic warfare, and in many adventurous pursuits. In his military career he has commanded infantry company groupings of up to 140 soldiers, and served in intelligence duties at local to global levels leading small teams of highly motivated specialists. He has worked effectively with the people of many different nationalities and cultures—both Asian and European.

On arrival in Australia in 1991 he joined the sales division of a major US-based fast moving consumer goods company, and subsequently worked as an Executive Search Consultant. Having seen the 'leadership gap' in the vast majority of candidates at all levels of management across many industry groupings, Jeremy founded his company 'Leading initiatives' in Sydney to address this need. Leading Initiatives' purpose is not only leadership and management development; but the Leading Initiatives team ensures that recruitment, selection and performance management systems, and organisational structure allow leadership and teamwork to flourish.

Jeremy has three reasons for writing this book; firstly to satisfy a desire to write, second because the subject is a passion, and third, and most importantly, because he wants to provide some principles and processes for practical application to replace the failed fads of management gurus and the muddled thinkers that have influenced some views of leaderless or self-directed teams.

His personal interests include off-shore racing (he has competed in the Sydney-Hobart race), shooting, rock-climbing and mountaineering, fencing, bush walking, malt whisky, New Orleans Jazz,. and he sings with the Sydney Amateur Sailing Club Shantymen.

ACKNOWLEDGEMENTS

There are so many people and institutions to which I am indebted that it seems fairest to work chronologically through the list.

Firstly, I must express my gratitude to my parents for giving me every opportunity to make a sound start in life and every support in all my endeavours. To my schools, notably Welbeck College, particularly for their classical education and development of self-discipline and character.

To The Royal Military Academy Sandhurst and the members of its Directing Staff for its training for leadership and for life in general that has no equal, the benefits of which I am still realising. In particular I would mention certain characters who made such an impression on me during my training in Burma Company and subsequently Salamanca Company: Colour Sergeant L. Scholes Grenadier Guards, Company Sergeant-Major D. Laden Scots Guards, Academy Sergeant-Major P. Huggins late Grenadier Guards, Captain R. S. Grant MBE Royal Marines, and my Platoon Commander Captain Alan Coates The Duke of Edinburgh's Royal Regiment (Berkshire and Wiltshire) who taught me that British officers lead from the front and under whom I later served.

To the example of my first Commanding Officer, Lieutenant Colonel M. R. I. Constantine, who inspired me with his trust and confidence when I assumed command of my first platoon—8 Platoon, C Company, 2nd Battalion The Queen's Regiment, in Londonderry.

My thanks to the Officers, Warrant Officers and Sergeants of the Intelligence Corps and The Duke of Edinburgh's Royal Regiment (Berkshire and Wiltshire) with whom I subsequently served. In particular to Major Jim Tanner on loan from the Staffordshire Regiment, and Company Sergeant-Major P. McLeod and Colour Sergeant 'Trog' Truman who made my time as a company second-in-command and Acting Company Commander in B Company, 1st Battalion, The Duke of Edinburgh's Royal Regiment (Berkshire and Wiltshire) so relatively easy.

For my excellent commercial education I thank the various management consultants that I have worked with that have shown me how to succeed and how to fail. To Dr Elliott Jaques and Rebecca Cason for their contributions to this work.

To my business partner, Chris Le Coïc, for making both the book and my consulting/training company Leading Initiatives possible. To Charlie O'Connor, a former brother officer, for joining Leading Initiatives and contributing so much in our formative stages.

Every effort has been made to trace holders of copyright of material alluded to, or cited, in this work. To the various publishers and authors who have responded, I am most grateful. Their eloquence and insight have saved me much hard work.

Warren Bennis, *On Becoming A Leader*, Century Hutchinson Australia, 1989; and revised edition, p. 45, © 1989 by Warren Bennis, Inc. Reprinted by permission of Addison-Wesley Longman Inc. Colin Carnall, *Managing Change in Organizations*, Hemel Hempstead: Prentice Hall International (UK) Limited, 1995; Peter de la Billière, *Looking For Trouble*, London: HarperCollins, 1994 and reproduced with permission of Curtis Brown Ltd, London, on behalf of DLB Partnership Copyright © General Sir Peter de la Billière, 1994; Basil Fletcher, *The Challenge of Outward Bound*, London: William Heinemann Ltd, 1971, the Outward Bound Trust, United Kingdom; General Sir John Hackett, *The Profession Of Arms*, London: Sidgwick & Jackson, 1983; John Harvey-Jones, *Making It Happen*, London: HarperCollins, 1988; *Managing To Survive*, 1993, and *All Together Now*, London: William Heinemann Ltd, 1994, reprinted by permission of Peters, Frazer Dunlop Group Ltd, London; F. Herzberg, *The Motivation to Work*, New York: John Wiley & Sons, 1959; Elliott Jaques, *Requisite Organization: A Total System for Effective Managerial Leadership for the 21st Century*, Arlington, Virginia: Cason Hall & Co. Publishers, and to Rebecca Cason; *Motivation and Personality*, A. Maslow © 1954. Reprinted by permission of Addison-Wesley Educational Publishers Inc.; Garry Morton, *The Australian Motivation Handbook*, Sydney: McGraw-Hill Book Company Australia Pty Limited, 1990; *The Memoirs of Field-Marshal Montgomery of Alamein, K.G.*, London: Collins, 1958; Field-Marshal Sir William Slim, *Defeat Into*

Victory, 1956, and *Courage and Other Broadcasts*, 1957, both London: Cassell; James Strong, *The Australian Way* (Qantas Airways Magazine), October 1994, January 1995, July 1995; V. H. Vroom, 'Some personality determinants of the effects of participation', *Journal of Abnormal and Social Psychology*, 1959, pp. 322-327, published under the same title, Englewood Cliffs, New Jersey: Prentice Hall Inc; and to 3M for checking the content of the section on Innovation in Chapter 19.

In particular I wish to thank The Commandant, The Royal Military Academy Sandhurst, for the Academy's assistance and permission to reproduce certain material. There are elements of the Academy's teaching in all chapters, but notably Chapters 2, 3, 4, 5, 7, 9, 11, 14, and 16 are based upon the Academy's lessons. I should add that in no way does this book purport to represent past or current training or policy at The Royal Military Academy Sandhurst or in the British Army generally; it is derived from my personal experience of it.

I must also express my thanks to those people who contributed to this book by way of quotable discussion: Sir Robin Knox-Johnston, noted sailor and leader of the Clipper 96 ocean challenge race; Ian Kiernan, Sydney builder, businessman, sailor and founder of the 'Clean Up Australia' and 'Clean Up The World' campaigns; Robert McLean, formerly Managing Director, McKinsey & Co Australia; Malcolm Jones, CEO, NRMA Limited; John Quinn, Managing Director, Thorn Lighting Pty Ltd, Robyn Fitzroy, Division Director, Macquarie Investment Management Ltd, Macquarie Bank Group; Kathy Rozmeta, Learning & Development Manager, Coca-Cola Amatil Limited; Karen Lonergan, Education & Development Manager, Castrol Australia Limited, Chris Walsh, Operations Director, David Jones Limited, and those who wished to be quoted anonymously.

Thanks are also due to Jenny Winterton, Jo Dixon, Lynette Etheridge, Roni Miles, and Jacqui Wingle who have all helped to overcome my PC illiteracy and to implant my thoughts onto the PC's memory and to the publisher and to Robin Appleton, my editor, for her invaluable assistance.

While I have tried to acknowledge the original source of every idea or view in this book that has not always been possible. I would like to give credit where credit is due and should any reader know of an original and unacknowledged source I would be most grateful for the information.

To my partner in life, Kristina Czaban, without whose unfailing support neither the book nor the company would have evolved. To Kristina I am deeply grateful.

GLOSSARY OF KEY TERMS

accountability Those features of any role that the incumbent is required to do by virtue of the role. Accountability may be delegated downwards, but responsibility to the organisation for the outcome remains with the delegating leader and such responsibility cannot be delegated.

aim The aim is a positive, clear, concise and unequivocal statement of overall intent and its purpose, best expressed as 'to do (something) in order to (achieve something)'.

appointment A position or role held by an individual and distinguished by a specific title.

appreciation The logical process of reasoning by which a person considers all the relevant factors affecting a situation or problem and arrives at a decision upon the course of action to be taken to accomplish a task or mission.

authority The features of a role that enable the incumbent to legitimately carry out the work necessary to meet the accountabilities of the role.

benchmark A process of comparison between one product, system process, or result and another within the same company, or among companies in the same or different industries.

briefing The formal communication of information or a plan to those affected by it, normally carried out face to face, collectively, and following a standard sequence or format to ease the assimilation of information by those receiving the briefing.

business procedure The standard operating procedure that has the aim of launching employees into action as swiftly and as efficiently as possible, understanding what they have to do and why, and with what support.

campaign A campaign is a sequence of planned, resourced and executed operations designed to achieve a strategic objective within a defined time scale and geographical area, usually involving the synchronisation of different business units or divisions.

category of potential capability The combination of cognitive process applied to information complexity that defines the category of task complexity a person may work at.

category of task complexity A level of work defined by the combination of task and information complexity.

centre of gravity The centre of gravity is that characteristic, or capability from which a competitor derives its freedom of action, or corporate power such as distribution network or technology supremacy. A centre of gravity may not always be clear and may be an abstraction such as morale.

cognitive power The potential strength of a person's cognitive processes and, therefore, the maximum level of task complexity that can be managed by that person.

cognitive processes The mental processes by which a person is able to organise information to do work.

command The lawful authority vested in personnel in armed services (army, navy or airforce) by which leadership may be exercised by a commander over those subordinates in the unit or sub-unit. Command is the leadership of people and the management of resources and time to achieve a mission.

(ability to) communicate The ability to speak and to write effectively employing the principles of clarity, brevity and accuracy both up and down the hierarchy of an organisation.

competence A combination of knowledge, skill, and behaviour, required for success in a role.

coordination The coordinating function of leadership is about leaders' lateral relations within organisations. The aim of coordination is either to seek the cooperation of personnel not in the leaders' own teams or under their authority, or to link actions by two or more of their own sub-teams.

contingency planning Contingency planning is the process by which other courses of action are considered and options built in to a campaign plan to anticipate opportunities or reverses.

control Control is one of a leader's most important functions. Modern writers have given the word 'control' an unpleasant taste so let us be clear that we mean it not in the interfering and domineering sense, but being able to influence events and results. The control and evaluation functions exist to ensure that what ought to be done is done.

decisive points Decisive points are specific events, the successful effect of which are necessary for overall success.

decisiveness The ability to reach a conclusion or decision quickly and effectively.

discipline Discipline is a person's state of mind that leads to a readiness for willing, intelligent and appropriate conduct and the subordination of self for the benefit of the team.

directing. Directing means establishing through effective two-way communication with your subordinates what is required to be done and giving any guidelines that are necessary that relate to how it is to be done—although as far as possible this should be left to individuals' initiative. The communication may be through an informal chat, or at a formal briefing or meeting.

doctrine The framework of understanding of the nature of business that provides the foundation for the practical and intelligent application of the fundamental principles and procedures by which an organisation guides its actions in support of organisational objectives.

efficient organisation An efficient organisation is characterised by timely and productive systems and procedures. At its extreme it has no spare capacity to plan ahead or to respond easily to market changes.

enthusiasm The infectious dispay of zeal, energy, and interest, in a subject or task that creates a willing and positive atmosphere within a team.

effective organisation An effective organisation is characterised by the ability to pre-empt competitors, respond swiftly and efficiently to changing situations, and display agility in its structure and conduct of operations. It has efficient systems and procedures but has the capacity to anticipate and plan ahead.

evaluation This is a continuous process by which the leader judges progress in a task against its plan and it is a result of his or her control measures. Continuous evaluation brings the leader back to the (re)planning function and on through the other key functions of briefing, controlling/coordinating, supporting, informing and back to evaluating (see Chapter 5).

flexibility of mind The ability to adapt to changing situations and amending plans without the negative influences of preconceived and rigid ideas.

humanity The ability to appear human, to be available to discuss ideas or problems, to display empathy, and to understand the human effect of decisions.

integrity Integrity embraces the combination of the virtues of honesty, sincerity, reliability, unselfishness, and loyalty, and it is a person's adherence to a moral code of values.

initiative Initiative is a combination of seeing the need to take action and then taking appropriate action without constant reference to a superior authority.

intellect The ability to reason and to understand the significance of concepts, trends, and so on, the capacity to reduce problems to their fundamental elements on which all plans are based, and to ensure that absolute clarity of purpose is evident in all activity.

judgement The maturity and wisdom to balance conflicting advice in arriving at decisions and to adopt simple, pragmatic, and clear solutions.

knowledge (a) Knowledge in the context of leadership comes in three forms: business knowledge, knowledge of subordinates' strengths, weaknesses, and abilities, knowledge and understanding of self.

knowledge (b) A combination of facts, concepts, and information, about a role that is understood.

leader A person responsible for achieving objectives through the work of others and for building and maintaining the team of which he or she is a member.

leadership The capacity and will to rally people to a common purpose willingly and the character that inspires confidence and trust.

leader-once-removed (LOR) The relationship between the leader of a three-layer or strata grouping, and the subordinates of a subordinate team leader.

level of work The level of work of a role is defined by the complexity of the task and information, and the time span of the role.

loyalty Loyalty is being faithful and bearing true to allegiance to a person or institution; this allegiance is to superiors, subordinates, and peers.

manoeuvre To manoeuvre is to seek to get into a position of advantage within the market and with competitors from which corporate power may be applied.

mission Similar to an aim, a mission is a statement of overall intended action and the purpose it is designed to achieve by a particular grouping of people. An aim becomes a mission when it is stated by a leader to his or her team of immediate subordinates as their collective goal.

mission analysis The dynamic and continual process of review or re-evaluation of a task or mission that occurs whenever the circumstances from which that task or mission was derived changes. It ensures that subordinates' chosen courses of action remain consistent with the direction and overall intent of the subordinates' leader.

mission statement A mission statement is a template for a company's approach to doing business.

moral courage Moral courage is the daily choice of right instead of wrong; it is that which makes a person do something because it is the right, correct, and necessary, thing to do no matter that it may be difficult, unpopular or distasteful to implement.

morale The mental attitude and bearing of a team or person.

motivation That which stimulates interest in a job and induces a person to behave in a particular way.

objective It is a precise statement of a measurable, concrete goal that needs to be attained if the aim is to be achieved. It is usual for a number of objectives to be essential to achieving an aim.

operational level Joint campaigns and major operations are planned and directed at the operational level to achieve the aim of a strategic directive. It is the level that provides the gearing between corporate strategic objectives and all tactical activity within a geographical area of operations.

operational objectives These are the business objectives that need to be achieved in pursuit of business strategy.

operational pause Operations cannot be conducted continuously without inducing excessive human stress. Therefore, there may need to be periodic pauses during which the initiative has to be maintained through other means.

pride Satisfaction and a feeling of elation with the accomplishments of an organisation, team, and oneself that encourages the maintenance or improvement of standards.

responsibility Those features of any role that the incumbent is held accountable for by the organisation and his or her superior, whether the work has been delegated to a subordinate for action or not. Responsibility cannot be delegated.

self-confidence This is belief and faith in onself and in one's ability to achieve delegated tasks, and to overcome challenges and obstacles encountered particularly when faced with the unknown of change. Self-esteem, self-respect, self-discipline and moral courage are contributory factors.

self-discipline The subordination of self for the benefit of others and ability to do that which is known to be the right and proper thing to do. Self-discipline is a person's state of mind that leads to a readiness for willing, intelligent and appropriate conduct and underpins consistency.

sequencing Sequencing is the arrangement of activities within a campaign in the order most likely to achieve the desired conclusion.

skill The ability to apply learned techniques, processes and methods in a role.

stakeholders Those individuals, teams, or organisations with an interest in, or who may be affected by, the activities carried out by a person or team.

stratum A level within the hierarchical structure of an organisation containing roles of the same level of work.

strategic level Corporate strategy is the application of corporate resources to achieve corporate policy objectives.

subordinate A person at a lower level in an organisational hierarchy with less authority and fewer responsibilites than a superior to which that subordinate reports.

subordinate-once-removed (SOR) The relationship between the subordinates of a team leader in a three-layer or strata grouping, and the team leader's own superior.

superior A person at a higher level in an organisational hierarchy and with greater authority and responsibilities than the subordinates reporting to that superior appointment.

tactical level Activities within a sequence of major operations are planned and executed at a, tactical level in order to achieve the operational objectives of a campaign. This level is characterised by the application of integrated and coordinated units and people at the point of main effort to secure an objective. It is at the tactical level that most people are directly employed in business.

task A precise and measurable action to be carried out by a person or subgroup whose efforts contribute to achieving the mission of the parent grouping. An objective becomes a task when a leader delegates it to a specific person or sub-team as part of his or her plan.

task organisation The composition of a team dedicated to a specific task or project.

team A grouping of people in either a permanent or temporary arrangement, but with a common task or purpose.

tempo Tempo is the rate or rhythm of activity relative to other competitors in the market within all tactical activity and between major campaign or operational phases.

time horizon The maximum period that a person is able to anticipate ahead, to organise and to plan for and to achieve his or her aim.

time span The time span is the target completion time of the longest assignments (tasks or projects) that may be encountered in a role.

values A set of beliefs and ethics that guides people's behaviour and dictates their moral standards for thinking and judging.

vision A vision statement is a simple affirmation of what an organisation aspires to be.

willpower The enduring will to win and to see a task through to its completion through good times and bad. It requires determination, stamina, tenacity, self-discipline. It is a part of courage, decision, and initiative.

INTRODUCTION

Should anyone share the common perception that officers lead simply by ordering people around then I would simply say this: if you think that that sort of leadership builds the relationship of mutual trust, confidence, and respect that is necessary for a soldier to risk his life in following you when you are both being shot at, you are mistaken. That relationship is built up over time—in exactly the same way that it is with people in industry. This popular misconception is reinforced by Hollywood films that are anything but an accurate depiction of the profession of arms (in the British Army at least). I, like many of my former brother officers, have experienced the excitement, temporary confusion, and stress, of active service. My soldiers never failed to follow when there was nothing to force them to do it other than the relationship we had of mutual confidence and trust. I like to think that I was well trained and did the right thing while building that relationship and this book should help you to do the right thing as well.

This is not a book about leadership in the British Army. I have worked as an employee in one of the world's largest packaged consumer goods companies, and as a corporate 'head-hunter' and management consultant for more than 30 companies across six industry groups and have seen much in common in all large enterprises. In this book I have assembled the most useful concepts and tools of leadership that I have studied and have used, all of which complement each other, and which are applicable to any enterprise. I have even originated some ideas! So while you may think that I have a military perspective, I can assure you that I have filtered out anything that I do not believe is relevant to any organisation—it is simply that the army has evolved a very effective system during the last 350 years and is very clear and precise about what it does. Few, if any, companies have a history or evolution that is comparable; and indeed, the history of business management itself does not date back much further than the turn of the twentieth century. Anyone familiar with the excellent work of Dr Elliott Jaques,[1] author of *Requisite Organization* and other books, will be interested to know that in a recent facsimile to me he stated that the British Army 'was a perfect match' to his theory of the universal stratification of managerial systems. His theory of organisation, combined with the skills, knowledge and tools of leadership presented here, are the solution to establishing a self-perpetuating culture of leadership and teamwork in which innovation, continuous improvement, flexibility, efficiency balanced with effectiveness (see Glossary of Key Terms) and agility, are implicit.

A plethora of books on leadership have descended upon book retailers since the mid-1990s, and it is not surprising that few, if any, seem to say anything that is fundamentally new. We can read discussion about the 'new leadership' required for the next millennia and how the 'type' of leadership in current use is failing as if some new panacea to corporate ailments had been discovered. The latter focussing on the re-engineered, down-sized, right-sized, impersonal, soulless, and often political, enterprises that employ an increasingly cynical workforce that has learnt the hard way that loyalty to oneself is the only kind of loyalty that matters any more.

We have stood mute witnesses as many organisations that were regarded until recent years, as icons and models of success, spiralled helplessly towards extinction while shareholders looked on bemused. We are also witness to companies that are apparently successful (often technology or communications-based), but whose success is a result not of good leadership, but the fact that they are fortunate enough to be in a growth industry—the lack of leadership is often evident in a turnover of 25% of experienced managers. If they are profitable with such a problem, how much more revenue and profit could they produce if the problem were eliminated? What does this cost not only the companies in lost profits, but the country in economic stability, employment, and social harmony?

> If you would divine the future, study the past
>
> *Confucius*

My aim is to demonstrate that there is nothing new in leadership and that the 'practices' that have so far been described as 'leadership' by organisations and management book authors demean and devalue that word. Human nature has changed little over the millennia and, therefore, some well-established principles, concepts and 'leadership tools' that have been proven through history are equally valid today. They will remain valid until such time as our human nature changes, which may never happen. It is unfortunate that so little training and development have occurred in organisations and that, therefore, an existing wealth of knowledge has been ignored because it is 'not the current fad'.

THE AIM OF THIS BOOK

This book is devoted to developing leadership that ensures the moral component of commercial effectiveness (see Figure 1.1) is present. Thus:

> the aim of this book is to describe the essential knowledge, systems and processes necessary for effective leadership, in order to raise the quality of leadership provided by the reader to any endeavour in which he or she is engaged.

It is not possible for this book to develop your expertise in the use of these concepts, or to develop the leader's personal qualities of leadership—that can only be done with practical experience, challenging training, and honest feedback.

Given the fact that you are reading this book, however, it is reasonable to infer that you value leadership and have the will to lead. Assimilation of the knowledge and skills presented here can only increase your capacity to lead, and, therefore, your success.

In the dictionary, definitions of 'manage', 'manager' and 'management', are usually associated with control, administration, precision, continuation of unchanging processes, regulation, and so on. 'Lead', 'leader' or 'leadership', however, are associated with showing the way, guiding, taking to a certain destination, inspiring others to follow (after its Anglo-Saxon root). It is obvious that these two roles involve very different attitudes and objectives.

Indeed, I propose, that 'management' (defined as the 'ability to allocate, coordinate and control resources and to administer') is a vital skill subset of a leader without which the leader will fail, but leadership is not a subset of management: vision, concern for people and innovation cannot be subordinate to repetition of established processes. It is only with inspired leadership at every level that any enterprise's employees become more productive, innovative, creative, willing to use their initiative and able to take risks, committed to their customers and to the quality of their work, and timely in product delivery. If that is not achieved then we will not have sustainable business in both the domestic and highly competitive global markets. Thus, management and leadership are inseparable. As Professor Warren Bennis, a US Professor of Business Administration[2] states:

> The manager administers; the leader innovates.
> The manager is a copy; the leader is an original.
> The manager maintains; the leader develops.
> The manager focuses on systems and structure; and leader focuses on people.
> The manager relies on control; the leader inspires trust.
> The manager has a short range view; the leader has a long range perspective.
> The manager asks how and when; the leader asks what and why.
> The manager has his eye on the bottom line, the leader has his eye on the horizon.
> The manager imitates; the leader originates.
> The manager accepts the status quo; the leader challenges it.
> The manager does things right; the leader does the right thing.

Companies are generally ready to invest in research and development and recover the cost over time. A senior expatriate executive in Sydney of a US company providing information systems and technology solutions to companies outsourcing the information systems (IS) function late in 1996 asked me the rhetorical question, 'Why don't we see the need to invest in people in the same way that we do in technology?' A good question since the perception created by the marketing effort (in me at least) is that they offer the best technical solution implemented by the best people. I assume that 'best people' means well motivated, committed to the customer's best interests, able to use their initiative, and accountable for their actions (or lack of them). Surely implicit in this is well led?

Management gurus are largely to blame for the 'fad culture' in which aspects of management become the 'flavour of the month' for a short time before giving way to another idea. Many of these fads seem to me to be an attempt to realise the benefits of leadership at every level of people management, but without doing what is necessary to select, train, and retain, leaders and potential leaders. This is probably because the true nature and practice of leadership is not really understood—few managers or consultants have ever worked in an organisation where leadership and the teamwork it generates was all-pervasive, or possibly because it is just too hard—the benefits of any investment in the training and systems needed will not be seen overnight. Too many of our senior executives cannot, or will not, sustain the commitment necessary in the face of shareholders wanting the short-term profits from expedient decisions.

It is interesting that until the late 1980s few organisations invested in leadership training. One reason for this is because it is nigh on impossible to measure. Many organisations are still paying only lip-service to developing the leadership skills of their staff because so few 'decision-making' executives really understand not only the difference (or relationship) between leadership and management, but what sound leadership actually is and what it can achieve. Since good leaders develop others, it is not surprising then that with a lack of good leadership at the top of a company, few managers within it would have experiences of effective leadership and a crystal-clear view about what it is they seek to develop. Presumably the fact that you are reading this book is a positive indicator that you are doing something about this situation.

I must express my serious concern at the growth of the Human Resource (HR) departments within companies that use the HR department as a service provider to recruit, identify training needs and allocate course places, manage careers and career development, appraise performance and provide counselling services. While HR managers act as service providers and not as consultants providing advice, and only advice, to line managers, then conditions are right for busy and overworked managers to abdicate their responsibilities for, and to, their people. This is a complete failure of their personal leadership and anything that encourages line managers and supervisors to avoid their responsibilities must be eradicated if a culture of leadership is to be developed.

Another matter for concern is the habit that some executives and managers have on appointment to a new role of sacking all the incumbent direct reporting subordinates and frequently importing members of their own 'fan club'. Such sackings are perfectly acceptable, indeed necessary, when there is general recognition of existing subordinates' incompetence or a person is clearly seen to be in the wrong role and incapable of changing quickly enough for the company's needs. When this is not the case and the reasons can be reduced to the new appointee's personal preference, however, then the new appointee's leadership must be questioned. A good leader is able to get to know, understand, and develop new subordinates rapidly—there is no such thing as a bad follower, only a bad leader. Such sackings, particularly if followed by importing outsiders with no consideration to internal candidates, does nothing to develop confidence in the new leader or loyalty to either the leader or organisation.

A word on language. While language can assist in defining culture and has its own internal meanings, the language I have used is precise and not intended to imply anything other than that which it is defined as. The Glossary is comprehensive. Thus, when the term 'superior' is used it means a manager or leader at a higher level in an organisation; it is not intended to imply that such a person is a 'better person' in any way. Likewise 'subordinate' is meant in the sense of a person who reports to a superior leader; it is not meant to demean that person as an inferior being, it merely indicates that they are subordinate to someone else in the company's hierarchy.

At level A is a team of peers, all subordinate to their superior team leader at level B. The level B superior is in turn subordinate to the superior at level C. The superiors at level C report in turn to their superior at level D. Any three-tier grouping such as the relationship between the superiors at level D and subordinates at level B, and the superiors at level C to level A are termed leader-once-removed (LOR) and subordinates-once-removed (SOR).

It is essential that the LOR knows personally all the SORs in the various subordinate team leaders' teams if the LOR is to ensure the quality of performance management by subordinate leaders.

Developing leadership throughout society is the key to national stability and contentment. Field Marshal Montgomery once said that such training has to begin in our schools and universities for it is wasted on the older generation. Looking around industry and government it is evident that he was right. The irony is that the people who need such training most are the least likely to make the decision that they, and others, need to be trained. Will we have to wait for the current generation of 'leaders' to retire before we see major investments in selecting and training potential leaders? Can we afford to wait that long?

Figure   An Organisation As a Team of Teams

LEVEL IN ORGANISATION   LEVEL OF WORK

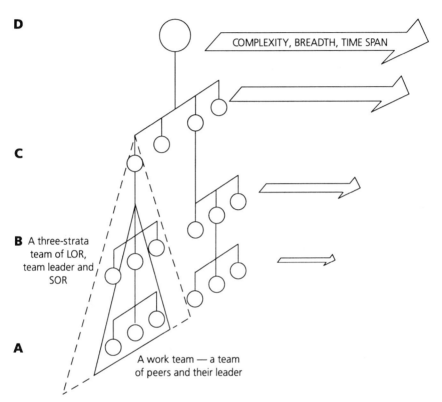

COMPLEXITY, BREADTH, TIME SPAN

D

C

B A three-strata
team of LOR,
team leader and
SOR

A

A work team — a team
of peers and their leader

Notes:
1. All personnel at one level A, B, or C are peers. All those in the same 'tree branch' at one of these levels are considered a peer team.
2. A peer team with their team leader (who comes from the level above) is considered a work team, as illustrated in the solid triangle.
3. The three strata grouping of leader-once-removed, team leader and subordinates-once-removed is illustrated in the dashed triangle.
4. The level of work is characterised by the length, breadth and the complexity of work; its scope.

References

1. Elliott Jaques, 1996, *Requisite Organization: A Total System for Effective Managerial Organization and Managerial Leadership for the 21st Century*, Arlington, Virginia: Cason Hall & Co. Publishers.
2. Warren Bennis, 1989, *On Becoming A Leader*, Century Hutchinson Australia.

CHAPTER 1

INTRODUCTION TO LEADERSHIP

A leader has got to learn to dominate events which surround him; he must never allow these events to get the better of him; he must allow nothing to divert him from his aim; he must always be on top of the job and be prepared to accept responsibility. He must endeavour to produce, on every level, commanders with the qualities of leadership which inspire confidence in others. These qualities are possessed in some degree by all men chosen as leaders but they need to be developed and trained.

Field Marshal Montgomery on leadership

Organisations are currently running at 20 to 30% of their potential and there is an opportunity to crank this up to 60% and higher still for short periods. The key to unlocking teamwork and higher levels of energy is to develop better leadership throughout an organisation. We see it happening at several levels in some companies, but I cannot think of an example where leadership is being developed at every level within an organisation.

Robert McLean, formerly Managing Director,
McKinsey & Co Australia

The quick fix is the answer adopted by too many companies, and we're learning that they don't work.

Karen Lonergan, Education &
Development Manager, Castrol Australia

Leadership is all about making more and better from less, there-fore, to improve means to change and to learn. Sir John Harvey-Jones, the former chairman of ICI, quite rightly said[1] that it is 'not about maintaining the status quo, but maintaining the highest rate of change that the organisation and the people within it can stand'. It is the leader's job to ensure that the separate fads of total quality, continuous improvement, mentoring, coaching and learning are integrated into day-to-day life as these **are all** part of everyday life. They are then part of the culture and become habit-forming in a positive sense.

Leaders and the people who follow represent one of the oldest, most natural and most effective of all human relationships. Effective leaders must be successful, for it is only with success that high morale can be achieved and through that, efficiency in the workplace.

'Leadership' is often thought of as the domain of the senior management team in organisations; it must be realised that the skills of leadership must be developed in any person who is responsible for achieving objectives through the work of others. What has often been overlooked in books and studies are the fundamental aspects of lead-ership that should be common to the factory supervisor and the Chief Executive Officer (CEO) both of whom have their own team to lead. What varies is only the degree of skill needed at that particular level, the complexity of plans and decisions, and their implications.

Unfortunately many managers have been given the responsibility of leadership without the career-long development that is essential. How can they assume a senior role and be effective in that role? How much damage have we witnessed ineffective leaders do to organisations by failing to seize opportunities, initiating change when it is needed and, perhaps most notably, by not listening to, and being responsible for, their employees' best interests? What does this lack of leadership ability cost organisations through staff turnover, retraining, lost oppor-tunities, poor motivation, unwillingness to change, and so on? Has there ever been a climate and attitude survey that has not highlighted the fact that most employees feel that they are not working at any level close to their full potential?

> The principles used to lead a large group are the same as those used to lead a small group. It is a matter of appropriate organisation.
>
> Sun Tzu, The Art of War

Managers often race into studying aspects of strategic leadership that they fail to implement successfully because they lack the basic understanding of what leadership is about. The 'nuts and bolts' of leadership is the focus of much of this book since the 'big picture' is a grouping of many 'little pictures'—what should be applied to the few, can be applied to the many. The application of simple and fundamental leadership concepts leads to the success of (feasible) strategic plans.

Too many senior executives seem only to consider 'strategic leadership'—yet most, if not all, have their own team of direct reports to lead. All too often the power of personal example is forgotten— thoughtless executives who pass a ringing telephone and ignore it are not setting examples of customer service that they would like their followers to adopt. The message 'it doesn't really matter' has been clearly sent, and will be understood to be the behaviour that is acceptable in those companies.

All would-be leaders are advised to remember a maxim of Napoleon's that 'there is no such thing as a bad soldier, only a bad officer'. Since the be-all and end-all of an officer's role is to lead this is offered as a valuable guide to your own conduct.

> There is nothing in life like a clear definition.
>
> *The Duke of Wellington*

Many books on leadership stress the need for clarity of vision, task, role, values, and so on, but frequently no clarity of meaning is established for the words used in those books, nor in any organisation's daily use of language and terminology come to that. If 10 different managers were to define the word 'aim', there would probably be 10 different answers. For such key words used, a definition of that word is given here. That word must then be interpreted only in that sense if the ideas presented in this book are to integrate into a complete winning concept.

How do we define 'leadership'? Let us think about some definitions of leadership given by leaders of the past.

> Leadership is the ability to elicit extraordinary performance from ordinary people.
>
> *John Harvey-Jones*

Sir John has highlighted the fact that leadership is about doing— making it happen—as he titled one of his books. This would seem to imply generating motivation and commitment—the harnessing and releasing of people's energies to achieve some purpose. This is vital— but let us continue in our quest to capture the essence of leadership.

> The art of leadership is getting somebody else to do something you want done because he wants to do it.
>
> *Dwight Eisenhower, US President 1953 to 1961*

Eisenhower emphasises the need to persuade people to follow or to enable them to see the need to do something for themselves. This implies a real knowledge of how followers perceive things and what their needs are, and for leaders to use this in communication and persuasion.

> The capacity and the will to rally men and women to a common purpose, and the character which will inspire confidence.
>
> *Field Marshal Montgomery*

This is Montgomery at his best—simple, succinct, and effective. He highlights the combination of personal qualities (character), skills and knowledge (capacity) and, most importantly, the will. I suggest that many managers in business often have the capacity—particularly in the functional skills—but lack the will and/or character for their role. This reflects not only their selection, but has implications for training and performance management. It is apparent to me among technical and accounting experts that promotion is frequently based on functional skills, yet the technical job that revolves around measurable and repro-ducible concepts could not be worse preparation for the leadership of people whose only common trait is their frequent unpredictability!

> A leader is best when people barely know that he exists, not so good when people obey and acclaim him, worst when they despise him: Fail to honour people, they fail to honour you: But of a good leader, who talks little, when his work is done, his aim fulfilled, they will all say, 'We did this ourselves'
>
> *Lao Tze 600BC*

Lao Tze sums up the need for a leader to build his or her subordinates' self-esteem by achieving the tasks set. He also touches on mutual respect that is a vital part of building trust.

> Leadership—that combination of example, persuasion and compulsion that makes men do what you want them to; it is an extension of personality. It is the most personal thing in the world for the simple reason that it is just plain you.
>
> *Field Marshal Slim[2]*

Slim stresses both personal example and personality—or character as Montgomery highlighted—and emphasises communication, implied by Eisenhower. The communication, honest and open, should usually be positive and persuasive, but despite much politically correct thought there are still people and occasions where 'a swift kick in the pants' or 'interview without coffee' are both necessary and effective. Even the best of us can become overconfident about our abilities and let our standards drop. The art of depersonalising such 'counselling' and giving full, frank, and objective, feedback must be developed, and that requires both the moral courage to grasp the nettle, and self-confidence to be assertive.

Of character or personality—the traits theory of leadership stresses the need for personal qualities, how do we define the list of essential qualities? Even if we define a list, not every leader has them all in the same ratio. Perhaps the answer lies in enough strength in a sufficient number of desirable attributes to make leaders acceptable to their followers. Such qualities are examined later in this book.

If you are able to develop and sustain such qualities in yourself, then you do increase your chances of gaining the respect, trust, and confidence of those that you would have follow.

In essence then, if leaders cannot communicate and persuade effectively, confused and incohesive teams are less likely to achieve the aims. Leaders lacking those qualities generally expected of them do not gain the trust and confidence of their teams and again are less likely to achieve the aims. Lack of discipline in teams (stemming from the individuals' self-discipline and sense of duty) lowers standards, the level of morale and trust, and result in incoherent action by groups of uncoordinated individuals.

With these views in mind, here are the definitions for 'leadership' and a 'leader' for use in interpreting this book.

Leadership: the capacity and will to rally people to a common purpose willingly, and the character that inspires confidence and trust.

This definition varies slightly from the one given by Field Marshal Montgomery. I have added the word 'willingly' to emphasise the point that people must want to do something if they are to perform to their best. While confidence depends on trust, there is a 'them and us' syndrome in organisations that is a result of a lack of trust. To quote an article by James Strong, Chief Executive of Qantas, a lack of trust 'gives rise to cynicism and suspicion at the motives and intentions of the company at every development'.[3] Building trust takes time, consistency and hard work; it is maintained by a balancing act, often on a knife-edge, and it is all too easily destroyed by a thoughtless word or action.

The above definition of leadership can also form a template on which recruitment, selection, training and development, and performance management, can all be based, giving the consistency and congruence that adds strength and continuity to any organisational culture.

Note that none of those definitions above specify the position or the level of a 'leader'. What is stressed is that a leader is a person who achieves objectives through the work of others. Hence, the definition of a leader below.

> Leader: a person responsible for achieving objectives through the work of others and for building and maintaining the team that he or she is part of.

Dr Elliott Jaques,[4] eminent in the field of organisation, structure, and hierarchy, points out that a leader does not exist *per se*, but exists in the context of a purpose—commercial, political, sporting, military, or social. A leader may formally be head of a team of direct reports, or may have an ad hoc role of leading a 'flat structure' project team. While the 'style' necessarily may change, the essential responsibilities and prerequisites for success vary little.

The word 'leader' is not qualified as managerial, military, sporting, or whatever since the concepts presented in this book are relevant to any type of organisation.

What has forced the current interest in developing leadership in managers?

Firstly, change. We are all familiar with the rate and unpredictability of change, but even this is speeding up to a point where we cannot keep up with its demands. Look at:

- The macroeconomic level in Europe through the European Community trading block, instability in the former USSR and in the Middle East.

- Changes in the aspirations, attitudes, and expectations of people, and an increasingly cynical workforce whose frequent experience of redundancy has bred mobility of employment and loyalty that is hard to retain. People quite rightly want, and expect, to be treated with more respect.
- The global paradox[5] of shrinking boundaries, increasing potential total market size combined with increasing 'tribalism' and an attendant desire to be treated 'differently' and the need for organisations to be able to be agile and to be able to act quickly. The break up of the USSR, Czechoslovakia, and Yugoslavia, illustrates this.
- The need for many organisations to grow through partnerships and strategic alliances (that require trust and confidence), rather than by acquisition. The success of expansion by companies like McDonald's with their supplier partnerships, Marks and Spencer (the UK retailer), and BT (British Telecom) and MCI's 'Concert' joint venture are good examples.
- The use and value of knowledge—the need to constantly train, to develop and to retain employees. The 'Big 6' chartered accounting firms, and information systems (IS) solution providers are organisations that clearly value knowledge and regard themselves as knowledge organisations.
- The paradox of communication. With IS, e-mail, voicemail, mobile telephones, and so on, senior managers demand more information than they used to and this results in interference and removal of decision making from the people best placed to make them. In days gone by, managers were forced to trust and to delegate because the luxury of such easy-to-obtain information was absent. Additionally, these electronic systems that should be used as a bulletin board for messages of a general nature are being used for important communication that should be done on a face-to-face basis. It is only face to face (or possibly over the telephone) that a leader can interpret directions, check understanding, motivate and impose some personality on the subject under discussion.
- The advance and implementation of technology.

It is this last point that is of particular interest because, as the technological gap among companies closes, the challenge becomes what companies do with the same tools where the only variable is the company's people, their motivation and commitment.

Thus, despite the assets, ready cash, investments, intellectual property, goodwill and distribution system, a company is no more than its people make it and, therefore, their leadership is of paramount importance. No company annual report has an opening statement by the chairman that does not recognise the employees' efforts. Why is it then that the focus on people in companies so often stops there?[1]

COMMERCIAL EFFECTIVENESS

Any organisation is judged by its commercial effectiveness, but this is not something that can be measured on an absolute scale. Comparison and benchmarking against others is the only way to gain feedback on our own effectiveness. What gives an organisation its commercial effectiveness is its corporate power. The components of this are shown at Figure 1.1.

- The physical component. The physical component provides the means to operate and it includes capital and cash flow, people and their training, logistics, equipment, products, the distribution system. In short, anything that can be bought or hired.
- The conceptual component. The conceptual component is the thought process behind what an organisation does and it includes 'The Principles Of Business' (see Chapter 20), and the fundamental doctrine that is the basis of an enterprise's operations.
- The moral component. The moral component is the ability to get people to work together to achieve company objectives. It is based on leadership that provides direction, a sense of purpose, and the climate in which people work at their best. Motivation, *esprit de corps*, and morale, are all essential parts of the 'moral component'.

Leadership is of the spirit, compounded of personality. It is a science to be studied, and an art to be practised.

The science of leadership cannot be learnt from reading a book or being taught in a classroom and then practised in a mechanical fashion. While certain concepts and ideas can be studied and do give an essential insight into leadership, science suggests exactness and repro-ducibility—and anyone who has worked with people knows that they can be most unpredictable. This is probably why so many people are frightened of taking a leadership role.

Leadership is an individual and personal ability that is born and is evident in some, but it can be developed in others who have the will and potential (how to identify this is examined later). It is an individual expression of long-established principles that have not changed as human nature has not changed over the millennia.

Figure 1.1 The Factors Affecting Commercial Effectiveness

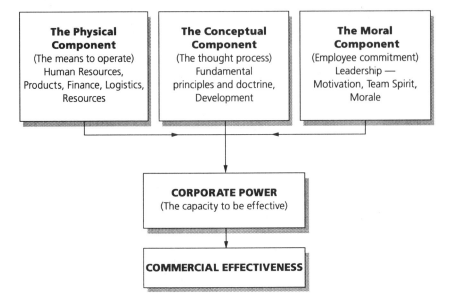

Leadership is not a skill in itself, but a combination of skills and personal qualities and the use of 'tools' that can be developed and can be applied with thought and common sense.

People do things for one of two reasons: either because they are forced to, or because they want to. If compulsion is to be replaced by inclination then working effectively together as a team to achieve agreed objectives willingly can only happen as a result of inspired personal leadership. Leaders create cohesive and effective teams and are vital members of those teams. This last point needs emphasising—leaders are not outside their teams, they are very much part of teams.

An awareness and the continuous development of leadership ensures team member participation, more thorough planning and preparation, clearer briefing and direction, and better people-management and building and motivation of the team. This can only lead to a stronger team and increased job satisfaction that, in turn, increases efficiency and productivity, lowers absenteeism and staff turnover, and increases 'service levels' and profitability.

> I do not believe that I have to know exactly where this company will be in 10 years time, but I do know that we need to have the systems in place to be able to anticipate and be able to respond quickly and do things in a different way. My challenge is to provide sufficient information to everyone in the organisation so that they can understand quite clearly how their role will lead to organisational improvement. For myself I want to see flexibility—policies and procedures must change from being rules to principles designed to achieve a purpose.
>
> *Malcolm Jones, CEO, NRMA Limited*

Figure 1.2 illustrates how developing leadership in every level of manager or supervisor—a culture of leadership and teamwork—is the key to ongoing innovation, organisational agility and responsiveness, and continuous improvement. Ongoing organisational development becomes both painless—planning and the ability to stretch replaces stress—and self-perpetuating; this is an organisational nirvana. At the CEO level the vision provides the direction around which all effort is united. The values dictate the code of acceptable behaviour and underpin all decisions. The example has to be set at the top because it is interpreted as the behaviour that leads to personal success within the company and is, thus, imitated down through the organisation. The values are the only certain thing in an uncertain world and provide 'security' to employees (Maslow's hierarchy of needs, see Chapter 12).

Leadership ensures that change is managed painlessly, communication flows, people are developed, and their needs satisfied, where possible. Learning, continuous improvement and innovation, become the norm and so they are not intimidating. Leadership inspires loyalty in staff, is reflected in their motivation, customer service and, therefore, leads to referred and repeat business.[6]

Karl Albrecht,[7] a managerial consultant, reminds us that one of the Pope's Latin titles is *Servus Servorum*, 'the servant of servants'. This point of view suggests that anyone in a leadership role, whether it involves formal authority or not, must lead by assisting others, not by driving them: today 'service leadership' is required. We see this as manufacturers 'add value' and competitive advantage to their product by continuously improving product quality and service; it will not be long before they see themselves as service companies, not manufacturers.

Figure 1.2 The Role of Leadership in Organisational Development

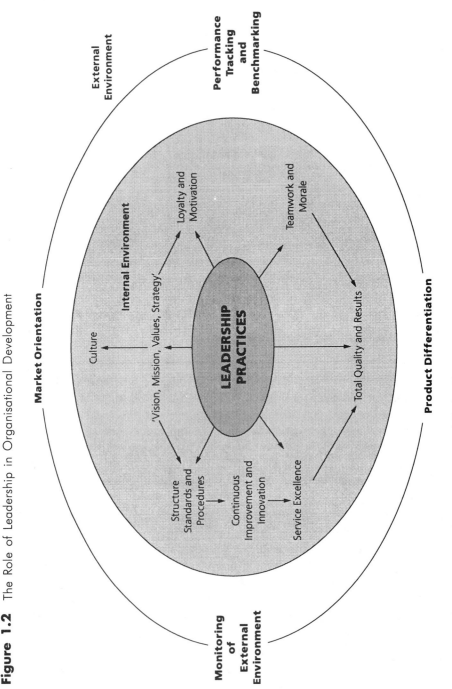

External Environment

Performance Tracking and Benchmarking

Market Orientation

Internal Environment

Loyalty and Motivation

Teamwork and Morale

Culture

'Vision, Mission, Values, Strategy'

LEADERSHIP PRACTICES

Total Quality and Results

Structure Standards and Procedures

Continuous Improvement and Innovation

Service Excellence

Product Differentiation

Monitoring of External Environment

© Adapted from an original by Jeremy Tozer and Shirley Harper

People in difficult and demanding roles need and expect effective personal relationships with their managerial leaders that help them to focus their energies, work at their best, surpass their expectations of themselves, and feel a sense of satisfaction at their contribution. Service leadership is the capacity to lead with a service focus:

- Service to the customer.
- Service to the employees—those who do the work in achieving the aim.
- Service to the organisation.

The point is that to provide service leadership you dedicate yourself to the interests of others and put yourself at the bottom on the list of priorities. This demands anything but a self-centred approach and there can be no room for playing politics and attempting to outshine other managers. You have to play a team game as a full team member to make your positive contribution. As with anything in life, the more you put into a job, the more you will get out of it—satisfaction and recognition (and reward) for a job genuinely well done.

It is interesting that the motto of The Royal Military Academy Sandhurst (established in 1812) where all regular British Army officers are trained and whose training has been reproduced in many academies worldwide, is 'Serve to Lead'.

No two people are the same and, therefore, leadership cannot be standardised into some convenient model that can be used on every occasion. Each leader has a pesonal style that takes into consideration common sense and an understanding of human nature, and such individuality requires a degree of freedom if the leader is to be identified as an individual and is to be successful.

This book pursues the view that there are two sides to the development of leadership potential and both are concerned with your relationships with senior staff members, peers, and team members. On the one hand, there is the practical side of demonstrating leadership, acting out its functions and showing that you, the leader, are actually leading, using certain skills or 'tools'. On the other hand, there are those traits and qualities that you need to display, so that others may recognise them in you—thus your superiors and peers will have confidence in your ability to lead and your team will trust and follow you.

TEMPLATE FOR TRAINING

Both these facets are explored later and this view of leadership is illustrated in Figure 1.3. Indeed, this view forms the template for training that is strongly recommended in which the practice of the skills and application of knowledge gives opportunities to develop participants' personal qualities of leadership.

The beauty and strength of this template is fourfold:

- It is simple, easy to understand and to relate to, and to implement.
- It is not a slave to any one theory of leadership; all the major theories are valid, but I suggest that none is complete in itself.
- It can be applied to any level of any enterprise—with the appropriate level of training given.
- It is derived from the definition of leadership already presented, and when applied to recruitment, selection, training and development, and performance management, gives the benefits of consistency and congruency in practices, policies and procedures, throughout the organisation.

There are many templates for leadership that are used and certainly these are relevant and effective within specific organisations. The Sandhurst template has much to recommend it and, thus, I put it to you to consider using it in your leadership development.

More of personal qualities later on, but in brief these are not developed in comfortable, easy and challenge-free conditions, but by placing demands on participants that produce spontaneous behaviour—behavioural evidence. To develop such qualities, personal limits must be extended and stress and pressure are necessary to do this. In this way, confidence, self-esteem (among other qualities) and personal attitudes are developed; and individuals learn about themselves and others' perception of them from the behavioural evidence. This might be termed 'personal development', concurrent with the assimilation of skills and knowledge. This is explored fully in Chapter 21.

. . .whoever wishes to foresee the future must consult the past; for human events ever resemble those of preceding times. This arises from the fact that they are produced by men who ever have been, and ever will be, animated by the same passions, and thus they necessarily have the same result.

Machiavelli

Figure 1.3 Template for Leadership Training and Development

Leadership = Leadership Qualities + Leadership Tools, Skills and Knowledge

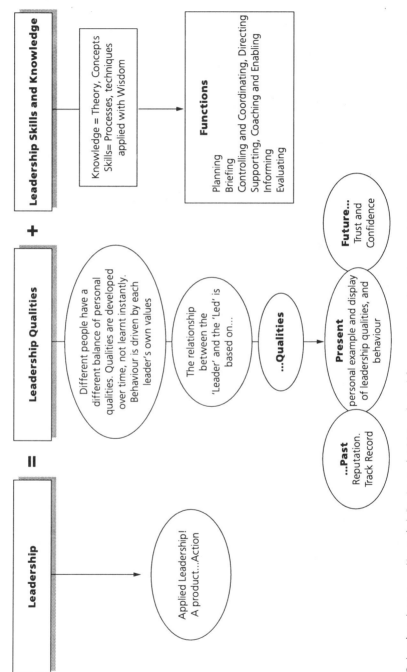

Leadership Skills and Knowledge

Knowledge = Theory, Concepts
Skills= Processes, techniques
applied with Wisdom

Functions

Planning
Briefing
Controlling and Coordinating, Directing
Supporting, Coaching and Enabling
Informing
Evaluating

+

Leadership Qualities

Different people have a different balance of personal qualities. Qualities are developed over time, not learnt instantly. Behaviour is driven by each leader's own values

The relationship between the 'Leader' and the 'Led' is based on...

...Qualities

Future...
Trust and Confidence

Present
personal example and display of leadership qualities, and behaviour

...Past
Reputation.
Track Record

=

Leadership

Applied Leadership!
A product...Action

Here are some 'philosophical themes' that are the cornerstones of effective leadership for your reflection and consideration in each of the following chapters.

- **Serve to lead.** To be the leader of a team is a privilege and you must constantly strive to be worthy of that privilege. This entails long hours, discomfort, and hard work. It means putting the interests of your subordinates, your organisation, and your customers above those of yourself. In short, it means being completely devoid of any sense of selfishness, personal greed, or excessive ego. Those managers who cover their own backs, seek to make themselves look good at the expense of others and overwork their team for their own greater glory do not deserve to be described as leaders.
- **Leaders have authority by virtue of their appointment, the leaders' power is given to them by their followers.** The extent of this power is a reflection of their acceptance of leaders. Leaders cannot force anyone to do anything. You cannot gaol or shoot someone if they say no to you, as leader. To keep their jobs, people probably do what you ask—but the degree of willingness and application of intelligence and initiative (and hence, quality of work) that is applied reflects your leadership power. If leaders rely on authority for their power to get things done, the organisational machine carries them only so far, but the leaders' relationships with their subordinates is weakened. Under stress, the strain may be too much for relationships that will break down completely and leaders fail.
- **Authority can be delegated, responsibility cannot.** Leaders may delegate authority to take action to their subordinates, but if they fail, it is the leaders' failure. The leaders' teams' successes are recognised as the leaders' successes by the leaders' superiors, so must be the teams' failures. If leaders takes the glory on good days, and apportion blame on the bad, leaders will never gain the trust, confidence or respect of teams—and can never be considered leaders because ultimately they will fail.
- **The function of leadership cannot be discharged on one side without a requirement to be led on the other.** As Australian-born General Sir John Hackett, one-time Professor of Classics, King's College, London,[8] writes:

The leader has something which the others want and which only he can provide. The man who can show the tribesmen where the water-hole is has a special knowledge: he can direct those in need to the place where their need can be satisfied. But you would call him no more than a guide and not a leader unless something else were present. This something is partly the ability to find an answer to a problem which the others cannot solve. But there is also the power, when difficulties have to be overcome, to help people over them. A capacity to help people in the overcoming of the difficulties which face them in a joint enterprise is one of those things which distinguish the person who is a leader from the person who is no more than a guide. What the leader has to give is the direction of a joint effort which will bring success. That is what he is there for, and he must have sufficient mastery of the techniques involved to do what is demanded of him by those he leads.

In this way the leader 'adds value' by his or her presence.

- **The relentless pursuit of excellence.** This way of life, or value, based on the desire to excel ensures that innovation, continuous learning and striving for continuous improvement, becomes a way of life. It is attainable.
- **Maintenance of the highest standards of self-discipline.** Practising self-discipline allows leaders constantly to display the personal example that can inspire others; applying self-discipline leaders do not 'cut corners', overlook detail, bypass effective, efficient and logical processes and systems, or overlook the needs of their teams.
- **Humility.** Leaders may hold superior positions in the appointments that they hold within the hierarchy, but this does not make them superior beings. This must be borne in mind in all dealings with other people.
- **Seek long-term sustainable performance, not short-term expediency.** Western businesses, by and large, ignore this principle that is so adroitly used by their Eastern competitors. There are obvious implications in decision-making style, if this is remembered. So many decisions can make the current balance sheet look good, yet stifle future performance, or even existence. This is particularly evidenced in down-sizing to the point where there is no employee trust, morale, capacity to innovate or even just to think ahead.
- **If you would divine the future, study the past (Confucius).** There are many great lessons to be learnt from the study of business, political, and military history. Technology and the employment of systems and processes has changed markedly over time and leaders in different periods of history may be isolated by

time, yet all leaders are united by the responsibility that they have shared and the principles that they have used. Most great leaders have studied the campaigns and personalities of other great leaders in history and have learnt much from it. General de Gaulle was always acutely aware of the links of leadership through-out history and in 1934 he wrote[9] that: 'whatever the time and place there   is a philosophy of command as unchangeable as human nature. When Charles XII wept at the recital of Alexander's exploits, when Napoleon poured over the Frederick the Great's campaigns, when Foch taught Napoleon's methods, it was because they were impregnated from the feeling of this permanence.'

In 1905 Colonel G.F.R. Henderson, military historian, wrote:[10]

. . .military history offers a more comprehensive view of those processes than even active service. . .the art of war is crystallised in a few great principles and it is a study of history alone that makes such principles so familiar that to apply them becomes a matter of instinct. . .The study of history results in the accumulation of facts and the understanding of knowledge and facts however wide constitutes experience.

While it is useful to have the precedent of experience to fall back on, there are circumstances when you will be faced with the new or unexpected where experience cannot help you. Often, as a leader, you must rely on your knowledge and understanding of yourself, your team and their capabilities and limitations, to ensure the success of your leadership.

Remember that you must want to lead. If you have no desire or motivation to lead, it will be difficult for others to follow—your lack of commitment will show. It will be particularly difficult to lead in times of stress. If your will is lacking then for your benefit, and more importantly your team, you are urged to reconsider your career direction.

References

1. John Harvey-Jones, 1988, *Making It Happen*, London: HarperCollins.
2. Field Marshal Sir William Slim, 1956, *Defeat into Victory*, London: Cassell.
3. James Strong in *The Australian Way* (Qantas Airways Magazine), July 1995.
4. Elliott Jaques and Stephen Clement, 1991, *Executive Leadership*, Arlington, Virginia: Cason Hall & Co Publishers.
5. John Naisbitt, 1996, *The Global Paradox*, Sydney: Allen & Unwin.
6. Frederick F. Reichheld, *The Loyalty Effect: The Hidden Force Behind growth Projects, and Lasting Values*, © 1996 by Bain & Company, Inc. Boston: Harvard Business School Press.

Karl Albrecht, 1994, *The Northbound Train: Finding the Purpose Setting the Direction Shaping the Destiny of Your Organization*, New York: Amacom, a division of American Management Association.

7. General Sir John Hackett, 1983, *The Profession Of Arms*, London: Sidgwick & Jackson.

8. General de Gaulle, 1934, *The Army Of The Future*, n.p.

9. Col. G.F.R. Henderson, 1905, *The Science Of War*, London: Longmans.

CHAPTER 2

PERSONALITY, SELF-CONCEPT AND SELF-PERCEPTION

In Chapter 1 I explained that there are two sides to the concept of leadership. There is the practical side of taking charge and of getting the team to do what you want them to do willingly, using the skills and tools of leadership, and there is the more abstract, but no less vital, aspect of the character and behaviours that you need to display if your superiors and subordinates are to have confidence in your ability to lead and to instil trust and confidence in others.

Here, in some ways, a bridge between these two aspects of leadership is placed to give you a basic understanding of how everyone develops and becomes what they are, and of the consequences of this. Take the opportunity as you read to look at yourself and to think about the factors that have influenced your own development. Until you have learnt to lead yourself, it is unlikely that you can be entirely successful in leading others.

In discussing personality you do quickly find that it is rather like leadership itself. Again everyone knows what the word means, but each has a slightly different definition. To make the point, here are two contrasting ones, from the technical aspect:

> Personality is the dynamic organisation within the individual of those psychophysical systems that determine his unique adjustments to his environment.
>
> *Allport*

to the drawn-out, yet easy to read:

> . . . the way a man looks and talks and thinks and feels, the things he likes and the things he hates, his abilities and interests, his hopes and

desires, the way he wears his hat or whistles a tune or throws a ball...The fact that a man is fat is as much a part of his personality as the fact that he has a deep voice. If his greatest desire is to play big-league baseball, that's as much part of his personality as his politics. If he loves sweets, rich des[s]erts, if he hates his mother-in-law, these things are also his personality. Personality simply means the total person . . .

Anonymous

Thus, there is no clear-cut definition of what personality is. The last sentence of the second definition, 'Personality simply means the total person', is perhaps the less contentious statement even if it tells us very little about the subject. What we know is that everyone differs from everyone else because of the unique combination of heredity and learned experience. Thus, individuals may well react differently from other individuals in precisely the same circumstances. As a leader you have to be aware of this constantly.

GENETICS

We all start life with a set of characteristics created, we now know, by the biological inheritance from our parents; no two people have the potential to grow up into the same person, not even identical twins. That certain aspects of our genetics influence our personalities, are beyond doubt. To take a gross generalisation think of how many people of short stature seem to be aggressively inclined, presumably to compensate for lack of height. Bonaparte, Hitler, and various contemporary high profile people are such examples!

Each of our physical characteristics and our basic intelligence, aptitudes, muscle coordination and dexterity, and so on, can all be attributed to our genetics. It is how we develop and use these endowments that is determined by us. For example, someone with a superb physique will only become an expert athlete by putting sufficient effort into training under the right conditions—willpower and self-discipline. Consequently, there are many with the physical potential of becoming great athletes who do not develop the capability because they do not wish to, or because their environment does not encourage it. Conversely, some of us will overcome physical shortcomings by sheer determination to succeed. This is well demonstrated on the 'sailors with disabilities' yacht seen racing offshore from Sydney, or in the Paralympic Games.

THE BRAIN

The most significant of the physical endowments is the brain. It is our mental capacity linked to the versatility of our bodies that provides us with the almost limitless variety of responses to our surroundings. The capacity to reason and to analyse is a more powerful asset than our physical abilities. It is through these capacities that we have been able to overcome the physical limitations of our bodies to conquer space and to walk on the moon, and to explore the depths of the oceans.

But why do individuals often act so differently from each other in the first place? The answer is that we each think differently. Our mental processes provide us with a wide range of different options for actions, based on our thoughts, our feelings and our responses to past experience.

ENVIRONMENTAL INFLUENCES

From the moment of birth we are influenced by our surroundings. Some psychologists suggest that we are not born with our minds completely blank with only the instincts to breathe and feed, but rather we are born with a whole range of primitive instincts. It is the cultural climate and home environment in which we experience early infancy and childhood that suppress and modify these instincts so that we develop our own personal ways of coping and thus each of us becomes an individual.

This then is an explanation for why two brothers can turn out very differently. There is plenty of evidence that first-born children are different from subsequent children and this is very likely since the new parents' experience of having and bringing up the first infant is likely to be considerably more stressful for them—than second-born and later children and, of course, the environment for the subsequent children includes the presence of the older brother or sister.

It may seem strange to be concentrating on the very early environment of the child in personality development, but it is beyond question that the child's experiences during the first four or five years of life are crucial in the formation of personality.

Learned Experiences

One of the great controversies of modern psychology has been among those who believe that genetics and environment are the foundations of personality and those who believe that a genetic and environmental mix has nothing to do with it and that personality is based wholly upon what each of us learns as we experience life. As in many great theoretical arguments, it is impossible to prove one way or the other, but what is certain is that as we as individuals grow up we learn from our personal experiences in life.

Learning can be described as 'a change in behaviour, based on experience'. It can be unconscious or conscious, and it greatly affects the ways in which we think, feel and act, our beliefs, values, and objectives. Whether we are loud or quiet, submissive or dominant, passive or assertive, how we attempt to fulfil our needs, make adjustments to our frustrations and resolve our conflicts are affected by learning. Through learning we form, in large measure, a concept of self and of the world in which we live. Biological drives and instincts remain important, but in modern life the ways in which we satisfy these drives and instincts are often determined by learning. You must beware, when thinking of learned experiences of assuming that, because the word 'learn' has connotations of school and conscious efforts made to commit information to memory, all learning is conscious. This is not so and many of the learned experiences that contribute to personality have an influence on the individual below the level of consciousness.

Values

Values, 'a set of beliefs and ethics that guide our behaviour and are so deeply held that they are not subject to proof'. It is usually difficult to prove that one set of values is better than another—just compare differing political ideologies. Yet the strength of values and beliefs can drive countries to war, or to self-destruction. While it is usually considered wrong to stereotype people—people are all individuals—John Wareham, the eminent head-hunter says values come in related clusters where they can be thought of as 'books of opinions in our archival library'.[1] For example, if someone were to say that he is a Conservative (in the UK) or Liberal (in Australia), we could safely assume that that person believes in the profit motive. . .based upon self-interest, and is likely to have a low opinion of egalitarian policies that might stifle initiative and reduce everyone to the same level. As Wareham says, '. . .values, not educational or technical qualifications, are the prime determinants of both life goals and professional competence'.[1]

The values that most determine personality are unconsciously learned experiences absorbed from people and events in closest proximity to us during our childhoods, and that the earlier in life that a value is acquired, the less it is likely to change. It is possible for us to have values that conflict with each other and these are resolved within us by an in-built 'sensor' that only allows congruent values to appear at any one time.[1]

EMOTIONS

We all have emotions or feel strongly about some subjects. These feelings are the result of our learning experiences and have a very significant effect on the way we behave. Our emotional reactions to a given situation might have no basis in logic or rationality, but it is no less important to us because of that. Some subjects do not generally create strong feelings in us one way or another. For example, a person usually reacts rationally when dealing with such subjects as mathematics, chemistry or physics, but that person might react on a purely emotional level when discussing politics, religion, football teams, trade unionism, motor cars, or feminism, and so on.

These are some of the characteristics of emotionally charged actions.

- We are reluctant to accept that our thoughts are influenced by emotion and insist that we are thinking logically. Yet thoughts based on emotion probably outnumber logical thoughts.
- We find it very easy to make associations between an emotional view and other unrelated subjects. For example, a proud father can easily relate any subject to his new son.
- For each of us our feelings are strictly related to each of us only. Other people may have similar feelings; but never identical feelings.
- Emotions insist on being expressed: they simply refuse to lie dormant. They continually influence our perceptions, thinking and actions, though sometimes they may be disguised in circumstances where others would find them intolerable.

SELF-CONCEPT

The concept of personality, then, is extremely complicated. Yet because leadership is about people it would be foolish to pretend that all individuals are the same and so it is necessary for us to have at least a basic understanding of what can lead to personality differences. We need to give the best performance ourselves and to get it out of other people and to do this we need to know what makes them 'tick'.

A useful starting point in achieving this understanding is for leaders to be aware of their own personality make up and how it affects their behaviour. Unless you can do this it is unlikely that you will be able to understand what makes other people behave in the way that they do.

The unique nature of individual development that we have talked about leads to individuals showing varying degrees of these characteristics, except perhaps integrity which, it can be argued, is absolute. You either have integrity or you do not, it cannot be qualified. Personal qualities are important because there are grounds for proposing that the personality of successful leaders will demonstrate a mix of these qualities without losing their individuality.

Individuals and Individualists

Individuals are simply people, and individualists are those people with a particular sense of identity—someone with an indivisible personality existing as a distinct entity. While individualists can make effective team members they are well suited to working on their own; however, leaders must be aware that excessive individualism inevitably leads to a break in cohesion within the team. There is a distinct difference between Western and Eastern culture in the emphasis on the individual or the collective body, and the degree to which some cultures require people to submit their own interests to the collective good needs no introduction and yet individualists do rise above that collective body. In the former USSR Mikhail Gorbachev is one example.

It is not easy to lead strong individualists because it is not easy or natural for them to subordinate their personal interests to the common interests or purpose of the team to which they belong. Individualists do not react positively to any routine or bureaucratic way of being led. They especially need to be recognised and to be treated as individuals, and to be made to feel special and, therefore, good leadership is essential to get the best out of them.

Individualists only really contribute to the team if they see value in the common task, recognise that some of their personal needs can be met by successful completion of that task, and realise that only a joint effort—teamwork—itself will succeed. As Professor Adair,[2] points out individualists do not 'sustain their place in working teams unless they are prepared to discipline themselves to accept—and perhaps go beyond—the standards of the group'. Such self-discipline can seem attractive to individualists because its self-imposition signifies their own liberty—the discipline has not been externally imposed.

Personal Coat of Arms

The personal coat of arms is a useful exercise that avoids using psychological assessments that you can do with a few others to gauge your own self-concept and the way that others perceive you. Take a look at Figure 2.1 and list in each section of the coat of arms:

Figure 2.1

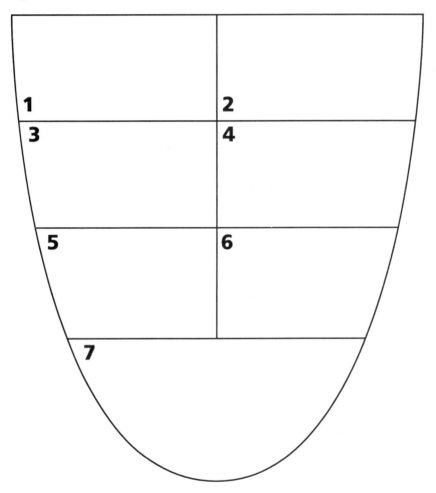

Section 1: Your three greatest strengths as a leader.
Section 2: Your three greatest weaknesses as a leader.
Section 3: Three words that describe what motivates you to succeed.

Section 4: Three famous leaders who you wish to emulate.
Section 5: Your three most important values.
Section 6: Three words that describe how you react under pressure.
Section 7: Three words to describe how you see yourself in 10 years time.

Now give a blank shield (Figure 2.1) to a few colleagues and ask them to complete the exercise honestly with you as the subject. The comparison will make for interesting reflection.

Using the same coat of arms template, now select every person who works with you, or for you, and list the ways in which they differ from other people in the team. Do this under the following headings:

1. History and Background
2. Values and Beliefs
3. Perception
4. Motivation
5. Personality and Character
6. Abilities and Knowledge
7. Aspirations.

You have now made a start in understanding your peers and subordinates.

PERSONAL CHARACTERISTICS

Leadership studies were about investigating the qualities and traits displayed by recognised leaders. The lives of acknowledged leaders, Churchill, Rupert Murdoch, Thatcher, Wellington, Kennedy, and so on, have been studied and assessments made of their most important personality characteristics. This was found to be both time-consuming and not very productive because of the vast range of characteristics and descriptions produced. Estimates vary, but between 17,000 and 20,000 words exist in the English language that can be used to describe some facet of personality. Certain characteristics are desirable in leaders and these are looked at more closely in Chapter 6.

Self-esteem and Self-confidence

Many psychologists and personality theorists state the importance of self-esteem and self-confidence. In general their research reveals that:

• A lack of self-esteem in the sense of insecurity, helplessness and failure to accept responsibility underpins many undesirable or negative behaviours and attitudes.

- People with high self-esteem are more likely to assume an active role within social groups or working teams, and they usually express their views more frequently and with greater assertiveness and effect than others do.
- People lacking self-confidence and self-esteem frequently view themselves as helpless and often inferior as well, unable to improve their situation and lacking the mental robustness and resilience to tolerate stress and minimise the anxiety caused by many everyday events, changes in work, pressures, and so on.
- Many people who are plagued by self-doubt, lack of self-confidence and self-assurance, experience problems in forming 'normal relationships' with other people because they are frightened that such exposure will reveal their inadequacies.

While employed as a corporate head-hunter, I have frequently observed the effects caused by candidates' lack of self-esteem and self-confidence. Firstly, executives deficient in these two attributes are far less likely to employ the best candidates available for a job because they feel threatened and lack peace of mind about the security of their own jobs. They do not realise that by hiring the best available talent they can bask in the reflected glory of their team. By hiring inferior candidates this syndrome cascades through the organisation, resulting in a spiral towards oblivion.

Second, people lacking self-confidence and self-esteem, in spite of whatever 'skills' training they may receive, find it difficult to face change because they do not trust in their capacity to manage the unknown—they have no faith in their ability to succeed. They are, therefore, unable to stretch beyond their comfort zone.

Conversely, when people have self-esteem and self-confidence, these characteristics frequently lead to increased levels of energy, initiative, and flair. It is also essential that leaders have these characteristics if followers are ever going to follow out of confidence and not curiosity. It is, therefore, essential to develop these attributes in everyone within the organisation if they were not developed earlier in life.

While head-hunting, I have often noted the correlation between high self-esteem and self-confidence and the activities pursued by candidates in their free time or earlier in life. Without exception, those who pursue an adventurous or demanding team-based activity, such as ocean-racing, climbing, Rugby, hockey, and so on, are particularly aware of 'people' in general, aware of their environment, and are at ease with themselves (attributes required in every leader in every form of enterprise). The greater the level of risk or adventure that has to be overcome, the greater the level of self-esteem and self-confidence that is developed. This is one of the basic tenets of Kurt Hahn's Outward Bound training and has been proven in the personal development gained by thousands of people in the schools that operate in more than 40 countries. Much contemporary leadership training, by necessity, is focussed on producing this personal development that really should have been experienced in younger life, although methods of achieving this vary (see Chapter 21).

References

1. John Wareham, 1980, *Secrets Of A Corporate Headhunter*, New York: Atheneum.
2. John Adair, 1986, *Effective Teambuilding*, Aldershot: Gower.

CHAPTER 3

PERCEPTION

Perception is reality

Anonymous

In the last chapter I discussed the main factors that influence the conscious and unconscious development of personality. We now need to understand how personality affects our approach to life, our understanding of problems, the way we see things, and our reactions to events and other people; this is 'perception'.

Perception is 'the process by which we become aware of what is happening around us'. Our senses provide us with information about our surroundings, but what we believe is happening, our 'perception', is a result of selecting, organising, and interpreting, this information in a very personal and unique way. Clearly personality and perception are very closely linked. Any organisation should focus on its people and on the demanding circumstances surrounding a competitive market. On neither count is there room for perceptual misinterpretation—'getting the wrong end of the stick'. Both people, including your competitors, and the flow of the battle for market share, are unpredictable. Correct answers to problems are never reached unless leaders think both widely and deeply; it is not enough merely to look at one point of view or just to look superficially at an issue and then gloss over it. In this chapter we consider the nature of perception principally by using visual illusions to make the point that things are not always what they seem.

THE REASONS FOR THE UNIQUE
NATURE OF PERCEPTION

This individual view, or perception, of life grows from our past experiences and from what we have learnt at home, in school, with friends (and enemies), in our current organisation and in previous jobs. Our current situations also have major influences on how the world is seen. Ambitions, expectations, age, status, and health, all play an important part in the way in which we respond to our surroundings. Our immediate environment, including people we live and work with, have a very significant effect on our perception of both people and events. Many of these influences are the same as those that shape our personalities.

WHY IS IT IMPORTANT TO UNDERSTAND THE NATURE OF PERCEPTION?

To assume that everyone around you sees the world exactly as you do is to invite, at the very least, misunderstanding and, at worst, to lead to a total breakdown in communication. Here are some fairly common examples of this.

- An employee who may be viewed by one manager as confident, but by another as arrogant.
- The same sports team may be considered to be beyond criticism by one person while another person might think of it as being just lucky.
- A junior manager walking around the factory floor may believe that it is a very pleasant organisation to be a part of, but a trainee apprentice with domestic problems that need his attention may view it as being similar to a prison.

Leaders who seek to understand, influence, control, and motivate, those around them, should be aware of the nature of perception. Try to understand and anticipate why individuals tend to see things differently from each other and from you; and through this understanding and anticipation try to avoid unnecessary misunderstandings, mistakes, and breakdowns in communication and trust.

The key to understanding perception is to realise that it involves an **interpretation** of a situation. We all are, to some extent, like artists who are painting pictures of the world that represent their own views of reality. In many cases these pictures may be abstract or emotional in nature and bear no resemblance to reality.

HOW PERCEPTION WORKS

We perceive when our attention is drawn to something in any way— visually, by listening, or by reading. We then select, organise, and interpret, the information we receive and then we act upon that interpretation, if necessary. But what is it that catches our attention? We notice things when their form or shape makes them stand out from their background. Although it may not be possible to identify what the shape is immediately once the object has been identified it always seems to be clearly demarcated. There are times when we are faced with situations where there are two equally understandable interpretations, however, the perceiver is unable to disentangle the shape from the background. Look at the illustrations in Figure 3.1 and Figure 3.2. How do you view the different representations in the same figure?

Figure 3.1   What do you see first, the vase or the faces?

Because of the many and varied things that happen all around us for much of the time we are forced to be selective about what we choose to take notice of when dealing with a given situation. Things tend to come to our notice for a number of reasons.

- **Intensity or degree of attentiveness**. An observer's attention is always quickly focussed on 'bright' objects.
- **Size**. The larger an object the easier it is to make it stand out from its background. Try looking for a needle in a wisp of hay, never mind a haystack; however, a steel bar is quickly distinguishable from the strands of hay.
- **Contrast**. Things that are unexpected stand out and are noticed.
- **Motion**. A moving object in an otherwise still environment ensures, that it stands out from the background and is readily recognised. Many wild creatures, hares, for instance, freeze when danger approaches in the hope that they are not spotted.

Figure 3.2   What do you see first, the old crone or the young lady?
Source: Two of the Rorschach ink-blot tests.

- **Novelty versus familiarity**. New objects in a familiar setting or familiar objects in a new setting tend to be picked out quickly.
- **The degree of threat**. People always tend to notice things that appear to threaten them, for example, a competitor launching a new product. We return to threatening circumstances later to look at the ostrich syndrome.

These properties of the object itself tend to emphasise how easily it is distinguished from its background and help us to perceive it. There are also a number of influences within the individual, however, that affect the way he or she interprets what is seen; things that may indeed distract his or her vision.

- **Previous learning or experience**. Very often we see or hear what we expect to as a result of previous experience, rather than what is actually to be seen or is being said.

- **Motivation.** Sex, survival, ambition, and social needs, all influence the degree of importance we attach to things. What page of the newspaper do you turn to first and why?
- **Values.** The learned experiences of each of us gives us an individual set of values about a job, spare time, our families, friends, morals, and so on. All these values are likely to influence the way we react to any situation.
- **How things are presented.** For example, an appealing advertisement or speech, or effective merchandising of a product attracts our attention and influences our thinking and our decision making.

You might be wondering why I am spending so much time discussing visual perception when clearly perception, in general, should concern itself with all the senses. There are two reasons for concentration on vision. Firstly, a vast percentage of the information we obtain about the world around us comes to us through the eyes, thus, visual perception is clearly a vital sense to all sighted people. Second, it provides an easy means of demonstrating perceptional effects.

The following influences on perception while having some visual context are probably more easily explained as being 'popular preconceptions' and even myths.

- **Grouping.** If we are not very careful there could be a tendency to consider similar people as identical and put them into convenient categories: for example, ethnic groups, trade unionists, 'management'. It is important to remember that each person is an individual. The tendency to stereotype is very evident in the way many of us think of foreigners.
- **Context.** You recognise the background so well that the object stands out. Broadly speaking, it is important to be aware of what is going on around you so that you can quickly identify something out of the ordinary.
- **Defence.** Now for the 'ostrich' syndrome, we often prefer to ignore or to reject information that we should sense as threatening to our position or to our idea. There has been more than one managing director who has rejected well-founded market intelligence and research reports because these did not match his or her own interpretation of the competition. At a more mundane level some people buy houses in highly unsuitable locations under airport flight paths, on the edge of motorways, and so on, because they do not accept the evidence of their eyes and ears if the property seems ideal in other respects, and they sometimes live to regret it.

- **Halo effect**. We sometimes make overall (blanket) judgements about people that are based on insufficient evidence. For example, an attractive female job applicant may be thought of as ideal simply on the evidence of her looks to a male hiring manager—sexism in action!

DELIBERATE DISTRACTIONS

These unconscious distortions of reality by the perceiver are bad enough, but they can be made worse by the deliberate distortion of reality. An artist can set out to deliberately distract the eye of the perceiver, either by distorting the perspective, or the contrast. Artists can visually distort logic in a much more subtle way (see Figure 3.3).

Figure 3.3 *Source: After the artist Esher*

This is the visual equivalent of the film director's portrayal of events—something that we can accept while in the cinema, but that cannot exist in real life. For us, a much more real problem is the tactic of deception as practised by a competitor. At the simplest level this amounts to just good camouflage. Will we be fooled by it, or will our perception enable us to see through the deception? Can we 'think competitor'? Look at Figure 3.4, what can you read:

Figure 3.4   What can you read?

If you cannot read Figure 3.4 easily look at the white space, not the black. Why do we automatically look at the black first? Our conditioning tells us to, and hence, our initial perception is that we cannot see a word. By changing our perspective we can read the word 'Fly'.

WHAT LEADERS CAN DO ABOUT PERCEPTION

You can see that perception is a complicated matter. You might think that life would be a lot easier if we all perceived things in the same way—your way; however, it has to be accepted that we cannot influence the rest of the world, so that everyone has the same point of view as our own. At the same time because individual perception lies at the heart of everything that we do, and consequently at the heart of many problems, we cannot ignore it.

WHAT LEADERS CAN CONTROL

If leaders understand the nature of perception they find that it is possible to influence situations, so that many misunderstandings can be avoided. Firstly, leaders should be concerned that the pictures of the world that they have painted are as close to reality as possible. This can be done by checking that they are aware of the factors, for example, directions from superiors that are influencing leaders, and that leaders are satisfied that their own views of the situations are distorted as little as possible by misunderstanding. At a personal level knowledge of your own personality is, of course, a help. Are you forgetful, naturally optimistic, or pessimistic? Impetuous, or overcautious? You need to take account of your own tendencies.

As far as other people's perceptions are concerned, leaders can, to some extent, control external factors that influence those around them such as the time and place of meetings. Through a knowledge and understanding of those people you work with, you should be able to understand, and even anticipate, their reactions to the internal factors—their personalities—that influence them. Through this understanding leaders can control the disruptive effects of different perceptions to some extent.

ATTITUDES

When we describe the way a person 'acts' we often refer to the attitude: the person is lazy, or industrious, or ambitious, or friendly, or lacks confidence, and so on. Remember that a person's attitude to life and work is the direct result of his or her personality. It follows, therefore, that to change someone's attitude means changing his or her perception and to do that it is necessary to know what has influenced that perception in the first place, and to have the skill to change those influences for the better when necessary and where possible.

To draw together all the threads of the sections on personality and perception consider what these pieces of elementary psychology mean to leaders. They mean four things: firstly, all the people in your teams will be different; second, that they see things largely in their own way—their perception differs from yours; third, situations are many-sided and are not be taken at face value; and fourth, the competitor, in whatever form—is worthy of perceptive thought. You should start cultivating thought processes now that are both broad and deep. In short—look, listen, and then think—before you speak or act.

CHAPTER 4

TEAMS AND GROUPS: THEIR CHARACTERISTICS AND DYNAMICS

> By far the best outcome of people acting together in an organised fashion is the greater achievement possible from a team, beyond the sum of the individuals involved. Only combinations of people can cover the scale, complexities, specialisation and geographical spread required today in many areas of business, government or other activities. It is always a delight to observe a group of people displaying true teamwork, with each person performing a designated role but combining together with others through disciplined performance.
>
> *James Strong, Chief Executive, Qantas Airways*[1]

The understanding of teams and groups is fundamental to leadership. Leaders need to understand the dynamics of teamwork to be able to harness the strengths and energy of their teams and to know and to minimise the effects of their likely weaknesses. We all know the value of teamwork from observing the example of sports teams, yacht crews, orchestras, and effective armed services. We see the way these teams react to support each other and to accept as normal their dedication to training, rehearsals, and discipline to maintain their effectiveness. It is strange, therefore, that so many businesses do not encourage the same practices.

I have never seen a leader-less team so it is one of the those things that I am not quite sure whether or how it can work. I have seen situations where several people assume leadership roles for specific parts of a project in addition to the leader. By thinking about purpose and performance you have an opportunity to allocate a number of leadership roles to different people and at the end of the day get more out of the team than you would if you simply delegate tasks. But the team still has a leader.

We recently had an example of a company that tried to suppress leadership to form leaderless teams. They tried to go through a set of routines where people seek to agree and forge consensus or vote on everything and they got extremely bogged down. They were not able to progress any issues in the time frames necessary to be successful.

Robert McLean, formerly Managing Director, McKinsey & Co Australia

From the moment of birth we are all vitally affected by the influence of other people. Initially it is our parents with whom we have contact, but gradually, as we develop we need to expand our contacts and to be able to interact socially with others. The family is probably the first group to exert its influence upon us and our behaviour and gradually the horizons expand as friendships and more formal groups such as school classes and working groups come to exert their influence on our lives.

In this chapter we consider group dynamics, the characteristics of teams, and the stages of team development, so that you can recognise and better manage your own teams, whether at work, or on the sports field.

GROUPS

People join groups as membership satisfies their need for companionship, affection, friendship, status and, sometimes, even power (more of which when we discuss motivation). The formation of groups depends on such things as the ability of members to communicate and to get on with each other; the fact that all members are substantially in agreement about important matters; and that it is possible for the group to develop rules or norms on acceptable behaviour. Consider for a moment how the factors evidence themselves in:

- A Hell's Angel Chapter
- A church choir.

A group, therefore, can be said to exhibit the following characteristics:

1. It has a definable membership of two or more people.
2. The members share a sense of comradeship and loyalty to the group and to each other.
3. Members share common goals or interests.

We have all experienced membership of groups. We also know the frustrations in trying to organise, say, a social event for a group of friends—people have different ideas of what to do, what to bring, what to eat. The same frustrations are not found in an efficient and high performing team. There are, therefore, some additional minimum characteristics a group must have to become a team:

4. A specific task or mission around which the team can unite and direct their effort.
5. A leader (elected, appointed, or de facto) to direct, coordinate, resolve conflict, and control, as necessary.
6. The imposition of restraint on behaviour—discipline or rules, whether from an internal or external source.

THE MISSION

The existence of a mission or a task is what primarily defines a team. In industry, all groups are faced with a constant stream of differing tasks. To cope with these, the members of a team must create an atmosphere of cooperation and trust, so that the basis of a team is formed. This is not sufficient, however, because, for a team to continue to work together in happy cooperation, it must perceive itself to have more successes than failures in the tasks undertaken. To ensure this success all the evidence of life indicates that the team needs sound, clear, effective leadership.

LEADERSHIP

There is no such thing as a Self Directed Team. This term means to me an absence of leadership and there are no results without leadership. You cannot create a leadership vacuum that will last. Nature will fill it. You cannot say 'you are empowered' and suddenly have empowered people. It's leadership that promotes confidence and initiative.

Chris Walsh, Operations Director, David Jones Limited

The idea that self-directed teams exist is false and ignores a fundamental fact of work and human nature. Firstly, no team is self-directed since this implies that it works in isolation. Aspects such as rostering, leave, allocation of minor duties or tasks, and so on, may be self-managed by agreement, indeed, a leader probably has no place dictating such detail, but in every organisation a team has to be coordinated with others in their work. They cannot be inward focussed or they only attempt to satisfy their own needs.

Second, no one can say 'you are empowered' and expect to see 'empowered' people. 'Empowerment' is a recently used word specifically to describe the confidence and moral courage to take the intiative. This is only developed and promoted by effective leadership.

Third, leadership is more than daily and routine episodic leadership (for leadership given in minor episodes of life—see Chapter 14). Leadership involves taking responsibility to ensure that people's welfare and needs (both as a team and individually) are met. That means participation, training, career management—that responsibility cannot be abdicated to each individual if any sort of loyalty or team spirit is to be expected. This is summarised in the functional approach to leadership in Chapter 5.

Fourth, from experience, four people is the maximum number that true democracy seems to operate in and that only applies when all the members are highly trained, motivated, and of equal intellect and ability—and even with four a casting vote might be necessary. It is for this reason that Special Air Service (SAS) teams work in teams of four since they operate in very tough conditions behind enemy lines with little support and they need each team member to be totally committed to a course of action. This phenomenon has also been observed by Dr Belbin, formerly chairman of Industrial Training, Research Unit, now a private company, once part of University College, London.[2]

It is not possible for a large team of, say, 12 to operate without a leader or, in the case of one company that I have encountered, with leadership actively suppressed. Teams need leaders who can ensure that the aim is achieved and the tasks completed, and that can operate within the ground rules, the disciplinary code.

All teams look for leadership and if it is not present because no leader has been appointed then a natural leader will emerge to fill the vacuum. Each team needs someone to both:

1. Take responsibility for looking after the interests of the individuals within the team.

2. Take responsibility for the continuation of the team to ensure the team's survival.

It is expected that an appointed leader will undertake all these responsibilities. That person must see that the job gets done and must look to the good of the team and the well-being of the members by always putting the interests of the team before his or her own.

When an individual's personal objectives coincide with those of the team, then individual commitment and motivation will always be higher. So leaders must know individual team member's needs, aspirations and values, and where possible, link them to those of the team.

LEADERSHIP AND THE HIGH PERFORMING TEAM

Figure 4.1 illustrates the key features in addition to the six characteristics mentioned earlier that differentiate a team from a high performing one. Note that the development of these features is a function of leadership. A leader usually satisfies all of the following requirements since the absence of any induces stresses that eventually erodes the effectiveness of the team

- The necessary number of members to achieve the mission and to perform the tasks allocated in the timescale needed.
- Members with the competence (behaviour, skills, and knowledge) that matches their job.
- Well-motivated individuals whose interest is stimulated and whose needs are satisfied by the type of work undertaken and the climate in which it is conducted. This could include internal rivalry or competition to raise standards. Keeping a perspective on competition and cooperation prevents destructive competition developing.
- Open, honest, and clear communication that prevents misunderstandings and promotes trust. Implicit in this is the moral courage and confidence to face up to weaknesses and say what you would like to without fear.
- Reciprocal confidence and trust among members—timely and firm conflict resolution, the integrity (honesty, unselfishness, sincerity, and reliability) of individuals, reciprocal support and encouragement to help others within the team and loyalty are implicit in this.
- Clarity of individual role and team task and mission that prevents wasted effort and resources and assists in building trust.
- Sound training to ensure that the team and its members remain fit for the team's role.

Figure 4.1 Characteristics of Teams

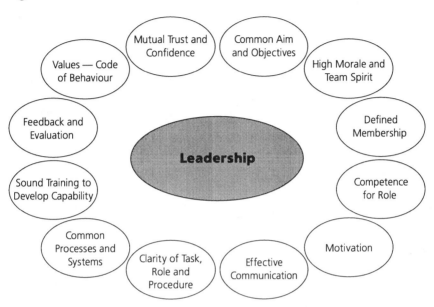

© Leading Initiatives (Australia) Pty Limited 1996

- Regular reviews, feedback and evaluation to ensure clarity is maintained, a continuous passage of information, recognition of effort and performance, and to raise standards.
- Common processes, systems and terminology, especially a common problem-solving and decision-making process, to promote the efficiency of the team.

THE ROLE OF DISCIPLINE IN THE CREATION OF A TEAM

> The best form of discipline is the subordination of self for the benefit of the community.

Discipline, or restraint on behaviour, is highlighted as one of the necessary elements in converting a team from a group of people. It is explained in more detail in Chapter 16.

'LIBERTY IMPLIES DISCIPLINE'

Slim uses the example of choice.[3] You can take your car or bicycle, you can choose where you want to go, your own destination. This, he says, is liberty! But, as you drive or ride through the streets towards your destination, you will keep to the correct side of the road. That is common sense and self-discipline. It ensures that you follow the convention of keeping to the correct side of the road. This illustrates the link between liberty and discipline. You accept this convention because it ensures your own safety and it is accepted by others for the same reason.

For the system to work, however, everyone has to trust in the common sense of others to follow. We also recognise that we can be charged for failing to adhere to the convention.

There are, thus, four reasons why you keep to the correct side of the road:

1. Your own advantage.
2. Consideration for others.
3. Confidence in your fellows.
4. Fear of punishment.

> Whenever we put a curb on our natural desire to do as we like, whenever we temper liberty with discipline, we do so for one or more of those reasons. It is the relative weight we give to each of these reasons that decides what sort of discipline we have. And that can vary from the pure self-discipline of the Sermon on the Mount to the discipline of the concentration camp—the enforced discipline of fear.
>
> *Field Marshal Slim[3]*

The road safety analogy gives a clear indication of the vital importance of having clear rules to get everyone in the team working effectively to achieve whatever task has been set.

Leaders should ensure that the rules are kept and use rules to assist them in keeping teams together. If you lack moral courage to apply the rules to all the members of your team consistently by letting things slip you lose respect of the team members who do maintain the standards and you risk the disintegration of the team.

It is this personal acceptance of the rules and your commitment to the group that, as leader, you must strive to obtain from every single member of your team.

GROUP DYNAMICS

Whenever a number of people are thrown together, whether by accident or design, as in a team, it is inevitable that friendships are formed. Those with similar interests or background get together and within the formal organisation of the team there are numbers of informal groups whose membership and, often, interests change over time, but that settle into patterns of behaviour that are acceptable to each other. Recall these groups from your own experience in business, at school, or at university? This development of informal groups of association is known as 'group dynamics' and in a well-led team the leader who understands group dynamics can take advantage of them because:

- The informal groups can blend well into the formal organisation to get jobs done by interpreting 'rules' in a practical, rather than a slavish, way.
- They can accept delegation and thereby lighten a leader's load.
- They can sometimes be useful as unofficial communication channels.
- They can encourage cooperation among individuals.
- They can be helpful in the planning and introduction of change.

In this competitive age competition drives us to improve standards. Leaders need to ensure that informal groups can recognise and can identify with the aims and missions of the teams. In this way the informal groups will cooperate to get the task in hand completed. Competition is natural among groups and one way for leaders to harness this competitive spirit is to identify to teams an 'outside enemy'.

Competition or a healthy rivalry among teams within the same organisation can be used to raise standards, but cooperation among these teams is vital, so the leader must ensure that constructive competition does not become destructive or hinder progress. There is a fine line that leaders must be aware of between constructive and destructive competition. Remember that ultimately you are competing against an external business rival, not each other.

In a poorly led organisation the informal groups can create problems by:

- **Resisting change.** You must be aware in yourself of a certain resentment when, for whatever reason, a new routine or working practice is imposed upon you. Whatever it is, when the change occurs, until you have settled into the new routine, you feel resentful. Badly handled group dynamics can lead to resentment growing, rather than diminishing.

- **Conflict of aims.** The informal groups provide members with social satisfaction. These social groupings can develop aims that conflict with the organisation's own. For instance, group members may find their own social interaction so rewarding that they begin returning late from tea breaks or they may be continually looking for opportunities to 'slope off'.
- **Rumour.** Informal groups often set up a 'grapevine' to communicate with one another and this can lead to the circulation of rumours and distorted information.

THE TEAM APPROACH

My most important discovery was of how valuable it is, in any project or operation, civil or military, to enlist the help and ideas of other people . . .

General Sir Peter de la Billière[4]

Working in teams in which participation by all is encouraged and discussion is welcomed produces the best results in certain kinds of situations, such as:

- Problems that have many different facets, or that require different skills, information, and knowledge.
- Decisions that require judgement, rather than factual analysis.
- Pooling and building on different ideas before reaching a decision.
- Gaining acceptance of a decision and commitment to its implementation.

The excessive participation of all the individuals in a team in decision making may be less productive for:

- Simple routine tasks or problems.
- Problems that have a 'correct' solution.
- Problems where it is difficult to demonstrate the solution to members.
- Problems requiring subtle logical reasoning.

The use of teams not only has implications for making decisions, but also for their implementation. We are more likely to carry out a decision that we have been involved in making. But, beware of all talk and no action.

Your employees might be members of several teams—in addition to their permanent role they might have temporary places in project teams. We give of our best when we are involved in the decision-making and planning process. The degree of the involvement depends on our ability, the nature of the task, and the time available for debate before action is needed. So it is in teams.

While poor leadership abounds people naturally want to be consulted in all matters. When an effective and capable leader has the trust and confidence of his or her team it is not unnatural for team members to be happy to participate less in minor decisions—they know that the right decision will be made. This reduction in discussion makes the team more efficient. A benevolent dictatorship can work, but only with highly effective well-trained leaders that are trusted by, and who have the confidence of, everyone within their teams!

STAGES OF TEAM DEVELOPMENT

The task of building and leading a team is made much easier if we are aware of how they develop over time. All teams are living entities or organisms; they are dynamic—continuously developing and changing in response to certain factors. Those factors are either internal or external and include:

External factors
- Changing markets and business needs.
- New organisational structures.
- New technology.

Internal factors
- Changes in team membership—people leaving or joining.
- Changing relationships within the team.
- The personal growth or maturation of team members.

Researchers such as Tuckman and Jensen[5] investigated this developmental process and suggest that any group or team usually evolves through several well-defined stages in the process from initial formation to full maturity. Only when a team reaches its mature stage can it be fully effective in successfully achieving task requirements through the

Figure 4.2

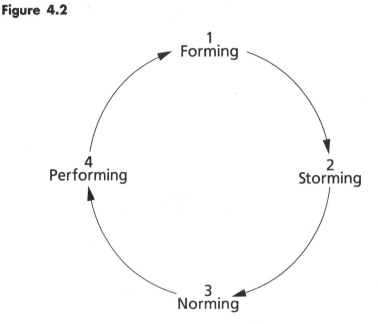

coordinated efforts of committed team members. This process becomes cyclical since leaders always want to improve performance and that means ongoing evolution of the team. Those stages of development that become cyclical are, to use Tuckman and Jensen's terminology:

At each of these stages the team must resolve issues about both the task and their social relationships.

Forming

During the forming stage the leader brings the individual team members together. Frequently, some want to impress his or her personality on the team while its processes, team composition and organisation, are being established.

Individuals try to learn about each other's attitudes and abilities, background and experience, and also any established norms of the team. Many people are cautious about introducing new ideas and respect the established way of doing things; they do not want to appear radical or unacceptable to the team. The mission or task, aim, and objectives, may be unclear.

Storming

The storming stage often involves some conflict, open or concealed, among individual team members. People might question the aim, objectives, 'rules', and norms. In a new team, or on a new project, this can be beneficial since more realistic things could emerge and trust starts to develop among team members.

There is likely to be disagreement within the team about some issues. Possibly there could even be a split within the team.

Norming

After the storming, as mutual trust and confidence grows, the team starts to settle in. People identify with the team and consider themselves full members. With good leadership this becomes devotion, pride, and loyalty. Higher standards, new and different procedures and roles may evolve and become accepted. These enable the team to carry out its task and enable its members to work in harmony as a cohesive team. Communication permits an open exchange of ideas and members are willing to listen and to respect the views and perspectives of others. Figure 4.3 illustrates a template for teamwork, that is, the factors that permit a team to perform to its potential.

Performing

By this stage the team has resolved both task and working relationship issues, and has established a flexible and functional way of doing

Figure 4.3 Tozer's Teamwork Template

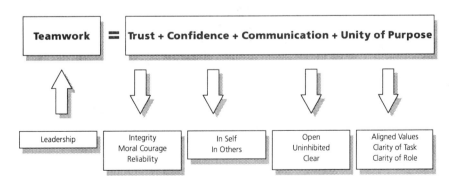

© Leading Initiatives (Australia) Pty Limited 1996

things. Personality clashes, if not reconciled, are understood—not everyone likes everyone else, nor do they have to, mutual respect, however, is necessary. The leader can now channel all the team's energy into the task.

Reforming

By establishing a culture or daily way of thinking that promotes learning, continuous improvement, innovation and change, ever higher standards can be reached. This may involve changing the composition of the team, or the role of its members in which case the process starts again, but should evolve to maturity rather more rapidly. Indeed the more frequently people go through and understand this process, the easier and quicker it becomes.

Cohesiveness

Cohesiveness, in essence, is the attractiveness of the team to its members. It determines the extent of the members' contributions to the team and the efforts that they will make on the team's behalf. The factors affecting cohesion are:

- **Contact and communication.** The opportunity to make regular contact with one another, their physical proximity in relation to each other, and the flow of understood open, and clear communication, based on facts, not assumptions or rumours.
- **The similarity of the work.** Similar work produces similar challenges around which people can unite and bond.
- **The incentive system (individual or team).** The way people are remunerated and are recognised can stimulate self-centred, or team-centred, behaviour.
- **Compatibility of individuals.** People like people who are like themselves. Homogeneity of values, social expectations, and so on, adds to compatibility.
- **Size of team.** Too large a team (usually more than 10 to 12) makes activities impersonal and does not lead or assist in providing 'the tribal identity' of smaller teams.
- **External threat.** A common threat always unites a group of people. Consider the effect of disparate people in the USSR or UK in the Second World War.
- **Leadership.** The magic word that this book is all about.

Highly cohesive teams support and protect their members, especially against any influence from outside the team. They also have more influence over the behaviour of team members as the general level of conformity to norms increases with the level of cohesiveness. This cohesion may show itself in united team action that can be used to the advantage or disadvantage of the organisation.

It is possible for a team to be too cohesive; too concerned with its own maintenance, membership and priorities, and focussed solely on its own needs. It can become dangerously blinkered as to what is going on around it and may confidently forge ahead in completely the wrong direction. The leader has to watch for such signs and take corrective action. Some of those signs are:

- Destructive competition or negative thoughts about other teams in the organisation.
- Complacency and a sense of invulnerability—blindness to the risk involved in 'pet' strategies, or repeating 'proven' formulae.
- Rationalisation of inconsistent facts, blaming others for mistakes regardless.
- Moral blindness—the 'might is right', the 'we are never wrong' sort of attitude.
- A tendency to stereotype non-team members as 'enemies'.
- Strong team pressure to squash dissent and anything 'different'.
- Self-censorship by members—not 'rocking the boat', refusing to say what is right and what needs to be said.
- Perception of unanimity—filtering out divergent views that question what is the accepted 'norm'.

References

1. James Strong, *The Australian Way* (Qantas Airways Magazine), October 1994.
2. R. Meredith Belbin, 1981, *Management Teams—why they succeed or fail*, Oxford: Butterworth-Heinemann.
3. Field Marshal Sir William Slim, 1957, *Courage And Other Broadcasts*, London: Cassell.
4. General Sir Peter de la Billière, 1994, *Looking For Trouble*, London: HarperCollins.
5. B. Tuckman and M. Jensen, 1977, 'Stages of Small group development revisited', *Group and Organizational Studies*, pp. 419–427. Also see B. Tuckman, 'Development sequence in small groups', *Psychological Bulletin*, vol. 63 (1965), pp. 384–399.

CHAPTER 5

THE FUNCTIONAL APPROACH TO LEADERSHIP

> In looking at the bare essentials of leadership I think not in terms of personality but in terms of what the leader has to do, they have to communicate, they have to involve people, they have to be prepared to work as a member of the team. The big part of leadership is getting people on side, getting things done and making things happen whilst keeping plans simple.
>
> *John Quinn, Managing Director, Thorn Lighting Pty Ltd*

While most, if not all, approaches to developing leadership are valid, the functional approach is, from my experience, the most effective. The purpose here is to give you, the aspiring leader, an understanding of what a leader does—the leader's real role and full range of responsibilities—in order to help you train yourself, increase your own confidence, and develop further your own leadership potential. The functional approach provides you with a method of observing other leaders' performance critically and measuring your practical leadership ability against theirs. It provides a model against which skills can be learnt while personal qualities and character are developed. If it forms the basis for training and development, observations that are fed back to the trainee are objective, not subjective. (This can be considered 'a development centre approach; more on training in Chapter 21.)

THE FUNCTIONAL APPROACH

Firstly, here is some of the background to the model. The ideas that go to make up this approach to the subject were developed at The Royal Military Academy Sandhurst in the UK in the 1960s as a result of studies carried out on the leadership course that was being conducted at that time by Professor John Adair and senior instructors. That study revolutionised the understanding of leadership. The ideas spread worldwide, and were adopted by many military academies, business schools, and corporate organisations. In the UK it was adopted by the Industrial Society and renamed 'Action Centred Leadership'.

THE ORIGINS

The essence of the functional approach has been an analysis of studies of group behaviour to extract exactly what it is that leaders do.

During the past 50 or so years there have been many studies of the behaviour of people who are grouped together, both voluntarily and compulsorily. You have already read about 'Groups and Teams' in Chapter 4 where you were introduced to the idea that the interaction among individuals produces forces and stresses that are often put together under the heading of 'group dynamics'. Within this framework of group behaviour certain patterns repeat themselves whatever the behaviour of the group leader. It seems that people in a group need a leader and there is always someone who, to some level or other, emerges to demonstrate the necessary behaviour to satisfy the group at the time. It was with the identification of these leader behaviours that John Adair produced his theory of functional leadership.

THE THEORY

Adair proposes[1,2] that working groups are like individual people in that they developed their own unique character sharing specific needs in common. He states that there are three main areas where a leader has to act to satisfy the requirements of a group for leadership. These three areas coincide with the pattern of needs generated by the group.

Firstly, a group needs an external focus, normally a task to complete that, unsurprisingly, should be successfully achieved. Failure introduces pressures that, in a group with no formal or disciplined structure, can lead to members leaving or, in the worst case, can lead to the complete disintegration of the group. If opportunities to leave do not exist you get an increase in personality conflicts within the group, a decline in general morale, and a falling-off of efficiency. You do find that both the team and individuals' real strengths and weaknesses—their true character—are more vividly seen in conditions of adversity than in good times. The leader's function, your function, is to ensure that each task given to the group to complete is successfully completed.

Second, a group has certain needs if it is to survive as a cohesive social entity. In the first place, once a group has formed, the dynamics of the situation operate to hold it together. You might be aware of the strong bonds of loyalty that have begun to hold your own team together at work. Do you really, voluntarily, have much to do with the people in other work groups in your lunch breaks or do you remain with your own team?

If you are honest, you will probably admit that actually it is 'just that I seem to be happier getting on with the people in my team'. You see group dynamics are at work in your life. Thus, the leader, second, has to satisfy the needs of his or her group, it is the leader's task to ensure its survival. In realistic terms this means helping it to develop a corporate identity, to forge it into a 'winning team'. If there is a lack of unity or poor relationships within the team then, again, individual satisfaction and task performance suffer. Uniting to face a common external threat or to extinguish internal disruptive behaviour that contravenes 'the norms' is commonly seen as a way of a team maintaining its cohesion.

Third, you must remember that a group is composed of a number of individuals and that each of those individuals has his or her own particular needs in addition to those generated by the group. The task, remember, has to be completed by a group of individuals and they each need to feel that their contribution to the group is recognised and is important. Their individual need for status and responsibility has to be catered for, thus the leader satisfies their physical, emotional, and psychological, needs. This is considered in more depth under motivation in Chapter 12.

THE THREE CIRCLES MODEL

The three areas of a leader's function can be represented by three circles:

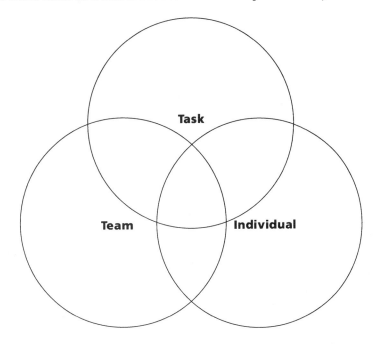

That the three circles overlap indicates their interdependence. If you cover the task you can see that sectors of both team maintenance and individual needs are also covered. In short, lack of a task, or failure to achieve it, leads to both:

    a. Increased disruptive tendencies within the team, and
    b. A decrease in individual satisfaction with membership of the team.

Thus morale, motivation, and discipline, deteriorate if this situation is allowed to continue.

Similar interactions can be observed by covering the other two circles in turn.

The converse is also true. When a team successfully completes a task the degree of group cohesiveness and identity increases, as does the level of individual satisfaction with membership. The moment of victory closes the gaps, emotionally and psychologically, among people and it always generates a rise in the level of morale, pride, and *esprit de corps*.

Therefore, when past success has raised the sustained level of morale and team spirit, the momentum has been generated that probably makes future success more probable. This also provides a healthy climate in which individuals can work.

The three areas of need must be balanced against each other; to satisfy one completely will probably be to the detriment of the other two. If this happens, a short-term focus on, say, task needs, must soon be balanced by a focus on satisfying the individual and team needs. The negative effects of continuous task orientation shown by staff turnover, loss of knowledge and expertise, lack of individual satisfaction or team cohesion, seem to have been recognised by some companies, although recognition of the fact is very different from tangible action.

The leader has to perform certain functions if he or she is to satisfy all the areas of need that exist; in short the leader must be continuously aware of the real scope of the role and its responsibilities. This is where so many 'managers' are lacking—through no fault of their own; no one has trained them or even explained the full range of responsibilities that a leader must, by definition, accept willingly. Recall in Chapter 1 that the notion that this book covers is two facets of leadership—what you have to be, the display of personal qualities and what you have to do, the basic functions of leadership—have been introduced. Here I outline this latter component of leadership. No matter what industry a leader works in, in addition to the role-specific job description, this functional check-list needs to be added, understood, and applied.

The functional leadership check-list is a simple matrix that shows the actions that need to be taken to satisfy the three areas of need—task, team, individual—during the six key sequential phases of any task or project (planning, briefing, controlling and coordinating, supporting and enabling, informing, evaluating) (see Table 5.1). For a one-off project this is the essential project management tool, for an ongoing task the check-list becomes cyclical. As soon as you have evaluated a result you may need to re-plan, re-brief, and so on.

At the lowest level of leader in an organisation, familiarity with this check-list does much to improve the aspiring leader's ability. A common use of this approach assists in closing the gap between 'management' and 'supervisors'. The check-list is also the foundation for all further leadership development since almost every other subject studied has application in one or more of the check-list 'boxes', thus, by understanding this entire book you have done much to acquire the

Table 5.1 The Functional Leadership Check-list

Phases	Achieve TASK	Build/Maintain TEAM	Develop/Satisfy INDIVIDUALS
	(a)	(b)	(c)
Planning	Define the task Obtain information Make appreciation of situation Make a plan	Involve team in planning Detail Groups Appoint sub leaders Recruit/select	Assess the skill potential of each person Use knowledge and expertise of individuals to assist in making the plan
Briefing	State aim Explain the plan	Give clear briefings Explain reason for task Set standards/priorities	Delegate Check that individuals understand the plan Perception
Controlling and Coordinating	Ensure that all activity is directed towards achieving the aim Monitor progress Re-plan if necessary	Coordinate Maintain standards	Maintain standards
Supporting, Coaching and Enabling	Provide resources	Maintain team spirit Build morale Coach the team	Encourage individuals Criticise constructively Ensure good administration Coach
Informing	Keep yourself informed of progress in all areas, and informed of the 'big picture'	Keep team informed of progress Ensure communication within the team	Thank and praise
Evaluating	Review tasking Has aim been achieved? Measure/compare benchmarks	Recognise success Learn from failure Identify training needs	Listen to feedback Assess performance Recognise and reward Identify training needs

knowledge that, with experience of practical application, will propel you towards greater leadership effectiveness.

In many teams the leader does not have sufficient time to exercise all these functions, nor is it desirable for him or her to do so—delegation is a great involving mechanism, motivator, and developer. The leader has to accept and to exercise responsibility, however, for ensuring that all these functions are completed.

As a leader you are also a member of the team, but somewhat removed from it. This has to be if you are to view the team in the context of the 'bigger picture' and take the hard decisions that inevitably arise. The inexperienced leader may try to be liked by his or her team, this is a serious error—the leader needs to be respected, but not necessarily liked. The leader relieves other team members from the burden of decision and of responsibility. This can never be given away nor shared and it is one of the factors that differentiates the leader and the led.

There are two further aspects of leadership that you must be aware of. Firstly, leading itself. All this theory and knowledge of how to organise a task is useless if you lack the courage to direct or to coordinate appropriately. You, as leader, must be prepared to take the lead. Some people find it difficult initially, but it does become easier with knowledge, confidence, and experience (which builds greater confidence), so take every possible opportunity to practise your leadership. Second, communication—this is an essential ingredient to everything a leader does. Without effective communication you cannot carry out many of the leader's functions.

- express yourself clearly, both orally and in writing
- be prepared to listen
- find out about your team and the individuals in it
- the state of your task.

This is all you need to know about the functional theory of leadership, but do remember that theory is there to provide you with an insight into your own, and others', behaviour when in positions of leadership and to offer you a method of planning how to lead a successful, well-knit team of satisfied individuals. Your own personal style and judgement develops with experience. For the present, the new or junior leader is advised to concentrate on the mechanics because even things that seem common sense in the tranquillity of thought can go sadly wrong in the heat of the moment. Use the check-list. Learn it so well that it becomes second nature to recall it mentally every time you find yourself in a leadership role. Why not make a small copy and keep it in your pocket at all times while you become familiar with it? After you have referred to it a few times it will soon be an automatic way of effectively handling any situation—when applied with common sense and a display of the qualities discussed in the next chapter.

References

1. Professor John Adair, 1973, *Action Centred Leadership*, London: The McGraw-Hill Book Company.
2. Professor John Adair, 1983, *Effective Leadership*, Aldershot: Gower.

CHAPTER 6

PERSONAL QUALITIES OF LEADERSHIP: INSPIRATION, CHARISMA AND TRUST

> We must endeavour to produce, on every level, commanders with the qualities of leadership and character which inspire confidence in others. . .we must then develop his good points and teach him to keep his bad points in subjection.
>
> *Field Marshal Montgomery on leadership*

PERSONAL QUALITIES OF LEADERSHIP

Leaders all have readily recognisable and distinguishing qualities. At the highest level John Harvey-Jones (former Chairman of ICI), Rupert Murdoch (News Corporation), Winston Churchill, or servicemen such as Montgomery, Patton, Slim, or Lord Nelson, prove this. That we think of the highest levels of leadership in this context is owing to the fact that these leaders are recognised by most of us and their lives are well documented. It does not diminish the necessity for these qualities at lower levels where the raw material of their profession remains the same—people; but it does magnify the effect of character or personality in the exercise of leadership. It must be remembered that the lower level is the training ground in which the seeds of future success are laid as leaders develop and prepare themselves for higher office—perhaps even the highest in their field of expertise.

Historically, 'leaders' in the services (officers) were expected to be 'gentlemen', indeed the Army Act in Britain still prescribes the penalties for 'conduct unbecoming the character of an officer and a gentlemen'. Wellington insisted that his officers were gentlemen: 'The description of gentlemen of whom the Officers of the Army were composed made, from their education, manners and habits, the best Officers in the world. . .' (quoted in E.S. Turner[1]) because inherent in the accepted meaning of that word are many of the qualities that are discussed in this chapter.

The notion that there are two facets of leadership—what you have to do and what you need to be is outlined in Chapter 1 and part of the template is described in Chapter 5. Here we consider the second part of that template, the personal qualities, or character, expected of leaders. The emphasis is on character (that part of personality that is valued by followers and by which a person is judged), not charisma. Charisma is explored at the end of this chapter. It is by displaying these qualities that you set the personal example for others to follow.

The problem with studying the qualities of leaders is that while all leaders have certain attributes that we can list, few leaders, if any, have the same qualities developed to the same level. But leaders usually reflect and exemplify those things that are expected in members within their team and that are demanded by the situation or context within which work is done. Hence, the earlier assertion that leadership is individual in its nature and in its application. Indeed, if we ask two leaders to list what qualities they consider important in leadership we would get two different answers.

A base level of certain qualities, however, is common: what varies is the strength of each component in the final blend. It is these qualities that leaders need to grasp the importance of and seek to develop by gaining an understanding of their own strengths and weaknesses. To develop such qualities is not easy without objective assessment and guidance from your immediate superiors and they would need to be experienced and capable leaders. How these qualities may be developed by training is discussed in Chapter 21.

> . . . leaders are largely made but the very good leaders have something a little bit extra in their character.
>
> *Sir Robin Knox-Johnston*
>
> We must remember that there are people who simply want to do a good job and get paid, they don't want the responsibility that any form of leadership entails. In Australia, we continue to take the best operator and make him or her the worst manager.
>
> *Karen Lonergan, Education & Development*
> *Manager, Castrol Australia*

Some leadership qualities are innate in each selected leader in different degrees; some must be learnt, and most can be developed by thought and practice. As we have said, many great leaders have drawn up lists, few are the same, but most include some or all of those attributes described in the following pages. While they are not in any order of importance, the first three, moral courage, integrity, and loyalty, are essential for reasons that will be shown.

MORAL COURAGE

> Courage is rightly esteemed the first among all qualities; it is the quality that guarantees all others
>
> *Winston Churchill*
>
> The daily choice of right instead of wrong
>
> *Aristotle*

Courage, in the sense of moral courage, is an essential leadership quality. It is important that we know what the differences between moral and physical courage are: physical courage drives someone on to risk pain, injury, and death. Everyone has at least some physical courage. In his book *Anatomy of Courage*[2] Lord Moran an adviser to Churchill, likened courage to a bank balance; you can draw on it, but if you overdraw, you break down—the strain has been too much. A person then has to be given time and assistance to recover.

Moral Courage is absolutely essential for long term success, the willingness to say 'something is not right therefore I will not do it' has led many good men to be dismissed but such an attitude is far more likely to win in the long term. The understanding of the meaning of moral courage comes from home, school and society.

Sir Robin Knox-Johnston

Moral courage is more important in managing relationships upwards rather than in leading those below you.

Chris Walsh, Operations Director, David Jones Limited

Moral courage stems from a cool, thinking approach that makes you do something because it is right, correct, and necessary, to do even if it is difficult, unpopular, or distasteful to implement. This is moral courage, but it needs to be taught and practised because it is not a natural part of most people's make up. Every time leaders display moral courage their characters are strengthened and it becomes easy to repeat in the future. Whenever leaders fail to exercise that quality, perhaps thinking that little things do not matter, they are less capable of displaying it when it is really needed—the stock of moral courage has not built up. Displaying moral courage is a deliberate and calculated decision.

Leaders must have the moral courage to take unpopular, difficult, but necessary, decisions and to implement them if they come from above as if they were their own. Of course, the 'reasons why' must be explained, but you must pass all decisions on as if they were your own and you must support them, as leader. To do otherwise is to display a lack of loyalty overtly to both your organisation and to your superiors.

To try to pass responsibility for arriving at and/or implementing such a decision does nothing to convince your team of the rightness and the necessity of that decision. Instead it shows that you, as a leader, lack willpower, loyalty to your superiors, and self-confidence. It is also a breach of your integrity and this will, therefore lead to the loss of respect of your followers for you. The result is a break in trust between you and your team. Leaders must have the courage of their convictions, stand their ground and fight their case; but when discussion is over, a decision is made, and action is to be taken then leaders have to do their duty however unpalatable it is—that is what leaders are paid for.

> Bad news in organisations is seldom received with much enthusiasm. It is all too easy to get people who will tell you nice things. . .
>
> *John Harvey-Jones*[3]

Leaders have to have and exercise considerable moral courage from time to time in maintaining standards because accepting sloppy standards is the start of a downward spiral that ultimately leads to a loss of existing accounts and future business opportunities. It is fundamentally wrong not to strive for improvement and improvement always takes courage and drive.

> To teach moral courage is another matter and it has to be taught because so few, if any, have it naturally. The young men can learn it from their parents, in their home, from school and university, from religion, from other early influences, but to inculcate it in a grown-up who lacks it, requires not so much teaching as some striking emotional experience—something that suddenly bursts upon him; something in the nature of a vision. That rarely happens, and that is why you will find that most men with moral courage learnt it by precept and example in their youth.
>
> *Field Marshal Slim*[4]

Junior leaders and inexperienced managers need moral courage particularly:

- When dealing with older subordinates that are not performing adequately and who often have strong personalities.
- Maintaining standards in a new team—despite what the previous 'boss' used to allow.
- In taking responsibility for passing on unpopular decisions that must be done with loyalty to the leader's superior and company.
- Giving honest feedback and in conducting performance appraisals.
- Speaking out in meetings when experienced managers, specialists, or senior executives, are present.

All leadership and management training is designed to develop our ability to manage the testing situations that come with the ebb and flow of business. Unpopular decisions have to be made, even though they may ultimately benefit the organisation. It takes moral courage to make and to pass on these decisions, especially to those who have to execute them. Moral courage is not the peculiar prerogative of business, political, and military leaders: indeed, the need for it constantly arises in any walk of life that demands acceptance of responsibility. The greater the responsibility, the greater the degree of moral courage demanded.

> I worked in a consumer packaged goods company that had problems with a brand that was a leader in other markets. It was failing badly because the variant sold in Australia was made in Japan and had four languages on the packaging—and English was not prominent. The sales force repeatedly passed on the customer and consumer view that the packaging was hated. All sorts of brand salvation measures were tried and the sales force was forced to continue to embarrass themselves by pushing something no one wanted. Eventually the product was withdrawn and after a considerable time lag, a US-manufactured version was relaunched. A combination of moral cowardice, exacerbated by an inflexible regional policy, were to blame for the pointless waste of time, money, energy, and unnecessary damage to the company image.
>
> *The author*

One can see the moral cowardice in action in the UK over further European Community integration, the common agricultural policy, and monetary union. Many rational economists would argue that fixing artificial prices and paying farmers not to grow anything is a recipe for disaster—no commercial entity pays employees not to produce anything, and a large percentage of voters are alarmed at their powerless loss of sovereignty. Yet no political party leader has the courage to give the people a choice via a referendum. There would seem to be too many vested interests at stake, yet a union can never succeed when one party is dragged screaming to the table. Unions among states occur when the countries' values and aims are in alignment and this cannot be legislated for, it has to happen naturally. No British political leader has come forward to say a mistake has, or may have, been made and provided an opportunity for the country to settle the matter.

Moral courage and integrity are closely linked—they are at the very core of leadership. You cannot be a good leader without both of these qualities. You behave like a good leader if your attitude and reasoning are based on sound principles; if you have integrity and practise moral courage you have a good start.

INTEGRITY

This is perhaps the trickiest area of all to discuss because of the nebulous and intangible nature of the concept. It is simple enough to look up the definition of the word. Indeed, three dictionaries in the library give:

- *Websters' Third New International Dictionary of the English Language*, G. & C. Merriam & Co., Encyclopaedia Britannica, 1981: 'Adherence to a moral code, artistic or other values.'
- *The Chambers Dictionary*, Edinburgh: C. Harrap Publishers Ltd, 1993: 'The unimpaired state of anything, uprightness, honesty, purity.'
- *The Concise Oxford English Dictionary of Current English*, 8th edn, Clarendon Press, Oxford, 1990: 'The character or moral virtue especially in relation to truth and fair dealing.'

As you can see, these authorities are not unanimous in their definitions, but make some reference to 'values', directly or indirectly, by talking of honesty and truth. Sometimes considering the roots of a word helps us to understand the meaning. 'Integrity' comes from the Latin word *integer* meaning 'whole' or 'untouched'. In this more abstract field of leadership, integrity's 'wholeness' takes the form of being 'untouched' or 'uncorrupted'.

Integrity embraces the combination of the virtues of honesty, sincerity, reliability, unselfishness, and loyalty without which the leader cannot gain the trust and respect of superiors, peers, or those people that the leader is privileged to lead. Integrity is absolute. It has to be innate and it is not something that can be taught late in life. Leaders' loyalty must extend upwards to support superiors, sideways to support peers, and downwards to look after the interests of subordinates. Your duty as a leader is to your team and organisation always before yourself—remember (Chapter 1) 'Serve to Lead'. Loyalty, a component of integrity, is treated separately here and in Chapter 17 as it is such an important subject in its own right.

Where does integrity come from? Every society provides its

members with a culture that derives from an overall set of beliefs, values, and standards. In most cultures these have become institutionalised within the predominant religion of the society. Thus Western countries conform to a set of principles that guides the formation of attitudes and patterns of behaviour of the people who are brought up there. This is not to say that attitudes and behaviours do not alter, but there is, throughout, an underlying knowledge within all of us of what is evil and wrong and also what is proper and right.

To a large extent it is the atmosphere and culture within which we grow up that moulds our attitudes and standards. Since some families hold stronger beliefs than others, and the social structure or norms that evolve from many government policies and public institutions also affect personal growth, varying standards can arise within a society as a consequence. Standards of behaviour and attitudes have, in many ways, relaxed since the 1960s, but the underlying values have remained constant and act as our frames of reference or conscience for the interpretation of experience. Such values control the perception of people and events and drive the behavioural and attitudinal response to situations.

In practical terms what are the implications for leaders? At its simplest we are interested in the choice between right and wrong. This might seem easy, but in the real world there are many pressures upon us to conform, to take an easy way out. The 'no compromise' case can be a hard one to put forward!

Often the issues in a case are not clear-cut but, even where they are, decisions based solely upon conscience can be lonely ones to make and are liable to misinterpretation and, often to attack by others. Take the hypothetical case of a young accountant who, on arrival at her job, found her 'boss was fiddling expenses'. Acting according to conscience she reported him and then found herself under pressure from the company to withdraw her statement as she had 'rocked the boat'. At the inquiry she was slandered by the Defence that suggested her actions were governed by spite. Even after the matter was closed she was unable to resume her normal career because she was 'seen' as the girl who had 'grassed'. Doubtless you are familiar with many real and similar incidents—society often seems to hold hypocritical standards.

In practical terms leaders' integrity revolves around scrupulous fairness, being honest, behaving honourably and sincerely at all times. Faith is strongly allied to integrity as the integrity of leaders generates faith and trust in them from both their subordinates and their superiors. Faith may not be religious: it may be faith in our own country, faith in the organisation, or faith in the justness of actions. Many of history's greatest leaders have a credo based upon ideals that are higher than the material.

Leaders' own standards of behaviour have to be beyond reproach because leaders set the example for others to follow. Leaders must always be truthful and must always feel that their superiors mean what they say. The key word is trust: if people cannot trust you you will never be a leader, either good or bad. To be trusted you must be respected and, to be respected, you must have integrity.

Characteristics of Integrity

Here is a summary of the characteristics of integrity.

- **Be straight.** Be honourable and reliable; be just and fair, do not say one thing and do another; avoid sarcasm or cynicism.
- **Be honest.** Do not give misleading statements, steal or 'acquire' other people's property, recognition or ideas, do not fiddle expenses or tax returns; do not avoid paying fares on public transport; do not buy obviously stolen property on the cheap.
- **Be humble and unselfish.** Confess and own up to your own errors or omissions and do not blame others; do not boast or make snide remarks; be generous in victory and defeat; think of service to others not self—place your own interests last.
- **Be sincere.** Be entirely yourself, honour your own faults, and be prepared to admit them and to try to correct them. People tend to follow sincere leaders even if they are mistaken, possibly through inexperience because the teams will try to help them along. It is not weak to accept advice, so long as the ultimate decision is the leaders'.
- **Be reliable.** Ensure that you keep to your word, honour any promises or guarantees that you have made, and ensure that you meet the expectations that others have of you. See things through—be accountable for your work and for solving problems that you discover on the way.
- **Be loyal.** Leaders must be loyal to their teams and accept members' errors or mistakes as their own—team members will not trust leaders if they 'pass the buck', likewise leaders must loyally support the decisions or actions of their superiors and peers if they are to retain their trust.

Loyalty

Loyalty is being faithful or true to allegiance, and is an essential part of integrity. Leaders have allegiance to their superiors, subordinates, and their colleagues. Ultimately though, their loyalty is to their organisations.

Directions, once agreed (you may agree to disagree), should be obeyed both in the letter and in the spirit. This particularly applies to unpopular decisions that you, as a leader, must pass onto your subordinates without criticism of your seniors as if they came from you. Only then can you expect the same loyalty from your subordinates.

There will be some directions or decisions with which you do not agree or which you think unwise. If time permits you should say so respectfully and try to get them changed, but there is a chance that you will find that the person giving the direction knows more of the situation or a 'bigger picture' than you and if he or she does not accept your views you should find him or her right after all. If you do not then you will doubt that person's competence and he or she will have lost your trust and confidence. Once your complaints have been rejected then, whatever your secret feelings, you must see the decision through loyally and to the bitter end and never, by word or deed, let others see that you do not wholly agree with that person.

Loyalty works upwards to your superiors—support them and obey them, but do not hide behind them, and never criticise them or their decisions in front of your team. Also be loyal to subordinates. Although your first loyalty must be to your organisation and then your senior, you are also responsible for, and must be loyal to, the people that you lead. Accept the responsibility for your (and, where appropriate, their) errors, and never let blame fall unfairly on your subordinates. Protect their interests, and state their case; however, do not try to protect a subordinate who is to blame and who deserves the consequences.

Loyalty also comes from the *esprit de corps*, or team spirit that your organisation and its culture develops. This is built partly on values, customs, and the reputation of the past, and partly on the efficiency and morale of the present. Together these breed the quiet determination never to let your colleagues down. Loyalty finally works sideways, so that your friends and peers can rely upon you.

So loyalty works upwards, downwards, and sideways. Sometimes, however, these loyalties may conflict and as a leader you must judge which to follow. On each occasion the choice is yours to make and advice cannot be given to cover every situation. Experience is the only sure teacher, but do not be too proud to seek confidential advice from a trusted friend or superior. Some general **guidelines, however, can be given:**

- Do not support what you know to be wrong (integrity again!)—this is mistaken loyalty.
- Do not cover up for your friends' errors as this is usually misplaced loyalty that, in the end, harms both them and you.
- Do not overstate the case or fight too hard for your team to the point of rigidity as this is often to their detriment.
- Do not overplay the traditions of the past when faced by the realities of present-day conditions.
- Do not forget that the end of the day loyalty to your superiors is your duty—you should not depart from that duty under any, but the most extreme of, circumstances.

Initiative

Leaders must plan, anticipate, and stay one move ahead of the competitors. By seizing the initiative, leaders force competitors to conform to the leaders' actions, not vice versa, that is, seeing the need to take action and doing exactly that and encouraging the use of initiative in their subordinates in all their routine or delegated tasks. If leaders wait for things to happen, they will, but the result will probably not be a welcome one.

The term 'empowered' is used to suggest the willingness of people to contribute by word or deed to their organisation's efforts, 'managers are to empower their staff', is the cry. Empowerment, it seems to me is merely the act of delegating, expecting the display of initiative, and creating the culture and atmosphere in which trust prevails and risk-taking is encouraged. None of this is new in leadership, and so there is no need to confuse the issue with words that become fashionable and then disappear.

The application of 'business procedure' by subordinates (see Chapter 8), and the application of the functional check-list (Chapter 5) and the display of leadership qualities by leaders do more to develop initiative in people than demands for people to 'feel empowered'.

> As a Captain serving with a multinational force on exercise in Turkey, I was chatting with a US 'Top Sergeant' (about the equivalent of my Company Sergeant Major) about different systems and differences among armies. We saw there was a problem with the nozzle of a petrol pump that was one of only two servicing a large number of vehicles. The Sergeant said that if one of his soldiers saw the problem,

he might report it and if that soldier attempted to fix something he had not been trained for, the soldier would suffer the consequences. He added that he admired us enormously because he expected my soldiers to simply cut off the nozzle, crimp the end with some pliers and carry on refuelling the vehicles—and he expected my soldiers would only 'lose their name' if they did not try to sort the problem out. I felt that he had paid an enormous compliment to us, and I realised then how initiative is encouraged and developed—through trust, confidence, frequent delegation, and example.

The author

INTELLECT AND CLARITY OF THOUGHT

The ability to reason and to understand the significance of concepts, trends, and so on, and the capacity to reduce problems to their basic elements on which all plans are founded, and to ensure absolute clarity of purpose in all activity, are essential characteristics for successful leaders.

Clarity, ownership of the objective and widespread knowledge of it only come from endless repetition and endless iteration and endless checking that the objective is still possible and relevant.

John Harvey-Jones[3]

The most striking quality people displayed by people such as John Harvey-Jones, Montgomery, and Wellington, is the ability to reduce any problem to its simplest basic components. Those leaders then focus all their energies on those things and those alone, and ensure absolute clarity of purpose and role among their immediate subordinates, taking great pains to ensure that the same thing cascades through their organisations. As Montgomery writes '. . .we are inclined to become immersed in details, and we often lose sight of the fundamentals on which those details are based'. Montgomery's biographer Nigel Hamilton writes that Montgomery's tactical concept of war was 'not spectacular for its novel ideas but for its unity of conception and the absolute clarity with which he put it over'.[6]

> It was delightful to see His Grace. . .in high spirits and very animated, but so cool and so clear in the issue of his orders that it was impossible not fully to comprehend what he said. . .
>
> *An officer describing the Duke of Wellington at Waterloo[7]*

If your brain is not clear you cannot control it and think logically and quickly and come to sound conclusions under the conditions of stress, urgency, and complexity that all modern enterprises face.

Intellect is also vital to developing 'time horizon' and the cognitive capacity to manage work of a particular level of complexity. This is discussed further in Chapter 9.

WILLPOWER AND DETERMINATION —THE WILL TO LEAD

Firstly, leaders must have the will to lead. No leader succeeds unless her or she genuinely wants to accept responsibilty for people in the most complete sense—that means operational deployment, work allocation, career development training, pay and administration, health and welfare, and anything else affecting a subordinate.

Leaders must have the enduring will to win; to see a task to its completion through good times and bad. It requires determination, stamina, tenacity, and self-discipline. It is a part of courage, decision, and initiative. If leaders do not impose their will on the surrounding events and situation then events dictate the courses of action to leaders instead of leaders dictating events. Note that the imposition of willpower is on events or circumstances—not people. Leaders cannot impose their will on teams without being dictatorial and this eventually leads to failure.

It is no use having all the skills, knowledge and other personal qualities of leadership if leaders do not have the resolute and unswerving determination to use them. Leadership requires mental fitness, and anecdotal evidence frequently suggests that this is aided by physical well-being, health, and fitness.

KNOWLEDGE

The first essential for leaders is to have the complete confidence of their subordinates. To have this they need three forms of knowledge.

Knowledge of the job and the business. Leaders must understand the job and the nature of the businesses and competition. If leaders understand the factors that affect their businesses, the extent and limits of the resources at their disposal, how those resources are best applied, and can plan soundly and deal with the unexpected calmly then they have made a start to impressing their team members with their professional competence. Knowledge of the job gives self-confidence to leaders that, in turn, enables teams to have confidence in their leaders. No one can inspire confidence in others if he or she lacks confidence. That is a truism that everyone has experienced if you wish to reflect on it.

Knowledge of subordinates. Any team leader must know the team both as individuals and collectively. To be able to guide their thinking—to know what will inspire—a leader must know how and what they think about the challenge to set them. If leaders know this they can communicate in language that subordinates understand and can predict and pre-empt their likely reactions. To get the best from teams, leaders have to lead them like an orchestra, using their knowledge of each of them to best advantage in achieving the common aim. (See Chapters 2 and 3, Personality and Perception.)

Figure 6.1 The leader's knowledge of individuals must include:

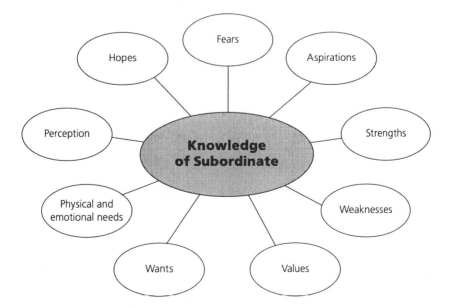

Know yourself. To lead others, you first need to learn how to lead yourself and to understand yourself. Are you excessively optimistic, or pessimistic, impetuous, or cautious, and does this affect your decision-making capacity? Do you jump to conclusions without establishing the facts? Are you sensitive to people's needs? In times like this it is helpful to remember Field Marshal Slim's advice that 'things are seldom as good or as bad as first reported'. No one is infallible, and many leaders require the occasional feedback from a loyal and trusted subordinate to remind them of the implications their usual style will lead to.

SELF-CONFIDENCE

Leaders need self-confidence in order to be decisive in action, calm in a crisis, and to be able to lead in uncertain times with faith in their capacity to overcome the unknown. Without self-confidence leaders lack the confidence of both teams and the leaders' superiors.

> The manager's greatest weapon is self-belief and the conviction that he or she can achieve the objective set. . .This self-belief can only be built up through a record of achievement. . .
>
> *John Harvey-Jones*[8]

Self-confidence develops as moral courage does. Once a person is shown that self-confidence is latent within and that it is possible to stretch, the inner voice of doubt, the imagination crying 'stop, danger!' should be ignored then all things become possible. Unless leaders can display continuous self-confidence (not to be confused with dogmatic rigidity or arrogance), teams do not follow. It is having confidence in yourself that inspires confidence in others.

> His personality, combined with his calm confidence had an electrifying effect on all; action was swift and orderly, and the panic which might well have set in was averted.
>
> *A subordinate describing Slim*[9]

Leaders who lack self-confidence tend to feel threatened by capable subordinates; there is a tendency then to try and conceal that subordinate or to not employ the best available candidates when recruiting from external sources.

As a head-hunter, the only time I was asked for a second short-list of candidates was on those occasions when I perceived that the client had not expected to be faced with candidates of the calibre presented. It was obvious that the client felt threatened and insecure, and instead of building the strongest possible team and basking in their reflected glory he was ensuring that he would only field an average team at best. No doubt this practice of hiring incompetents was continued down the line sending the department into a spiral of self-destruction.

The author

ENTHUSIASM

Enthusiasm must pervade all that leaders do. It is infectious and is reflected in teams, creating a positive attitude and a willing atmosphere.

Have you ever followed a leader, giving your full commitment to him or her, if that leader has not radiated enthusiasm for the task? Do recruitment advertisements ever ask for dour candidates? No. Enthusiasm is always necessary and has to be projected. Leaders' communication has to reflect their enthusiasm. It is shown in their pace of speech, tone, pitch and gestures must all be congruent with leaders' own natural enthusiasm. And it has to be natural zeal, otherwise leaders' insincerity shows through and trust begins to falter.

ABILITY TO COMMUNICATE

Teams must always be fully informed about what their tasks are, why they are to do them and how. Leaders must be able to speak and write effectively. Here are the principles of effective communication.

- **Clarity.** Clarity is a theme often mentioned here because it prevents wasted effort and overcomes perception by directing all action towards the common aim. It promotes the use of initiative and decisiveness because people understand how they fit into the scheme of things and what the superior's intentions are. It promotes understanding and effective relationships that lead to trust.

- **Brevity.** Everyone is busy and life is getting busier by the day. The fewer words that are used the less time it takes to digest the content. Brevity must be consistent with clarity—brevity must not lead to any form of ambiguity or confusion surely follows.
- **Accuracy.** Say what you mean and mean what you say. Do not skirt around issues, but come sharply to the point to prove the point. In relaying messages from above down the chain, say what you were told not what you thought you were told. Think of the story from the First World War about the message from the front 'send reinforcements we are going to advance' being corrupted to 'send three and fourpence we are going to a dance' by the time the message got back to the higher formation headquarters!

Leaders must communicate effectively upward to superiors, downward to subordinates and sideways to peers in language that can be understood and that inspires. At times you need to be exceptionally tactful and diplomatic, at other times you need to be firm and assertive. Your awareness and sensitivity to your surroundings and to what is happening about you should guide you in the style of your communication. Further guidance on this is given later in this chapter.

JUDGEMENT AND COMMON SENSE

Leaders must have the maturity and wisdom to balance conflicting advice in reaching decisions and must adopt simple, pragmatic, and clear solutions. Subordinates in diverse teams see things from their own perspective and have a narrower view of matters. Working close to the subject, they have detailed and intimate knowledge of matters within their area and have advice to offer. It is for the team leaders to balance their advice against conflicting advice from other team members or departments. This is where the maturity and wisdom of experience and common sense are needed in making a judgement call.

Your judgement also ensures justice in your dealings with your employees. People respect you if you are firm and fair, they do not if you vacillate, equivocate, and are unjust in your treatment of subordinates.

FLEXIBILITY OF MIND

Leaders must be able to adapt to changing situations without preconceived and rigid ideas in mind. As the Prussian General Von Moltke said more than 70 years ago 'No plan survives contact with the enemy.' In implementing plans all sorts of 'friction' and obstacles need to be overcome. Friction might be self-imposed, owing to poor planning or indecision, or simply from the sheer complexity and difficulties encountered in organising and deploying resources.

> The French Marshals plan their campaigns like a splendid set of harness which answered very well until it got broken: after that it was useless. Now I made my campaigns of rope. If anything went wrong, I tied a knot and went on
>
> *The Duke of Wellington*[7]

PRIDE

Leaders must have pride in their organisations and in the teams and their achievements. Your pride in your team and its achievements will be obvious to everyone. In extolling the team's virtues be careful not to claim credit yourself—the team deserves the recognition of its efforts. Your ability to weld it into an effective and cohesive team will be obvious to everyone. Do not let your ego take over and your vanity control you. Humility in the light of your team's great achievements will assist in projecting your humanity.

Never be so proud that you become vain and arrogant. Everyone is fallible and to openly admit to errors often endears you to your followers.

HUMANITY

Leaders must be approachable and be available for the team members to discuss their ideas or problems. Leaders must have empathy and understand the effect of their decisions on the teams. The ancient Chinese advice 'Seek first to understand then to be understood' holds good. Few great leaders have lost the personal touch, the ability to talk to the lowest employee one to one, away from the trappings and splendour of 'high office'.

> . . . The fact that we became a happy and efficient headquarters stemmed from the humanity of Slim himself. He was ready to speak to every man in the Corps from Divisional Commander to junior clerk or soldier. When speaking in English, Gurkhali, Urdu or Pushtu it was always as one man to another—never the great commander to his troops.[9]

The obvious concern for their followers and their families endears leaders to their subordinates. It closes the gap between levels and strengthens the bonds that define the leader–follower relationship. The actions of the individual leader and the policies of the organisation must support this approach.

DECISIVENESS

Leaders must be able to make decisions and have the wit and courage to make them at the right time.

It is indecision that hampers so much organisational growth and activity. All decisions are so complex and/or depend on so many other issues that an appreciation and subsequent decision cannot be made until other matters are confirmed. There is, therefore, a constant backlog of things to do that depend on someone else making a decision on another issue.

If an organisation is to retain flexibility, become more agile and globally competitive, then decisiveness has to be developed universally. The attitude that any decision, based on reasoned logic, is better than none has much to commend it. Decisiveness follows when subordinates have trust in the support that they are given if they happen to make a wrong decision. A culture that instils a fear of failure never develops initiative and decision.

Douglas McGregor, a champion of the human relations school of thought, worked as a consultant to many companies and eventually became President of Antioch College in the USA. He writes in one of his essays:[10]

> I believed . . . that a leader could operate successfully as a kind of adviser . . . I thought I could avoid being the 'boss'. Unconsciously . . . I hoped to duck the unpleasant necessity of making difficult decisions, of taking responsibility. . .

SELF-DISCIPLINE AND CONSISTENCY

> . . . I never cease to admire his calmness and courtesy when the strain of a 'touch and go' situation for long periods on end must have been wellnigh unbearable. His imperturbability did not stem from insensitivity, but rather from a superhuman self-discipline.
>
> *Subordinate describing Slim[9]*

Discipline is discussed in more detail in Chapter 16. Suffice it to say here that it is essential that leaders have a greater degree of self-discipline than those they lead. It both contributes to, and is derived from, moral courage and a sense of duty—the three are intertwined and almost inseparable. Self-discipline helps leaders to maintain their standards and to seek to raise them. When pressure and stress abound discipline helps leaders to go that little bit further and when things look bleak or tricky or uncertain it reinforces their self-confidence. Self-discipline helps leaders to face new challenges undaunted and to set the example that others will follow, and underpins consistency.

> A defeated general . . . In a dark hour he will turn in upon himself and question the very foundations of his leadership . . . And then he must stop! For if he is ever to command in battle, he must shake off these regrets, and stamp on them, as they claw at his will and his self-confidence. He must beat off these attacks he delivers against himself, and cast out the doubts born of failure. Forget them, and remember only the lessons to be learnt from defeat—they are more than from victory'.
>
> *Slim[5]*

Followers need their leaders to be consistent if they are to know where they stand and to be able to maximise their working effectiveness. This means that leaders' behaviour has to be consistent with organisational values, that what is acceptable within this code of conduct is not open to change for the sake of expediency. What is acceptable one day as a standard of work or a method of working does not change the next day because of some short-term crisis. Mutual expectations need to be constantly understood and met.

This sort of consistency is closely linked to reliability. The world is a changing and uncertain place and one of the few things that can give people security is consistency in their working relationships and daily expectations.

SENSE OF HUMOUR

Your sense of humour must be maintained when things go wrong! There has never been a successful leader who has made it to the top that did not have a sense of humour. Wellington and Churchill were renowned for their dry wit; Montgomery encouraged a happy atmosphere within his headquarters; and General Norman Schwarzkopf maintains a twinkle in his eye despite his ebullient manner. Leaders should take everything seriously, except themselves.

THE NATURE OF INSPIRATION

'To inspire: to stimulate or arouse people to creativity especially by supposed divine or supernatural agency. To prompt or give rise to.' (Combined dictionary definitions).

> Belief in a leader contributes strongly to the willingness to follow and the enthusiasm of the followers. Thus Nelson, Hannibal, Alexander the Great could achieve with smaller numbers what others with larger and equally well trained numbers could not.
>
> *Sir Robin Knox-Johnston*

The ability to inspire people is the mark of a successful leader. Most people would agree on this, but many would be at a loss to define it or to discuss its components or how it could be developed.

Think to instances when someone has inspired you, or does now, and you would probably agree that to be inspired by someone you:

- Trust that person; their integrity, sincerity, moral courage and loyalty are not in doubt and you, therefore, have a firm belief in the reliability and moral strength of that person.

- Are captured by their communication. The language, both verbal and non-verbal, and the style of the person convinces you that he or she is congruent with, or understands your own values, beliefs and needs, is enthusiastic and obviously sincere—the person's integrity again is not in doubt. This emotional appeal is verging on charisma.
- Are convinced that that person is committed to his or her cause or purpose (willpower), that 'the purpose' is the right and necessary thing to do, and that it is feasible—this is the intellectual component of inspiration.

Integrity, loyalty, and moral courage, have been discussed. Now we consider those other characteristics of inspiration.

COMMUNICATION

Communication is a vast subject in its own right, and it is not the aim of this book to consider it in depth. There are certain fundamental considerations, however, that the aspiring leader should employ in effective two-way communication.

- **Plan, prepare and rehearse.** To do this you need to know your audience as individuals, so that you can connect with their values and beliefs and demonstrate that, by achieving the leader's mission, some of their needs will also be satisfied. You must be clear on the aim of the communication, and structure it logically with a beginning, a middle, and an end. You must rehearse it, so that you can deliver the message with confidence and conviction. This includes both oral and body language signals.
- **Absolute clarity.** Choose unambiguous language that is understood by the audience. If you are confused, vague, or muddled, so the audience's understanding is; if there is any understanding at all! It must be impossible for anyone to fail to understand your meaning. Say what you mean and mean what you say.
- **Listen effectively.** The following hints will develop your own listening ability, and that of your team members.
  - There must be a reason why someone should listen to you.
  - Do not jump to conclusions when listening.
  - Rephrase the message in other terms to ensure understanding.
  - Listen to the whole message and observe and interpret non-verbal communication.
  - Show interest in what is being said.

- **Simplicity.** Why over-complicate things that, in essence, are simple? The simpler the plan, the more likely it is that it is remembered.
- **Impact.** Give your words life and character, engaging all the senses of sight, sound, touch, taste, and smell, where you can. Implicit in this is enthusiasm and the projection of energy.
- **Sincerity.** You must be yourself. Be natural and comfortable with what you are asking people to do and be congruent with the implicit values and beliefs that are inherently necessary to achieve the task. Use your own emotions and beliefs to control your manner of speaking.
- **Commitment and feasibility.** Your language, verbal and body, reputation, 'track record', overt willpower, determination and conviction, contribute to your obvious commitment to the plan of action that you propose. Your reputation will be based on past behaviour that must have demonstrated, consistently, the qualities of leadership, already discussed. The commitment that you generate from others to a plan will be all the greater if it is readily seen that what you are proposing while it may be challenging, is possible and necessary—this is where your communication of 'the reasons why' is so important.

CHARISMA

Charisma and personal qualities of leadership are frequently not understood. 'Charisma' I define here as 'an excessively strong blend of personal attributes that induces people to assign god-like status to the charismatic leader and follow his wishes without question.'

> With charisma, what you see is not necessarily what you get. You can be very compelling and appealing but many charismatic leaders fall down on delivery. I can't think of a prime minister that has not been removed from office, which maybe says a lot about how things can go to people's heads. You have to know when the time is right to both start and finish.
>
> *Malcolm Jones, CEO, NRMA Limited*

Aristotle says that virtue rests somewhere between two extremes. Like most things in life, anything that is done or possessed to an extreme can become a liability and needs to be counterbalanced by something or someone else. It is the same with the charismatic leader: such strength of personality often develops an ego that ensures that that person remains blind to reality or indifferent to advice that conflicts with his or her own preconceived ideas. Many charismatic leaders generate a band of sycophantic followers. If sycophants and 'cult worshippers' exist within his or her own immediate team, the charismatic leader has nothing to balance out his or her own excesses.

Charismatic leaders are often brilliant listeners who can synthesise what they hear and generate responses that appeal to their devoted followers; inspirational leaders tend to put more thought into their actions and are less driven by their egos. A smaller ego makes them more successful.

Robyn Fitzroy, Division Director, Macquarie Bank

Charisma is not a necessary attribute for successful leadership.

Chris Walsh, Operations Director, David Jones Limited

Charismatic leaders are extremely successful or fail badly. A lack of charisma, but not character, makes a leader more acceptable to a wider range of people and far less polarising.

Karen Lonergan, Education & Development Manager, Castrol Australia

---

According to Bass,[11] a US Professor of Management,

. . . charisma entails massive displacement of feelings onto the public stage by both leader and followers. The feelings are connected with a search for love. . .Acute and chronic crisis components are a necessary element in a theory about charisma. . .

The charismatic leader can be seen as a saviour from distress. The rise of Gandhi, Hitler, and Mussolini, are examples of this.

Charismatic leaders certainly inspire their followers, but inspiration does not rely on charisma. Inspiration, in our context, contains an intellectual component and, thus, differs from the raw emotion of charisma. If followers are drawn to a leader's purpose, the leader is inspiring; if followers are drawn to the leader personally he or she is charismatic. Which appeals most to a follower must depend to a large extent on the follower.

No doubt there are some successful charismatic leaders, but few endure. How many can you think of?

TRUST

When you have a situation where there is a high level of trust in the leader, the leader overcomes the largest component of organisational friction such as people impeding the ability to get things done. When you have trust you have an opportunity to make the best use of people's intellectual and emotional energy, this leads to high performance.

Robert McLean, formerly Managing Director, McKinsey & Co Australia

Some people can never be turned into leaders and some organisations continue to fall down because they still want to promote regardless of people's ability. Technical experts frequently fail as leaders because rather than trusting subordinates they are trying to take over a subordinate's job if it is within their personal area of expertise.

Chris Walsh, Operations Director, David Jones Limited

Trust is belief in a person's reliability and that is governed by their integrity, loyalty, self-discipline, and moral courage. It is interesting to remind ourselves that to gain the trust of others we first have to give it—for the leader this means taking a risk and trusting in others first. Table 6.1 shows common actions that build or break the level of trust.

Subordinates and subordinate leaders, once chosen, are entitled to their leader's trust and confidence, particularly when facing a difficult situation where they need support and understanding. Deciding whether to intervene and how in such situations requires wisdom and judgement on the part of the superior if his or her subordinates are not to have their own levels of self-confidence reduced. The risk of failure must be balanced against the unnecessary interference and the risk of possibly stifling initiative when decision and action are needed.

An article about trust written by James Strong, Chief Executive of Qantas Airways[12] is reproduced on pages 91 and 92.

Table 6.1

Building Trust	Breaking down Trust
• effectively listening	• not listening
• demonstrating empathy and humanity	• not considering others point of view
• sharing information	• withholding information for own purposes
• accepting differences between people—diversity	• criticising others, finding fault and making assumptions
• offering help	• looking after 'number one'
• delivering what you promised—reliability	• failing to meet expectations
• asking for feedback	• blaming others
• providing constructive feedback	• criticising the team to others outside the team
• being consistent in standards and behaviour	• inconsistency
• trusting others first	• expecting trust to be shown
• being straight	• being devious and playing politics
• putting others first	• being selfish
• accepting responsibility, maintaining loyalty	• acts of disloyalty, passing the buck

Trust. One of the most dangerous subjects to raise within a business organisation is 'building the level of trust' between people within the structure. 'Dangerous' because in many cases the reaction is almost certain to be cynicism, or a sarcastic comment, as if any discussion on the subject is certain to be insincere and a waste of time.

It is a sad commentary that all too often there is a low level of trust between the management and the people who are the organisation, and even between internal groups. At risk of generalisation, this seems to be more pronounced in Australia than in some other countries. **Negative Effects.** Whatever the causes, distrust is obviously a negative attitude which should not be merely accepted. It colours every aspect of the employment relationship. Suspicion as to motives and intention becomes automatic. People can and do reach the stage of automatically looking for a conspiracy theory on every development, and taking the worst possible interpretation of each event as a matter of course.

Why. There are obviously many contributory factors, some fairly obvious and virtually inevitable. Some people would leap to the view that this 'us and them' situation is created and fostered by trade unionism, where differences in interests are a fundamental proposition. More thoughtful analysis would indicate this is an overly simplistic view.

Where one person is employed to work for another individual or corporation there arises automatically a potential basis for 'conflict of interest' in the sense of benefit to one party may be to the cost of the other eg. higher wages/lower profits. So from the very beginning there are elements which can lead to distrust or divergence of interest.

Decline of Trust. But obviously more factors are involved. The quality of every relationship is a product of the extent of contact, communication, understanding and cooperation. This is easily maintained in a small organisation where people are in close contact, know and assess each other personally, understand why decisions are made and can have a basis for trust.

As soon as an organisation grows to larger size, communications and contact levels deteriorate, as does personal knowledge of individuals. With virtual certainty, trust declines.

Hard Decisions. Almost as inevitable as the growing gap between people with size is the fact that sooner or later actions will have to be taken which can be seen as harmful to people within. If some part of the business has to be closed down or sold, the size of staff reduced in recession by redundancy, costs cut or other cost saving measures implemented, this can be seen as being in the interests of the company and against the interests of its people.

In a small group it would be more likely that you could demonstrate that unless steps were taken to cut costs, all employment is at risk as the organisation may not survive. With a large corporation the interpretation is more likely to be that 'it could have been avoided' or 'there must be enough money to carry on through', and so on.

Remoteness. The more remote and impersonal at a distance are the management, the easier it is to dislike them and be critical in larger organisations. Every organisation of any size can be guaranteed to have a red hot rumour mill which thrives on negative possibilities and interpretations, with a conspiracy ready for any occasion. The worse the level and standard of communication between people, the stronger and more active the rumour mill to fill that gap.

Distrust is also fuelled by non-disclosure of information, by secrecy and a lack of openness. Many companies for many years have been very reluctant to discuss financial information, or operational statistics. The reasons are varied ranging from a tradition of believing this is the sole prerogative of management, to real issues of competitive secrecy necessary from opposition firms.

References

1. E. S. Turner, 1956, *Gallant Gentlemen*, London: Michael Joseph Ltd.
2. Lord Moran, 1945, *Anatomy Of Courage*, London: Constable.
3. John Harvey-Jones, 1988, *Making It Happen*, London: Collins.
4. Field Marshal Sir William Slim, 1957, *Courage And Other Broadcasts*, London: Cassell.
5. Field Marshal Sir William Slim, 1957, *Defeat Into Victory*, London: Cassell.
6. Nigel Hamilton, 1981, *Monty: The Making Of A General*, London: Hamish Hamilton.
7. Sir Arthur Bryant, 1971, *The Great Duke*, London: Collins.
8. John Harvey-Jones, 1994, *All Together Now*, London: William Heinemann Ltd.
9. Ronald Lewin, 1976, *Slim: The Standard Bearer*, London: Leo Cooper.
10. John Adair, 1983, *Effective Leadership*, Aldershot: Gower.
11. Bernard M. Bass, 1985, *Leadership And Performance Beyond Expectations*, New York: The Free Press (Division of Macmillan).
12. James Strong, *The Australian Way* (Qantas Airways Magazine), January 1995.

CHAPTER 7

MISSION ANALYSIS AND THE APPRECIATION: PROBLEM SOLVING AND DECISION MAKING

In reviewing the functional leadership check-list and Adair's three circles model of needs, note that the main task needs that leaders must satisfy are in defining the task, solving any problems, and producing a plan of action.

Leaders might not consider their tasks as the source of problems because tasks are simply a routine part of the job. Leaders may have followed similar procedures many times before in order to achieve particular ends. It is only when unexpected or unanticipated events occur and interrupt the flow of work in progress that 'problems' exist. Therefore, it is true to say that one person's routine task may be another's problem.

Not only is it vital to know how to tackle problems as they arise, but it is useful to understand how problems arise in the first place. Therefore, this chapter is in two parts. In Part 1 we consider how problems arise and are perceived and in Part 2 we look at a suggested structured way of thinking about problems that, if followed, leads to an optimum solution.

PART 1 TYPES OF PROBLEMS

IDENTIFYING THE PROBLEMS

In any task leaders might face there are two sorts of problem that could be encountered.

- **External problems.** Those that occur while actually getting the task done.
- **Internal problems.** Those caused by the individual demands or needs of team members and those presented in maintaining the team's cohesion.

This chapter deals only with managing external problems; for the solution to internal problems refer to Chapters 5, 10, 12 and 13.

PERCEPTION OF PROBLEMS

Following the chapter on perception we can surmise that we notice things because of the degree of attentiveness, size, contrast, motion, novelty versus familiarity, degree of threat. Our interpretation is then influenced by previous experience, motivation, values, presentation, grouping, context, defence, and the halo effect. The reasons for this can generally be explained by the following influences.

- **Simplification of perceptual clues.** Our senses can suffer from a barrage of perceptual data that is growing in volume in the 'on-line' data age. Think back to the day you joined your company and when you met all the people in your team. It is likely that it was several days before you could put names to faces or even remember names. Your senses were reeling from meeting people, absorbing the 'norms' and trying to assimilate into the new environment. The usual reaction of the brain to such information overload is to make gross simplifications and these can create distortions. Just how these distortions occur can be seen from considering two of the main reasons for them.
  - **Closure.** We make assumptions about a person or an event, based on insufficient evidence. Look at this example. You see two damaged vehicles parked by the side of the road, their drivers in discussion, your immediate reaction is to assume they have been in a collision. In fact the cars may have each been damaged in separate accidents and the drivers are friends with

one coming to tow the other home. In business terms we can exploit competitors' closure by the use of surprise.

- **Projection.** This is attributing to others what you want them to be or to do. This can be very dangerous, as under stress, a leader can have the tendency to make plans, based on false assumptions of what the competition and market are doing and how they will react.

- **The effects of personality.** As personality is derived from an individual's genetics, and the environment in which he or she is brought up, this mixture provides each of us with a set of different thought processes, three of which are relevant to the consideration of problems.

  - **Divergent—convergent thinking.** Some people seem to have a greater affinity for concentrating on the minutiae of a task and for logical thought; others seem to have an ability to make intuitive leaps and find solutions to problems in innovative and imaginative ways. The former are known as 'convergent thinkers', the latter are 'divergent' or 'lateral thinkers'. Much of Edward de Bono's writing is aimed at developing divergent thinking.

  - **Reflective—impulsive.** The reflective person likes to take time checking all the facts before reaching a solution. The impulsive person, as the name suggests, tends to come to quick decisions, acting on intuition, often without fully absorbing all the facts.

  - **Field independence—dependence.** This is used by psychologists to describe the fact that there are some people who can quickly grasp the nub of any problem, no matter the complexity of the background to it (field independence); others take longer to sort out exactly what it is that needs doing (field dependence).

As always, in considering personality, beware of assuming that people are either one thing or the other. People generally have degrees of all these dimensions within themselves, but one or other tends to predominate.

PART 2 DEALING WITH PROBLEMS

MISSION ANALYSIS AND THE APPRECIATION

Whatever perceptual traits leaders have, approaches to dealing with problems are needed that minimise distortions, perception, and personality effects and that increase the possibility of arriving at the optimal solution. Here is an approach to problem solving and decision making that should bring you to a logical solution to a problem and form the basis for a sound plan. This is called an 'appreciation' of the situation.

We tackle problems every day. Every problem derives from a situation. The solution involves an examination of the situation and it usually requires the selection of a course of action (COA). There is nothing inherently difficult in this problem-solving and decision-making process—for simple problems people do this instinctively. For example, in planning a weekend away we consider where to go, how to get there, the cost, and other factors.

The decision-making process (or appreciation) can be mental, oral or written. It is a logical sequence of reasoning, leading to the best solution to an operational, administrative, or even personal, problem. It is a process suitable for the supervisor and the CEO. What varies is only the complexity of factors and implications. This assists in providing consistency, common language and understanding across an enterprise, and a process that people can grow with as their careers develop. Remember that a decision maker needs self-confidence, sound judgement, and an understanding of implications as well as authority and trust and confidence in his or her subordinates to be effective and, thus, prevent bottlenecks in work flow.

No leader can delegate making the appreciation of his or her mission to a subordinate since only he or she is far enough removed to view the whole in perspective, and only the leader can conduct the mission analysis. A leader can and should, where appropriate, however, involve the specialist expertise of subordinates in considering the factors affecting a situation and the pros and cons of each possible COA.

When this consideration of factors is followed by a group, you have collective support, since the end result should be arrived at through logic, not through factional interests. If written, anyone reading the appreciation should arrive at the same conclusion—unless factors have been overlooked in which case it is easy for a reader familiar with the format to spot errors and it is relatively simple to make the necessary changes.

One of the greatest advantages of following the process described is that it develops awareness of 'the big picture'—which can be termed 'vision' in the CEO. This is where part of the appreciation's power lies when instilled as a way of thinking all of the time it provides the ongoing management development that results in well-understood, clear, and unambiguous, purpose and intent.

Appreciation is THE process by which all plans should be made. There are two types of appreciation.

- **Quick appreciation.** A quick mental or note-form appreciation carried out 'on the spot' for simple problems.
- **Formal appreciation.** This can cover any subject, often in much detail, and is written. It is this that which we look at now.

The essence of an appreciation is clear thought, critical examination, and logical reasoning. Approach the task with an open, unprejudiced mind, do not 'situate the appreciation', that is, form a convenient plan from preconceived ideas and then 'bend' the facts to fit it, but make a considered appreciation of the situation as it really is.

It is one of the paradoxes of human behaviour that as we get closer to making serious decisions the more we become assailed by doubts. Think of a time when you have been about to make a major purchasing decision such as buying a car or a house. At those times people always question their decision and seek reassurance when writing the cheque. A logical sequence of problem solving to help identify the best course of action would have provided some security (Maslow's needs, see Chapter 12) and confidence that the decision was correct. Using such a process minimises the negative effects of doubt and lack of confidence in the leader and his or her followers.

The appreciation is designed as a formal, but flexible, form of a logical thought process that enables leaders and their teams to arrive at conclusions under the stress of business and under the pressure of time. While it may feel cumbersome to use at first, with practice it simply becomes a way of thinking and dealing with issues on a daily basis.

If you can understand this decision-making process you are becoming proficient in one of the essential skills of a leader. Some people have an aptitude for clear thought under pressure, but this is something we must all develop.

FORMAT OF AN APPRECIATION

Break the problem down into its component parts, so that each may be examined in detail. There are four distinct steps in writing a formal appreciation:

Step 1, analyse what must be done and establish absolute

clarity (what is the aim, what do I have to do?) This is called 'mission analysis'.

Step 2, evaluate or analyse all the factors (a factor is information that contributes to, or has some bearing on, the outcome). As you do this you can make deductions about what needs to be done.

Step 3, consider all the practical COAs open to you.

Step 4, the leader's decision or selection of the best COA to achieve the aim or mission that forms the outline plan or concept of operations.

After appreciation is completed, the detailed plan, briefing and review follow. See Chapter 8 and the Glossary for: Aim, Appreciation, Objective, Mission, Mission Analysis, and Task.

These terms cascade down through an organisation. A regional executive's aim and mission might made up of a number of country objectives and tasks. The country objectives and tasks after mission analysis form the country manager's own aim and mission and his or her appreciation will produce a number of objectives or tasks for his or her subordinate leaders. And so this process continues down through the layers of the organisation. Consider Figures 7.1 and 7.2.

Mission Analysis

Figure 7.1

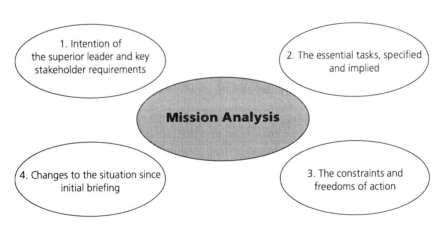

Evaluating the Factors

Figure 7.2

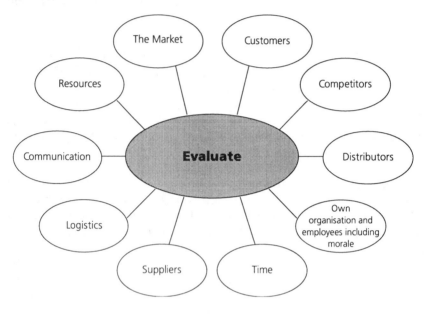

CONSIDER THE COAs

State all the COAs in outline. List the advantages and disadvantages of each to make comparison easy.

THE LEADER'S DECISION

Selection of the best COA to achieve the mission. Form the outline plan/concept of operations.

This methodical sequence prevents us from leaping ahead of ourselves and arriving at a solution without considering all the factors logically. The layout may appear formal and the contents may seem to be laid down rigidly. This, however, is inevitable because the appreciation is deliberately designed for use in the most complicated situations where the mind must be directed along a continuous, comprehensive and logical channel if the best solution is to be reached. There may be many different factors to be considered, so it must be a disciplined process.

METHOD OF APPRECIATION

The detailed application of the appreciation is outlined below and should be read in conjunction with the example at the end of this chapter.

Mission Analysis

This is the crux of the appreciation. In some situations the mission is given to you, but for other problems you may have to write an aim. Unless the mission analysis is correct the whole appreciation may be worthless. Mission analysis helps you clarify precisely what must be achieved, so that any actions support 'the main effort'. It is a dynamic process that should be continually applied to all tasks that are under way to determine whether any changes to plans are necessary.

1. **Analysis of the superior's intention.** It is essential to know and understand exactly what your superior intends to achieve and what your part is in his or her plan. This now allows you to carry out the intent because you know what is wanted and you can continue to act without constantly checking back. If you lose communication, you are still in a position to act in a positive and constructive manner. What is the superior's (= your partner's!) intention in the holiday problem? To go on holiday in order to wind down and to relax without the children.

2. **Key stakeholder requirements.** The needs of key stakeholders must be considered as this inevitably highlights additional implied tasks.

3. **Identification of essential tasks.** The tasks given by the superior and implied by consideration of stakeholders must be analysed in order that the essential tasks can be identified. Some tasks may be specified by the superior; alternatively the tasks may be implied. The junior leader needs to identify and to extract these implied tasks, based upon his or her knowledge and understanding of how the 'operation' is to be carried out. The essential tasks of the holiday problem are: one week's holiday abroad this year and the children are not to accompany the parents. The implied task is that a babysitter is needed.

4. **Constraints/freedom of action/risk.** It is often difficult to decide what should be set down as constraints. The rule is that constraints are those imposed upon you by your superior. They are not those things that you decide should limit your actions as a result of considering the factors—this would be 'situating the appreciation'.

The holiday constraints are that the food and weather should be good, if possible. By identifying the constraints you understand what freedom of action you have, and to what extent you can take risks to enable you to achieve your task.

5. **Changes in the situation.** Has the situation changed since you received your last briefing? Sometimes, while you are carrying out your appreciation something could change. For example, if your parents'-in-law world cruise is cancelled or delayed, you could have one of three answers:

   a) Yes, the situation has changed, but your plan is still good.
   b) The situation has changed, your original mission is still possible, but you need to amend the plan.
   c) Yes, the situation has changed, your original mission is no longer valid. You should then consult your superior, but if you cannot you should support your superior's main effort (to go on holiday for one week abroad without the children in this example).
   d) Write an aim if you have not been given one.

I believe that within two weeks of learning about mission analysis, just by asking 'has the situation changed?' when looking at a problem I saved the company half a million dollars. We had been working on a project for a year and were about to continue and invest more money in it and I asked the question. The situation had changed and we cancelled the programme as a result which we wouldn't have otherwise done.

Consumer Goods Information Services Manager

Evaluating the Factors

Evaluating the factors and the deductions that can be derived from them means that all the relevant information must be weighted critically, not only in relation to yourself, but also in relation to the competitor. Remember that factors stem from the best information available to the leader at the time. Typical factors include: the market, competitors, distributors, suppliers, time, surprise, communication, morale, people, assessment of tasks, logistics.

Discuss each factor in relation to the aim and this should lead to one or more deductions affecting the attainment of the aim. A good test of the factor is to ask 'so what' to indicate what you should do about it. If the answer is 'so nothing' the factor should be discarded since it blurs the issue. Examine each factor exhaustively. Subject deductions to the 'so what?' test. If the answer is 'therefore. . .needs to be done', draw a further deduction, and so on, until you have exhausted that particular line of argument.

Ideally, arrange various factors in a logical order, starting with the most important or over-riding factor, so that the discussion of one factor leads logically to the discussion of the next. A summary of major deductions can be a useful heading to include if the appreciation is complex. (Refer to step 2 of the solution to the holiday problem to illustrate a few key factors and deductions.)

It is usual for a 'scientific linear approach of cause and effect to be taken in considering factors', but in long-range strategic planning particularly, unexpected forces and chaos may impinge on events, making their outcome unpredictable (but understandable in hindsight).[1] A wider ranging type of thinking is then required (see Chapter 9, Requisite Organisation Stratification theory[2]).

Preliminary assessment of tasks. This factor comes at the end of step 2 and is sometimes awkward to grasp. It is the assessment of what is needed to achieve all the tasks that fall out of the deductions of the factors; in effect it is a shopping list of 'jobs to do'. It is likely that, when concurrent actions are totalled, there are insufficient resources to carry them out. Two options are open: divide the task into phases or stages; or set ruthless priorities and go for economic courses of action.

Consider the COAs

Here you list, in outline, each practical COA left open to you. Against each COA you must also list the advantages and disadvantages. Take a look now at step 3 in the holiday problem.

It would be very unusual (or even wrong) to arrive at this stage with only one COA open. If this happens to you you have probably wrongly dismissed a practical COA.

The Leader's Decision

Selection of the best COA. This section of the appreciation is the culmination of the whole argument. Now weigh one COA against another, and if the previous section has been fully and clearly argued it should not be difficult to make this comparison briefly. The more concise and direct the argument, the more convincing it will be. The comparison among COAs should be developed logically so that the selection of the best COA, the leader's decision, becomes the natural conclusion. This section must finish with a definite recommendation of the COA—the mission—to adopt.

OUTLINE PLAN

The selected COA dictates the outline plan. The plan must be clear and definite and written in concise and positive English. It should give enough general direction to enable someone to issue a 'warning brief', so that preparations can be made by as many people as possible. Possible headings for a warning brief are:

1. Task organisation/Team composition
2. Mission
3. Execution
a) Concept of operations (or General outline)
b) Grouping and tasks
c) Coordinating instructions.

The detailed plan should follow the format outlined in Chapter 8.

SUBSEQUENT REVIEW

After completing the appreciation it should be reviewed to ensure that it stands up to the following tests:

- Is the reasoning valid?
- Is the sequence logical?
- Is everything in it relevant to the mission aim, and has anything been forgotten?
- Is it free from vagueness, ambiguity, and prejudice?
- Is it accurate?
- Will the plan achieve the mission?

Pitfalls. We need to look at three areas of difficulty in order to make sure that you start learning the appreciation process in the right way.

- **Factor—deduction.** Many people state a series of facts (especially under the 'competitor' heading), but do not make deductions. Make valid deductions. It is these deductions that affect your achievement of the aim. Remember to test each factor and all subsequent deductions with the words 'So what?' and 'Therefore?'

repeatedly, in order that you squeeze out all the implications and likely tasks that may affect you.

- **Allocating time.** If you are given a time by which a task must be complete or you face a constraint, then you must work backwards from that time through all the steps until you reach the present. If you do not have enough time you must either telescope the original allocations, or cancel some activities. The result should be a workable programme. If you cannot make savings then a further deduction must be made to establish the effect of insufficient time. The penalties point to either further revision of timings, or to delaying the decision until COAs, and selection of best COA —leader's decision.
- **Situate the appreciation.** Avoid the strong temptation to favour one COA, trying to justify it and playing down the deductions and advantages of other courses. This is a common pitfall—it achieves nothing. You must remain objective, impartial, and employ balanced logical thought.

CONCLUSION

An appreciation is a sequence of logical thought and sound reasoning. Whether written or not, do not allow it to become a theoretical process; it should be a flexible means for the orderly and practical consideration of the factors affecting the solution of any problem. Do not be disappointed that after your appreciation the situation changes, apparently undermining the validity of your work. Simply run through the mission analysis again as the appreciation is designed to be a cyclical process, so you can react to changes.

In business terms, particularly in a highly competitive market, there is often no opportunity for reassurance for your own decisions. Making a decision can be painful, the bigger you perceive the decision to be, the greater the uneasiness you are likely to feel. Knowledge of this 'dissonance' should help to reassure the inexperienced leader that having doubts is natural. Leaders need to be aware that doubts afflict both themselves and others, so that they can develop the confidence to minimise its effects on themselves and to be aware of the need to support subordinates at times of decision. Remember that these feelings of doubt are normal.

FORMAL APPRECIATION EXAMPLE

'THE HOLIDAY': NARRATIVE

It is 1 January. You are an expatriate married person with two children younger than school age and you are working in the UK. Your home town is Hobart and you find the UK weather to be similar to that of Tasmania—often sunny, but sometimes cold and wet, in other words variable and unpredictable. In reent years, however, the UK has had some very good summers. It has been a very busy period and you have been working late with pressures and stresses. Your partner (and you) need a break to wind down and relax. Your partner had been badgering you for some time to go on holiday for one week this year where, if possible, the food and weather are both good, but not on any account taking the children, and it must be abroad. (The children could go to their English grandparents at any time except August when they are on a world cruise. If the children cannot go to the grandparents then there are lots of couples in the company who would look after them, except during the Easter leave period.) You agree to look into the idea and subsequently visit the local travel agent. He tells you that the only holidays now available are as follows (costs for one week for two people):

Place	Total Cost before 31 May (£)	Total Cost after 31 May (£)	Remarks
(a)	(b)	(c)	(d)
Austria	350	480	Food good, but dull Weather changeable, but normally better in August
Cyprus	700	900	Food unpredictable Weather always good
France (Brittany)	450	600	Food superb Weather similar to the UK
Morocco	420	550	Food doubtful Weather always good
Cornwall	180	210	Food variable Excellent surfing and cider

106

You then go to see your boss and find out that the best times for leave are:

22–29 March   Easter Leave.
1–14 May   Gap between two peak periods.
3–21 August   Someone else can stand in for you.

You check your finances and find very little in your account and discover that a bank loan cannot be used to pay for the holiday. By living frugally the following can be saved:

by   22 March   £250.
by   1 May   £500.
by   3 August   £700.

MISSION ANALYSIS

What is the intention of my superior and what is my role in the overall plan? My partner's intention is to go on holiday abroad this year in order that we can relax without the children. The children (stakeholders) need to be cared for. My part in the plan is to organise the holiday.

What am I required to do, or what tasks do I have to complete in order to achieve the mission?

Specified Tasks:
Organise a one-week holiday this year.
The holiday must be abroad without the children.
Implied Tasks:
Organise babysitters for the holiday.
What constraints are there on my freedom?
The holiday must be this year.
If possible the weather and food must be good.
Has the situation changed in principle?
If the grandparents' world cruise is cancelled after this appreciation then the implication of it must be considered.
Aim:
To go on holiday abroad this year in order to relax without the children.

EVALUATION OF FACTORS

• **Leave**
The three leave periods are:
22–27 March.

107

1–14 May.
3–21 August.

Deduction
A holiday is only possible during one of these periods.

- **Finance**

A bank loan cannot be used to pay for the holiday.
By living frugally the following can be saved:

by	22 March	£250.
by	1 May	£500.
by	3 August	£700.

Deduction
Savings are the only source of funds.
I can afford £250 by the first leave period, £500 by the second, and £700 by the third.

Total costs

Place	Before 31 May (£)	After 31 May (£)
(a)	(b)	(c)
Austria	350	480
Cyprus	700	900
France (Brittany)	450	600
Morocco	420	550
Cornwall	180	210

Deductions
I cannot afford Cyprus and Brittany before 31 May, but I can afford Austria or Morocco before 31 May.
As Cornwall is not abroad this option is discounted.
I cannot afford Cyprus after 31 May, but I can afford Austria, Brittany, or Morocco after 31 May.
As Cyprus is unaffordable this year it is discounted.

- **Babysitters**

My wife's parents can look after the children at any time except August when they are on a world cruise.
Other couples in the company would look after the children at any time, except during the Easter leave.

Deductions
Babysitters are available for all leave periods.

The children would be happier with their grandparents, therefore, a holiday outside August may be best.

- **Food and Weather**

Comparison

Place	Quality of Food	Weather
Austria	Good, but dull	Changeable, better in August
Brittany	Superb	Similar to the UK
Morocco	Doubtful	Always good

Deduction

Austria would be acceptable in August, otherwise the weather is not good.

Brittany would be acceptable from July–September when the weather is better.

Morocco is not preferred—dodgy food.

Holiday before 31 May is not preferred as good food and weather are not available.

- **Summary of Deductions**

Timing. A holiday is possible only during:

22–29 March.

1–14 May.

3–21 August.

Funds. I can afford a holiday costing no more than:

£250 by 22 March.

£500 by 1 May.

£700 by 3 August.

Affordable. The following holidays are affordable:

Austria and Morocco before 31 May.

Austria, Brittany, and Morocco after 31 May.

Babysitters. Babysitters are available all year, but grandparents (the preferred choice) are not available in August.

Food and Weather

Austria is acceptable in August.

Brittany is acceptable in August.

Morocco is least preferable unless an alternative source of food is available when it is acceptable all year.

A holiday before 31 May is not preferred because good food and weather are not available.

CONSIDER THE COAs

The mission analysis constraints are:

- A one-week holiday this year.
- The holiday must be abroad without the children.
- If possible the weather and food must be good

The COAs satisfying these constraints are summarised below.

Serial	COA	Advantages	Disadvantages
1	Austria in August	Cheapest option in August Babysitters from the company are available Food is good Weather is better in August	Grandparents not available Food good, but dull
2	Brittany in August	Affordable Babysitters from the company are available Weather similar to UK with some recent good summers Food superb	Affordable, but expensive Grandparents not available Good weather not guaranteed
3	Austria in March	Affordable Grandparents can babysit	Food good, but dull Weather changeable
4	Morocco in March	Affordable Grandparents can babysit Weather good	Food is doubtful
5	Morocco in August	Affordable Babysitters from the company are available Weather good	Food doubtful Grandparents not available

LEADER'S DECISION

I will select Course 2 (Brittany in August) because it offers the best combination of food and weather within the time and financial constraints.

PLAN

Mission. To organise a holiday abroad this year for my wife and me in order that we can relax without the children.

Execution

Concept of operations/general outline. The holiday will be in Brittany for one week between 3 and 21 August. A couple from the company will look after the children.

Costs. £600 that will have to be saved.

References

1. Richard Luecke, 1994, *Scuttle Your Ships Before Advancing*, New York: Oxford University Press.
2. Elliott Jaques, 1996, *Requisite Organization: A Total System for Effective Managerial Organization and Managerial Leadership for the 21st Century*, Arlington, Virginia: Cason Hall & Co Publishers.

CHAPTER 8

PLANNING AND BRIEFING

I keep six honest serving men
(They taught me all I knew)
Their names are What and Why and When
And How and Where and Who.

Rudyard Kipling

In Chapter 7 we discuss in detail how to approach solving problems.

- By firstly defining the aim and ensuring complete clarity about your purpose, what it is intended to achieve and where it fits into higher level plans, that is, 'mission analysis'.
- By making an 'appreciation' by considering every factor and making valid deductions.
- By outlining every possible COA.
- By comparing the advantages and disadvantage of each COA.
- By deciding upon the best COA.

The selected COA is an outline of what you, as a leader, intend to do, that is, the outline plan. What leaders now need to do is to add detail to the plans and to communicate plans to those who need to know about it. When planning leaders should think 'two levels down'. This does not mean that they should interfere with a subordinate's own planning or conduct of operations, but it does give leaders an appreciation of the problems that may be faced by subordinates.

At senior levels in the hierarchy senior executives may make their appreciation and produce 'concepts of operations' that are then given to their staff or functional advisers to have complex detail added. This must always be overseen by CEOs or project leaders with direct access to the senior executives and who clearly understand what the senior executives wish to achieve and why, and what those plans may be the precursor to.

THE PLAN

I have a simple formula for success:

- A good idea
- Careful timing
- A simple plan
- Effective communication and inspired leadership

Ian Kiernan, sailor and founder of Clean Up Australia

Described below is a series of headings that need to be addressed. It provides a logical way of adding the necessary detail to any plan for any situation that leaders may encounter. It can be used at every level of the organisation, only the amount of detail varies; the headings remain relevant. If the list is adopted company-wide, as people move into different roles they can use a familiar process, designed to ensure that nothing is overlooked. Its use also facilitates speedy planning and rapid reaction.

It is in formulating the plan that leaders need to consult with their team members, invite their participation, and maximise use of their specialist knowledge and experiences. Their participation leads to commitment to the plans. Leaders, however, may have to exercise their judgement in assessing conflicting advice from within their teams. The headings, in the order in which they should be covered, are given below.

1. Mission
2. Execution:
   a) General outline
   b) Grouping and Tasks
   c) Coordinating instructions
3. Administration and logistics
4. Control and coordination.

Mission

The mission is derived from your appreciation of tasks allocated to you, as leader, by your superior. It helps to ensure clarity in your own mind if you start by reminding yourself of your mission in your detailed planning notes. (See 'Mission Analysis' in Chapter 7.)

Execution

a) **General outline.** In this paragraph reproduce your outline plan, that is, the selected COA. Doing this helps to crystallise your own thoughts and is useful in briefing others as you will see later.

b) **Grouping and tasks.** Under this heading list any sub-teams or subgroups that you need to establish or that already exist within your own team, or additional individuals or teams that have been temporarily attached to your team. Allocate precise tasks (derived from the objectives that you need to attain) to each sub-team that include any constraints, limitations, or extra authority that you are delegating. This assists subordinate leaders to make their own appreciation of tasks delegated to them that then become their own subgroup's mission as the process cascades down.

c) **Coordinating instructions.** In this section include any activity or measures that are vital to understanding the plan. Timings, preparatory action, control measures and action to be taken, should anticipated events occur, are usually best given here.

Administration and Logistics

In this section detail any distribution of resources, administrative issues such as changes to normal routine, and so on, that are necessary.

Control and Communication

This heading is designed to give clarity to: who is controlling or who can authorise what, or who is to coordinate what. Changes to normal reporting procedures or additional reporting that is essential, changes to authority for decision making, and so on, can be addressed here.

WARNING BRIEF

The leader now knows how exactly he or she and the team are going to accomplish the task. As soon as the plan has been formulated the leader should send a 'warning brief' to all those involved in the plan that:

- specifies who is to attend the briefing
- the time and place of the briefing
- the scope of the plan
- and any action that subordinate leaders should initiate immediately.

This warning brief should tell people all that they need to know to start implementing their 'business procedure'. The sending of a warning brief should not be delayed until the leader has had the full brief, if earlier on he or she has information that will help his or her subordinates anticipate and 'aim off' for what may come next. Once a warning brief has been sent, the plan then has to be communicated to the team in a way that leaves them in no doubt about the task and how they should approach it, and that will promote confidence and enthusiasm among them.

BUSINESS PROCEDURE

Business procedure is a standard operating procedure that every leader at every level should understand, the aim of which is to initiate activity as rapidly and efficiently as possible and to ensure that every person understands what he or she needs to do, why, and what he or she is to do it with. It is a way of operating that promotes organisational responsiveness and agility, the use of initiative, and reduces reaction times. The principles are:

- **Maximum concurrent activity.** When any action is being planned a warning brief passed to all who may be involved enables them to make whatever preparations they can, and this saves time later on. This requires a clear understanding of the responsibilities and duties of their role (see Chapter 9).
- **Anticipation at all levels.** Some projects may involve standard operating procedures or routine action. When people know the scope of a task they can anticipate what they are required to do and make their own dispositions accordingly.
- **Thorough knowledge of the briefing group system.** This means that everyone understands what briefings they need to attend as a matter of course, and that nobody (or no team representative) is absent from important briefings. This principle can only be applied when there is a clear organisational structure (see Chapter 9, the 'Requisite Organisation').

- **Efficient processes and procedures for all routine action.** This ensures economy of effort (see Chapter 20, 'Business Principles') in all work.

THE BRIEFING

We now discuss a method of maximising the effectiveness of your briefings—occasions in which you, as the leader, explain a plan to your team. For any task a leader must ensure that everyone in the team knows at all times:

- What is going on and why.
- When it is going to occur.
- How it is going to occur.
- What their part within it is.
- What action they should take if the task does not go according to plan.

The manner in which you convey this information must be clear, concise, unambiguous, simple, and inspiring. Rehearsals, frequently overlooked by leaders who think that they will get it right 'on the day', are strongly recommended. The briefer needs to be confident in delivery, totally familiar with the script or notes, and familiar with the layout of the venue and use of any audiovisual equipment. If the briefer has rehearsed and is able to make the presentation flow naturally, succinctly and clearly, he or she need not worry about the script, but can concentrate on how it is being put over and the audience's reaction to it. Most briefings fail because a confused briefer is unable to get the message across clearly, concisely, and in such a way that the audience is confident of success.

Sequence of a Briefing

The ideal briefing will follow the sequence:

1. Preliminaries
2. Introductions
3. Description of task
4. Situation:
   a) Market
   b) Competition
   c) Your own organisation
   d) Attachments and detachments to your own organisation.

5. Mission
6. Execution
   a) General outline
   b) Grouping
   c) Detailed tasks
   d) Coordinating instructions
   e) Summary of execution
7. Administration and logistics
8. Control and communication
9. Questions.

Always give briefings in this sequence because:

- The sequence is logical, easy to follow and to remember
- Subordinates know what is coming next when this becomes the norm
- It becomes habit and tired or stressed leaders are less likely to omit important points
- Subordinate leaders and team members can grasp concepts and details quickly and make relevant extracts on which they can base their own briefings.

Preliminaries

The leader needs to make any necessary preparations to be able to give the brief. This includes availability of location and any audiovisual aids, production of notes and handouts, and so on.

Introductions

Ensure that everybody needed is present and then introduce 'strangers' who may be attached to your team, or who may simply need to be aware of what you are doing, to the briefing so that everyone present knows one another. It is not only polite, it is a simple human fact that if a person knows a face and what a person's job is, it greatly aids cooperation and enhances teamwork later.

Description of Task

Simply outlining, in a sentence, the nature of the task helps subordinate leaders orientate their minds to what their part in the task is likely to be. They become aware of what is about to be covered.

Situation

Explain the context in which the task is to be carried out. This can include geographical, demographical, economic and market influences, and so on, as sub-paragraphs and can usually be extracted from your appreciation. There is no need to read out the appreciation in full, including all your deductions.

a) **Market**. State the relevant facts for the market in which you are working.

b) **Competition**. Outline the state of play about competitors, their strategy, and their expected next actions.

c) **Own organisation**. Brief the team on the higher level organisational plan so that they understand their team's role in the 'bigger picture'. As a rule of thumb brief two levels above your own, so if you are briefing at area level give a national and regional overview. Share information, it makes the team feel involved.

d) **Attachments and detachments to your own team**. For 'project work' outline any temporary additional people working with your team or detached from it.

Mission

Your mission stems from your appreciation of tasks allocated to you by your superior. This must be clear, concise and unambiguous. If you express it in the infinitive it conveys a sense of action that is what you want to happen. This should be followed by the purpose so people understand the reason why it is going to happen. For example: To launch an extension to XYZ product range in order to increase brand equity and market share. When briefing, state it slowly and repeat it. Missions are best given as 'To do something (action) in order to achieve (purpose).'

Execution

a) **General outline**. Explain your outline plan or concept of operations, in simple terms, by phases including the objectives necessary for overall success.

b) **Grouping**. Explain the composition of any sub-teams that are to work together for this exercise.

c) **Detailed tasks**. Brief each individual or subgroup leader by stating his or her name and looking at the individual while you do it, maintaining eye contact. Allocate the specific tasks, include any constraints or additional authority and resources allocated. Ensure that each person understands his or her role, or sub-team's role, by asking each one before you address the next person.

d) **Coordinating instructions.** Include timings, preparatory actions, and so on, only giving details that are essential at this stage to understanding the plan and that are applicable to most, or all, of those present.

e) **Summary of execution.** Summarise the plan to give the individuals clarity on the 'bigger picture', and their part in it. Use this opportunity to stress the importance of each person's task, generate commitment, and enthusiasm.

Administration and Logistics

The execution paragraph should only include detail essential to understanding the plan and each team member's part in it. Other detail can now be covered.

Control and Communication

Ensure the team is clear on who is controlling and/or coordinating the various aspects of work, and brief the team on any changes to normal reporting. Include how progress is to be measured, and how feedback is to be shared.

Questions

To ensure absolute clarity and understanding, ask those present if they have any questions and give them a few minutes to read through their notes before you expect questions to be asked. After this, asking questions yourself can confirm people's understanding of the 'big picture' and their part in it.

CASCADING PLANNING AND BRIEFING

As leaders, you could have subordinate leaders reporting to you who make up your own briefing group. These subordinate leaders need to be able to extract from your briefing their own task(s), make their own appreciation of how they are to carry out the task(s) and then brief their own direct teams. This process needs to be cascaded down through the organisation until the lowest team leader is briefing the front-line operator. Figure 8.1 illustrates this cascading of the extraction of briefings sequence.

People at every level need to understand the 'big picture' for relevance to their own level, hence, the concept outlined of briefing people on the situation 'two levels up'. As a leader you attend your superior's briefings and are given his or her team's mission; you also receive your own detailed tasks. Mission analysis of your detailed tasks will lead you to state your own mission to your own team, allocating subordinate leaders their own detailed tasks. This process is repeated as they, in turn, convert the tasks that you have given to them into a mission, and then allocate their own tasks.

Figure 8.1 Cascading of Briefings: Extraction and preparation of briefing information

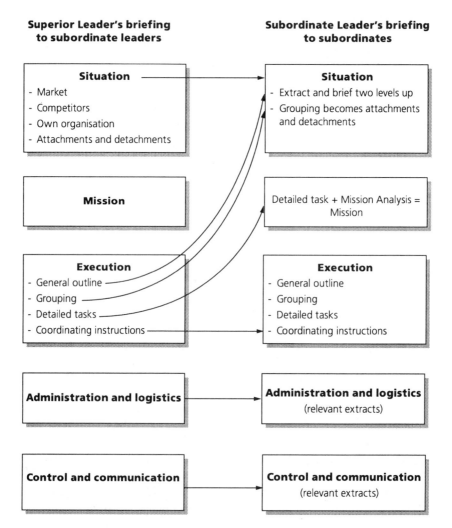

DO'S AND DON'TS WHEN BRIEFING

- Make your briefings **clear, concise, and simple**.
- Give your subordinates a thorough understanding of your intentions and explain the concept of your superior.
- Integrate all subordinates in coordinated action.
- Allow subordinates the maximum freedom of action consistent with the need for coordination.
- Do not try to give detailed instructions covering every possible contingency.
- Remember Von Moltke's maxim that 'No plan survives contact with the enemy.' Things can, and do go wrong, but your planning has reduced the chances of that happening to the minimum.
- Be aware that over-detailed instructions stifle initiative, restrict flexibility, and are time-consuming to prepare and deliver.

COMMUNICATION AND INSPIRATION

For the factors to remember and the principles to apply when briefing see Chapter 6. At this point it is worth re-reading that chapter, but the key words are:

- Clarity
- Simplicity
- Impact
- Sincerity
- Commitment to a feasible plan.

As an example of an inspiring briefing, one of Montgomery's speeches is reproduced in part below.[1] Montgomery was appointed to command 8th Army in the Western Desert in 1942 shortly before the Battle of El Alamein (one of the war's turning points) and found a rather demoralised organisation with little sense of direction and thoughts only of further withdrawal. A reflection of his predecessor perhaps? This was his first address to his headquarters staff on assuming command and was designed to dispel doubt, instil confidence and initiate the rebuilding of morale in the whole army:

> I want first of all to introduce myself to you. You do not know me and I do not know you. But we have got to work together; therefore we must understand each other and we must have confidence in each other. I have only been here a few hours. But from what I have seen and heard since

I arrived I am prepared to say, here and now, that I have confidence in you. We will then work together as a team; and together we will gain the confidence of this great army and go forward to final victory in Africa.

I believe that one of the first duties of a commander is to create what I call 'atmosphere' and here in that atmosphere, his staff, subordinate commanders and troops will live and work and fight.

I do not like the general atmosphere I find here. It is an atmosphere of doubt, of looking back to select the next place to which to withdraw, of loss of confidence in our ability to defeat Rommel . . . All that must cease. Let us have a new atmosphere.

. . . If we lose this position we lose Egypt . . . Here we will stand and fight; there will be no further withdrawal. I have given orders that all plans and further instructions dealing with withdrawal are to be burnt at once.

. . . What I have done is to get over to you the 'atmosphere' in which we will work and fight; you must see that that atmosphere permeates right down through the army to the most junior soldier. All the soldiers must know what is wanted; when they see it coming to pass there will be a surge of confidence throughout the army.

References

1. Nigel Hamilton, 1981, *Monty: The Making Of A General*, London: Hamish Hamilton.

CHAPTER 9

THE ROLE OF ORGANISATION IN LEADERSHIP

Organisation, structural and procedural, is something that armies have constantly been studying because of the need to deploy mobile units rapidly over long distances that can operate effectively immediately. They need enough leaders to provide adequate command in action, but not so many that leaders get in each other's way. Businesses have the same needs, but these are not so obvious since the consequences of failure are not so immediately obvious and bloody.

Organisation has various meanings. We can say 'I'll organise lunch', meaning to take responsibility for ensuring that it happens, we can use the word in the sense of giving order to, and making arrangements for, an activity, or it can be used in the sense of a structured, systematic, and disciplined, collective body.

So far we have been largely concerned with the leadership of people to achieve tasks. In most circumstances, however, people need to be grouped into permanent or temporary teams within the organisation and other resources need to be deployed and so we need to consider leaders' role in organisations. This chapter considers the way leaders can best deploy their teams to manage the resources available effectively for the accomplishment of tasks.

Analysis of the performance of efficient, productive, and profitable, enterprises generally allows observations to be placed into one of four categories (that can be compared to Adair's functional approach to leadership):

1. Planning
2. Organising

3. Controlling, coordinating, and directing

4. Evaluating.

Planning is considered in detail in Chapters 7 and 8. Planning is all too often paid cursory attention. Leaders at every level must remove themselves from day-to-day detail to think ahead, to reduce problems and challenges to their basic components, to clarify what is essential and what is not, to anticipate events, to make appreciations and plans. Developing foresight and thinking about the 'what ifs' should be second nature to you as a leader. Directing, coordinating, controlling, and evaluating, are subjects in Chapter 11.

ORGANISING IN ORGANISATIONS

My Lord, if I attempted to answer the mass of futile correspondence that surrounds me, I should be debarred from all serious business of campaigning. . .So long as I retain an independent position, I shall see no Officer under my command is debarred by attending to the futile drivelling of mere quill-driving from attending to his first duty, which is and always has been, so to train the private men under his command that they may without question beat any force opposed to them in the field.

Wellington writing from the Peninsular to the Secretary of State[1]

Many recent ideas have been put forward to eliminate hierarchical structures under the names of 'leaderless' or 'self-directed' teams, quality circles, matrix management, and so on. A hierarchy, however, remains because some form of hierarchy is essential to every efficient organisation. It is because many organisational structures have grown with too little thought about the principles that we consider below that has led to the desire to replace hierarchical structures. It is not the removal of the concept of hierarchy that is important, but removing the causes that stifle initiative, impose bureaucratic 'red tape'; lack clarity, decision-making ability and the concomitant authority, and autocratic behaviour.

The right structure helps to speed up the effective completion of tasks and to provide the framework in which clarity of role, authority, and accountability, aids in promoting sound working relationships and trust. In thinking about structure remember that over-flat structures often lead to:

- poor direction and lack of clarity of task and role by everyone
- poor decision making by superiors who have no firm grasp of the issues facing their diverse team members
- insufficient time spent developing subordinates
- insufficient planning and anticipation
- lack of career paths that lead to staff turnover and politicking, despite the 'lateral growth concept'
- little time for thinking and innovating by the superior
- relentless crisis management.

In contrast, excessive numbers of organisational layers lead to:

- lack of 'head-room' and freedom of action for subordinates
- stifling of initiative
- slow decision making
- inefficient communication channels
- a bureaucracy that hinders, rather than facilitates
- costs of unnecessary employment.

It is, therefore, essential to get the balance right. Balance is stressed because in the 1990s down-sizing or re-engineering seems to have swung the pendulum too far to the lean flat style. This has resulted in a vicious cycle, high staff turnover, and loss of knowledge and experience, higher stress, more crises, and less training and development (as there is no time). The net result of all this is a decrease in innovation of levels of customer service and, therefore, a reduction in the numbers of loyal customers.[2]

> An interesting fact of large industrial organisations is that there is always a nearly unanimous clarity amongst those involved at lower levels about who is actually keeping the thing going.
>
> *John Harvey-Jones*[3]

There are frequently three 'types' of organisation in an enterprise. Firstly, there is the formal organisational structure that appears on organisation charts that shows the reporting structure. Second, there is the ad hoc organisation that a leader of a team may temporarily adopt when presented with a task. This could include only specific individuals from the permanent team, or it may include other 'temporary' or 'project' team members. Finally, there is the informal organisation. In healthy enterprises where there are leadership and teamwork at every level it is a preferred social grouping; in inefficient organisations that lack leadership it is the collection of personal relationships that actually gets things done.

PRINCIPLES OF ORGANISATION

There are certain principles of organisation that should be employed. These do not exist to produce an inflexible bureaucracy, but to assist the speedy and successful completion of tasks. All interpersonal relationships occur within a social system and a dysfunctional system produces dysfunctional working relationships; the right organisation stimulates the growth of healthy and effective relationships. These should be viewed as first principles to be considered in all situations and applied as the leader's judgement and wisdom sees fit. See Figure 9.1.

ROLE OF ORGANISATION IN LEADERSHIP

Unity of Leadership

In a really effective organisation there is one 'boss'. Thus, at every level, one person is responsible for an area of work, and everyone knows to whom to report and who reports to him or her. The often ill-defined matrix structures are inherently dangerous as no one can effectively serve two leaders as conflicts of interests and priorities of work are bound to arise. Unity of leadership is the basis of an effective organisation.

> People do not like being told that things need improvement from people outside their immediate team. It has to come from their own leader first, from within the chain of command so to speak. Otherwise it is not really accepted.
>
> *Karen Lonergan, Education & Development*
> *Manager, Castrol Australia*

If a person is temporarily detached from his or her permanent team and leader and attached to a project team and project team leader, then the two leaders' accountabilities must be defined and understood by

Figure 9.1 The Role of Organisation in Leadership

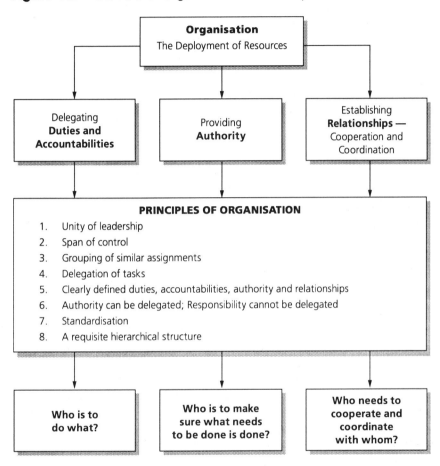

Source: Adapted from an original at The Royal Military Academy Sandhurst with permission

that person as well as those two leaders. If this division of duties is constantly adhered to then everyone knows what to expect as it becomes habit and is not overlooked.

The project team leader should be responsible for:

- all work allocation
- task delegation
- routine project performance feedback
- discipline within the project team.

The permanent leader remains responsible for:

- assessment of potential and management of all career development
- training course nomination
- welfare
- formal annual performance assessment
- pay reviews and other forms of recognition and reward
- other disciplinary matters.

The permanent leader should seek input into the annual performance assessment from the project leader during, and after, the project. If the project has been lengthy an 'insert' for the review may be written by the project leader. Naturally, the permanent leader takes an interest in detached subordinates and talks with them frequently.

Span of Control

There are limits to the amount and quality of 'overseeing' that a leader can exercise effectively. Those factors are number of personnel, distance, and time.

Personnel. The number of direct and indirect relationships multiplies as the number of subordinates increases: seven subordinates produces more than 100 relationships for a leader to manage. It is hard for any leader to effectively have more than seven subordinates and manage the number of relationships as well as devote enough time to understand, in detail, what is happening in each subordinate's area of responsibility, and, therefore, resolve conflict or make decisions from the whole-team perspective while planning. Fewer than three subordinates can often lead to over-supervision that, in turn, leads to frustration on the part of the team members.

Additionally, a student of group dynamics would observe that people are often happier working in smaller groups (often four to eight people), rather than in large groups, and that if no subgroup leader is appointed one frequently emerges who will represent the group to the team leader. Remember that four seems to be the maximum number of people that can belong to a truly democratic leaderless team (motivated, well-trained people of equal capability is implicit). As soon as five is reached the dynamics change and a leader will emerge. Belbin[4] refers to this phenomenon in his examination of management teams.

The capability of the individual under the leader's control affects the total span as a leader needs to spend more time with less capable subordinates and that affects management of the team.

Distance. Personal contact is vital to effective leadership and if subordinates are spread out over a large geographical area the leader cannot exercise leadership over a large group. Therefore, he or she may only be able to lead a smaller span of control.

Time. Some tasks or functions are excessively time-consuming, and again the leader may not have time to do justice to a full 'span of control'. This depends entirely on the nature of the work being done.

This principle may be summarised by saying that the span of control decreases as the number of variables, the complexity of situations, and the absence of the leader from his or her subordinates increases.

Grouping of Similar Assignments

Grouping similar or closely related tasks together in an organisation must be balanced against the need both to develop agile business units capable of working with little need for additional support, and the need to develop leaders' breadth of vision and leadership capacity by giving wide-ranging responsibility for as many functions as possible, as early as possible.

Delegation of Tasks

Refer to the Glossary for definitions of Task and Authority.

A good sign of a healthy organisation is the way authority is delegated within it. The larger the organisation, the greater is the need to set up a clear and efficient delegation system that enables the leader to exercise his or her influence over all. The hints below will assist you in delegating effectively.

Reasons for delegation

The reasons why delegation is necessary in successful leadership are as follows:

- Leaders, as organisations grow, cannot cope with the various problems at every level. They need the help of others.
- Subordinates must be taught how to accept and how to cope with responsibility to prepare them for higher posts in the organisation.
- People are required to make a more personal contribution to their work, and, therefore, the delegating of tasks provides motivation for high performance standards.
- Leaders, by delegating routine tasks to subordinates can spend more time on some of the more important functions of leadership such as planning and decision making.

> As a recently arrived and newly appointed company second-in-command in 1st Battalion The Duke Of Edinburgh's Royal Regiment in Northern Ireland, and with a Company Commander on loan from another regiment (The Staffords) to whom I was an unknown quantity, I marvelled at the operational accountability that was rapidly delegated to me in the first month in addition to the 2ic's admin role.
>
> It not only rapidly established a close and trusting relationship between my boss (Major Jim Tanner) and me, but stretched and challenged me in a way that was truly satisfying. It was as if I were the company commander—but without the pay!
>
> It prepared me so well for the next step up that, as a fairly junior Captain, I was appointed Acting Company Commander and left to my own devices for four months or so in the province while the boss was away on a career course. That acting appointment in an operational theatre again was the most wonderful opportunity for personal development. It was sad to learn through experience that that aspect of leadership would be so lacking in my first corporate employer.
>
> *The author*

What and what not to delegate:

A leader should delegate the following to subordinates:

- Tasks—routine and minor.
- Tasks that others can handle as well as, or better than, he or she can, so that the specialist skills of subordinates are used.

A leader should not delegate the following to subordinates:

- Matters of exception to general policy and routine procedure.
- Matters with potentially serious consequences.
- Tasks requiring the 'status' or 'position' of the leader.

Why are some leaders reluctant to delegate?

- They are insecure and hence, wish to retain the decision-making power (lack of self-esteem and self-confidence).
- They feel they are more competent than their subordinates.
- They are unable to define objectives clearly.
- They are afraid of being thought incapable and in need of assistance.
- They fail to realise that trust and risk are inseparably linked.

Why are some subordinates reluctant to accept delegation?

Most people like to have responsibility delegated to them because recognition of ability satisfies ego needs. There are some, however, who prefer responsibility not to be delegated to them because:

- They fear criticism if they fail.
- They lack confidence in their own ability.
- They find it easier to ask the leader for a solution, rather than think it out for themselves.
- They believe leaders are paid to accept responsibility, rather than to delegate it.
- They do the work while the leader gets the credit.
- They lack identification with the organisation.

To whom to delegate

- Your direct subordinates, not to theirs.
- Those with the most unused time or capacity. Avoid delegating to the 'busy' (capable) person who always succeeds.
- Those needing experience and growth.
- The lowest level at which performance capability exists.

Unless the task has to be done in a particular way let the subordinate do his or her own thinking that leads to learning, judgement, and maturity.

Clearly Defined Duties, Accountabilities, Authority and Relationships

> One store manager was so confused about discipline and role clarity that she rang me to say the store was on fire and ask if she should report it to the fire brigade or whether that was my job. The result of misdirected discipline and the fear that stifles initiative.
>
> *Karen Lonergan, Education & Development Manager, Castrol Australia describing life in a previous retail company*
>
> Our aim is to develop the company as a team of teams and seek to avoid the confusion that terms such as 'self-directed teams' can lead to. Our teams seek to clarify their areas of responsibility. Some decisions are givens and non-negotiable, some are arrived at by

consultation, some are the team's responsibility, and some are 50/50 joint decisions between the team and by its appointed leader. This approach clarifies levels of authority and what decision-making approach is taken in which situation.

The team of teams' concept does not negate hierarchy, but accepts that leadership has different levels. Our hierarchy, however, does not preclude individual or team contribution. It gives clarity and structure to what we do.

Kathy Rozmeta, Learning & Development
Manager, Coca-Cola Amatil Limited

Refer to the Glossary for Accountability and Responsibility.
A leader's role includes:

- Responsibility for both his or her own work output and that of any direct subordinates.
- Responsibility for building and maintaining an effective team that adheres to corporate values.
- Responsibility for performance review and appraisal, and pay review of his or her permanent team.
- Decision upon attachments to, and detachments from, a subordinate's permanent team.
- And all those functions of a leader given about a task in progress outlined in Chapter 5.

As Elliott Jaques says[5]

Military commanders in combat know all about context setting. If they do not do so their subordinates are lost once the shooting starts and communications break down. . .

- Commanders who do not involve subordinates by setting context do not survive.
- The fact that managers do not get killed does not mean that failure to set context has no serious consequences: it means only that we can hide from the connection.

Leaders must be clear about their own work if they are to set the context so that subordinates understand where they fit in the 'big picture' and then leaders delegate work for others. Leaders must ensure that all subordinates have:

- Clearly defined authority for all delegated tasks.
- Clearly understood the purpose, context and objective of the role, routine duties and the standards against which results are to be evaluated. This goes for all work, including delegated tasks.
- Fully appreciated the resources available to them.
- Understood completion dates for all tasks.
- Recognised that they are accountable to the person delegating the task.
- Have well-defined freedom of action and constraints, so that subordinates know when, and when not, to refer to the superior.
- Understood with whom they should cooperate or seek assistance as necessary.
- Established a system of progress assessment and evaluation if the task is lengthy.

Jaques has stated[5,6] that managerial leaders need four minimum authorities if they are to be held responsible for the work of their subordinates. They are summarised as:

- Veto on appointment. Whilst not having free reign in making an appointment, a manager must be able to reject any candidate whom he or she judges as being incapable of doing the work required.
- Decide task assignment. The manager, not his or her manager, decides what work their subordinates are given to do.
- Decide personal effectiveness appraisal and merit awards.
- Decide to initiate removal from role. If after fair warning etc, the subordinate is not capable of performing then the immediate manager must be able to start proceedings to remove the subordinate from that role. This does not mean dismissal from the company as the person may be suited to work elsewhere in the organisation.

The authority accompanying a role should be able to achieve a satisfactory result, but will never gain the wholehearted and enthusiastic cooperation of people. This 'power' has to be earned personally by you, as a leader, winning the hearts and minds of your people.

In addition leaders who are once removed (LOR) have additional responsibilities to their subordinates once removed (SOR) (that is, the relationship between leader and subordinate leader's subordinates that covers three hierarchical layers or strata)[5,7] for which appropriate authority is required:

- Ensuring the quality of leadership provided by the subordinate leader to the SOR.
- Final decision making for dismissal, removal from role, promotion, transfers, appeals, and pay reviews initiated by subordinate leaders.
- Assessing potential of, and acting as mentor, to the SOR.
- Building and sustaining the three-strata team.
- Ensuring equilibrium of work, conditions, opportunities, and so on, across the subordinate work teams.

The quality of leadership provided by a subordinate leader can be assessed by:

- Asking the SOR to explain where they fit into the higher level plans and to describe their role and that of others in their team.
- Considering the frequency and quality of briefing sessions and team meetings (too many is almost as bad as too few).
- Determining how much crisis management happens, rather than planned work.
- Determining the level and frequency of coaching, feedback, and recognition.
- Assessing the quality of administration and induction of new employees.
- The level of delegation.
- The willingness of a subordinate leader to lose a team member to another team and role if it is in the career interests of the SOR who has the capability needed for the new role and who wishes to pursue it.

If LORs are to exercise these responsibilities then there are implications for the maximum size of the three-strata group, that is, the LOR, subordinate leaders and SORs. The LOR has to know each individual in the entire group personally. Jaques terms this a 'mutual recognition unit' and suggests that the limit is 300 people.

These LORs should refuse to accept and certainly not solicit views on their subordinates from the SORs as this breaks the trust that should exist for strata levels. When 360° or upward feedback tools are used, the subject leader must personally gather opinions and data about him or her from others and voluntarily distribute results.

The capable LOR should not really need such survey results about a subordinate leader if he or she is alert to what is going on and is ensuring the quality of leadership provided by his or her subordinate to the SORs.

> As a corporate head-hunter, it was often my job to take clients' briefs and turn them into position descriptions (PD) for the prospective candidate to read. I frequently used to wonder how companies managed to get things done with such vague ideas about roles, authority, and accountabilities. At a low point in that job I was heartened by a visit to United Distillers Australia to discuss a corporate recruitment systems consulting project in which I saw real clarity in the sample PD the HR manager handed to me. It gave me hope for the future and took the edge off my cynicism!
>
> *The author*

If these responsibilities are cascaded down through the organisation, then clarity, consistency, and the foundations of a healthy culture, have been laid.

Role description form

Any role or position description should outline the following at least:

- Position title, department, time span and stratum level (see principle 8 below).
- General description of role
- Reporting structure:
    - Permanent organisational reporting structure diagram
    - Project team and other working relationships
    - Key peers/contacts/and so on
- Role-specific duties:
    - Main tasks, duties, responsibilities and accountabilities.
    - Authority levels and constraints.
    - Budget authority.

Authority and Accountability Can Be Delegated, Responsibility Cannot

> Whitelaw. . .said: 'Peter, I want you to understand two things. The first is that if and when the operation is launched, I will not interfere in any way; the second is that if anything goes wrong, I will take the responsibility afterwards.
>
> *General Sir Peter de la Billière as Commander of the operation to assault the Iranian Embassy in London, 1980*[7]

135

Remember that while authority can be delegated responsibility cannot. Responsibility for the successful completion of tasks always rests with leaders irrespective of whether they have delegated authority and accountability to one of their subordinates to carry the tasks out on their behalf. This acceptance of responsibility by the leaders is the key to building trust, confidence, and loyalty. By force of circumstances leaders have to delegate authority to selected people to organise their units' resources, accounts, sales, and administration, and so on, and plan the training of their personnel, but overall if anything goes wrong leaders should accept full responsibility.

As a leader, you are delegated tasks by your superior. Some of these you will wish to carry out personally; others you will wish to delegate further down the line. Leaders cannot escape or abdicate their responsibility. Everything done by members of the team, including the complete outcomes and the results of their combined work is the team leader's responsibility. Individual team members can only be accountable for areas under their direct control. If a team fails, any failures or mistakes by those individuals are ultimately attributable to the leader's poor judgement of character, failure to provide the necessary information or training and there the buck stops, with the leader of that team.

In Londonderry in 1984, my platoon and I were patrolling the Gobnascale area of the city. The area had been relatively quiet and there had been no need for troops to fire baton rounds (plastic bullets).

I felt trouble was brewing when we entered the area and very soon our Landrovers were being petrol-bombed with the latest version—large confectionery jars filled with a mix of petrol and paint to make the petrol stick to the victim. We called them 'sweetie jars' and they were a real threat as one of our battalion's soldiers had been killed by one only a couple of weeks before. I wanted to prevent us being forced to use our rifles (which we were entitled to do in that particular situation) and I wanted the crowd to keep their distance.

I ordered baton rounds to be fired to cover our move through, and out of, the area. I was quite within my rights to do so, but I had heard stories of junior leaders 'copping the flak' for making necessary decisions on the ground that upset politicians and created media stories and I half expected trouble on return to camp.

> How little did I know my Commanding Officer at the time, I heard that 'he was asked questions' yet I never said more than writing the normal patrol report. I believe that he supported me to the hilt and with such confidence that he never even mentioned the subject to me. That was my first real lesson in shouldering responsibility.
>
> *The author*

Standardisation

Do not confuse standardisation with rigidity and unthinking slavish adherence to established procedure. Standardisation of the meaning of terminology in use, processes, reporting formats and procedures, internal stationery, and documentation, application of policy for pay, promotion, discipline, and so on. These all exist to make an organisation efficient and agile. In this way consistency of expectations across the company can be achieved, and new teams or groupings can be formed that require the minimum settling-in period to become operational.

What is essential is that decision making is retained at the lowest possible level and this is what keeps organisational flexibility and agility. Here is an example to illustrate the value of standardisation.

> As a sales rep with a major consumer packaged goods company, the State Sales Manager tried to show how our results compared to other States. This proved very difficult because we all used different forms and sometimes measured different things. God knows how the National Sales Manager knew what was going on!
>
> *The author*

A Requisite Hierarchical Structure

The starting point for establishing an effective hierarchy is at the top of the tree (as in everything about leadership), and the acknowledgement that the more complex the task, the greater the competence required to do it.[5] In considering organisational structure the principles of Jaques' *Requisite Organization*[6] are recommended; its guiding principle is:

137

> To have effective managerial leadership, a leader must be in a role one stratum higher than immediate subordinates, handle maximum task complexity one category higher, and must possess cognitive power one category higher.

The theory behind this is briefly outlined below.

Refer to the Glossary for Category of potential capability, Category of task complexity, Cognitive power, Cognitive process, Stratum, Time horizon, and Time span.

Summarising Jaques' research findings[5,7] to a few key statements:

- Real boundaries of managerial hierarchical layers or 'strata' exist at time spans of one day, three months, one year, two years, five years, ten years, twenty years, and fifty years.
- These time spans coincide with the desired number of strata in any large organisation.
- The levels or strata of an organisation are based upon the level of task complexity (itself affected by the level of information complexity), with each stratum containing roles of the same level of complexity faced by leaders within it.
- These hierarchical strata reflect the stratification of human capacity—cognitive capacity can be measured in levels of abstraction.
- The level of work of a managerial leader is based on the level of task or information complexity faced by the leader and it can be measured by the time span of the role (see Figure 9.2). The greater the time span of a role the greater the level of responsibility and the greater the pressure felt by the incumbent and the greater the effect on subordinates, that is, the greater its scope. The leader needs to have a time horizon and cognitive power to match the role.
- Human cognitive power, which defines a person's time horizon, follows a predictable pattern of growth or maturation.

Leaders at every stratum within organisations must be sufficiently greater in capability than their subordinates to add value, set context for the work, have the wisdom to judge the effects and implications of subordinates' proposals, and be sufficiently self-assured to get on with their own jobs leaving the subordinates to do theirs without leaders' oversupervising them. Leaders must be one quantum step higher in cognitive capacity and managing work one stratum of complexity higher than their subordinates to do this effectively. This quantum step can be addressed by considering cognitive processes, information and task complexity.

Cognitive processes. There are four levels of cognitive processing:

1. Assertive processing in which information is organised and direct associations and assertions are made in immediate situations. A reason may be given or statement made that is not connected to anything else.
2. Cumulative processing in which significant pieces of information, none of which are conclusive on their own, are combined and conclusions drawn. In interviewing, for instance, the interviewer builds a collection of clues from which he or she makes a judgement on the suitability of an applicant.
3. Serial processing in which information is combined in a linear and logical sequence, cause and effect studied, and predictions made, for example, 'X will lead to Y that will lead to Z.'
4. Parallel processing in which separate serial processes are held in parallel and are viewed in relation to each other. A number of scenarios and options are, therefore, to be considered.

As we mature we progress up these four levels of processing that are used to make sense of data and turn them into useful information. Just as we can employ more complex cognitive processes there are more complex variables to apply them to, that is, information complexity.

Information complexity. Let us now consider information itself and the four orders of information complexity:

A. First-order complexity: *concrete verbal.* The variables are clear and unambiguous, they are not tangled with each other and are relatively unchanging. This is the world of the adolescent and 'juniors' in industry—'use this tool', 'we start at 9 a.m.'
B. Second-order complexity: *verbal abstraction.* This allows work to be discussed and briefings given that enables products to be made, sold and marketed, accounts and information systems maintained, and so on. It is the combination of a myriad of concrete things.
C. Third-order complexity: *conceptual abstraction.* Ordinary second-order language is used to express concepts of ever-changing variables and to discuss intangibles by senior executives. To mean anything these concepts have to be illustrated with concrete examples such as corporate culture change, the effects of corporate 'values', the effects of government policy and foreign exchange rates, the bringing together of wide-ranging accounting categories on balance sheets, and the like.

Figure 9.2 *Source:* Elliott Jaques,[6] adapted with permission.

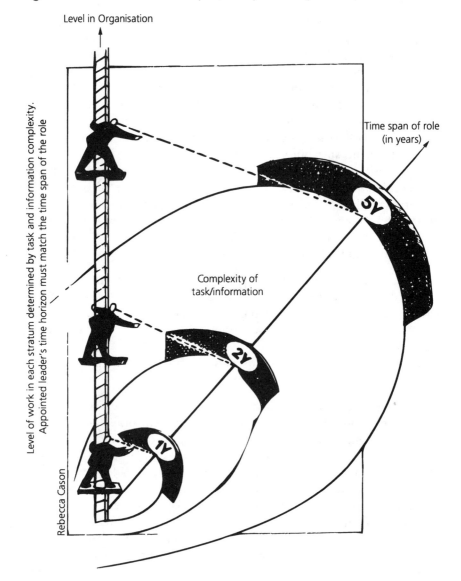

Level in Organisation

Level of work in each stratum determined by task and information complexity.
Appointed leader's time horizon must match the time span of the role

Rebecca Cason

Time span of role
(in years)

Complexity of
task/information

5Y

2Y

1Y

D. Fourth-order complexity: *universal abstraction*. Combining third-order concepts to make universal concepts for whole societal change, philosophies and ideologies, and so on.

With maturity we apply the four levels of cognitive processing, in turn, to increasing levels of information complexity, that is, we apply more complex processes to more complex information. *Our thinking moves from A1 through the categories of A2, A3, A4, B1 in a continuum and the mode in which a person operates may be termed his or her 'category of potential capability'.* This can be evaluated by the way a person behaves, approaches work, and discusses work. Different people mature at different times of their lives, so while the pattern is universal the timing is not. By the end of childhood we have generally moved through the four cognitive processes applied to first-order complexity information (A1 to A4) and start again at the second-order complexity (B1).

Task complexity. Jaques also says that there are four types of task complexity:

1. Direct action and immediate situational response. (Problems dealt with as they arise.)
2. Diagnostic accumulation. (Problems anticipated and resolved by collection, collation, and evaluation of information.)
3. Alternative serial plans. (Possible courses of action based upon cause and effect are evaluated and the best COA chosen.)
4. Mutually interactive programmes. (A number of interactive serial plans are implemented and are adjusted for timing and resources to keep the whole plan in line with the aim.)

These four types of task complexity are overlaid with the four levels of information complexity to produce categories of task complexity that again we may label A1, A2, A3, A4, B1, B2, B3, and so on.

The key to success in any role is that a leader's category of potential capability must be equal to the category of task complexity. Therefore, a person with B1 level of potential capability has a role that involves B1 level of task complexity. This match partly defines the selection criteria for people, and separates the strata of an organisation.

Thus the strata of an organisation are based upon the category of task complexity with each stratum containing roles of the same category of task complexity held by leaders within it who share the same category of potential capability. Jaques' work has shown that a maximum of eight levels are necessary in most large commercial

141

organisations, with fewer in smaller enterprises. The levels are: B1, B2, B3, B4, C1, C2, C3, and C4.

Type of Structure

There are five common structures employed by businesses that generally reflect their level of growth. None are absolute—they frequently combine elements of two or more of the types described, and all can be designed, based upon the time span of role already considered. They may follow the sequence described, but the complexities of operation may induce a leap one or two structures forward.

Table 9.1

Strata	Level Of Task/Information Complexity	Role Description
I (1 day–3 months)	B1 Direct judgement	Shop Floor Operator
II (3 months–1 year)	B2 Data Accumulation and diagnosis	First Line Manager Or Team Leader/Supervisor
III (1 year–2 years)	B3 Construct alternative routes to goals	Second Line Manager Or Unit Manager Or Unit Specialists
IV (2 years–5 years)	B4 Parallel processing and trade offs	Site/Functional General Manager (GM) Or Business Unit Specialist Managers
V (5 years–10 years)	C1 Judge downstream system consequences	Business Unit Managing Director (MD) Or Group Specialist Directors
VI (10 years–20 years)	C2 World wide data accumulation and diagnosis	Strategic Business Unit Group MD Or Head Office Specialist Directors
VII (20 years–50 years)	C3 Strategic options, alternative routes to make or transform whole systems	Executive Chairman Or Chief Executive Officer (CEO)
VIII (50 years +)	C4 World wide parallel processing and trade offs	Super Corporation Chairman/CEO

Source: Elliott Jaques, 1989, *Requisite Organization: The CEO's Guide to Creative Structure and Leadership*, Arlington, Virginia: Cason Hall & Co Publishers and Aldershot: Gower.

Usually the entrepreneurial structure is based entirely on the owner of the business. Employees are recruited as needed and little organisational structure or development occurs until change is forced by company growth, customer needs or market conditions.

The functional structure

Organisational growth from the entrepreneurial starting point often leads to a structure based on the company's main activities: sales, marketing, finance and product development, manufacturing, and so on. My fast-moving consumer goods employer was structured this way. This allows the enterprise:

- To develop functional expertise.
- To provide career paths for experts to lead people from the same functional background.
- To allow the effective use of resources across the company's activities.

However, functional organisation limits organisational agility and makes continued growth of product and service range in a highly competitive changing market very difficult.

The product and service structure

As a company grows people cannot devote enough time and energy to a wider range of products and services. Priorities are not easily decided and accountability is difficult to establish. Teams are established around a particular product (service) or product (service) group with their own specialists, and they are then responsible for use of their allocated resources. The teams may be supported by other parts of the company, organised on a functional basis (such as finance). The various product teams are then:

- More able to respond to market conditions through inbuilt flexibility.
- Able to focus specialists on to a product group and market needs. My recruit consultancy moved direct from the entrepreneurial stage to this structure.

Changes in the market lead to either a demand for more resources, or the disbandment of teams and their reallocation elsewhere in the business.

While this structure makes sense from the company's perspective, it may pose difficulties in maximising the service and product range delivered to customers. Instead of focussing on the customer and identifying the full range of products that can be offered in a value-adding integrated package, the product focus may prevent a supplier from identifying opportunities and limit the range of business done with a customer. A customer may be serviced by several different product sales personnel.

Account management, sales and marketing have to be focussed on the customer and on maximising the potential for business across the complete product range of a company—market-orientated management. As an example, Optus Communications changed from a product structure to a market segment structure in 1996.

The business unit and divisional structure

Continued expansion will overload senior executives with work across a diverse and complex portfolio. This forces senior executives either to ignore long-term planning, or to focus on such plans and leave a vacuum in the day-to-day operational leadership. It may then be necessary to create autonomous business units or divisions, serving particular products or markets or functions. The various divisions may cover sales, marketing and manufacturing operations with the personnel, IT and finance functions remaining centralised. Unilever Australia followed a similar approach in the early 1990s.

A divisional structure enables:

- Delegation of responsibility for performance to each division's leader, and further delegation throughout the group.
- Freedom of action for each group to respond to the market as necessary.

To promote total organisational agility, management and information systems should be retained at corporate levels.

The matrix structure

The matrix structure is often found in consulting engineering, construction, and information service-provider companies and other contract-driven organisations involving complex projects requiring specialists. It is an attempt to combine the focus on market and product, but this focus can be fraught with danger if leaders' and team members' duties and responsibilities have not been determined. Such structures allow:

- Maximum use and flexibility of specialist resources.
- Specialist professional development.

It is essential that LORs ensure the quality of leadership provided by permanent and project team leaders in matrix structures. It is very easy for specialists to become lost in the system, and not be led by anyone or to have constantly conflicting interests and priorities because they report to more than one person.

References

1. Sir Arthur Bryant, 1971, *The Great Duke*, London: William Collins Sons & Co.
2. Frederick F. Reichheld, *The Loyalty Effect The Hidden Force Behind Growth, Profits, and Lasting Values*, © 1996 by Bain & Company, Inc., Boston: Harvard Business School Press pp. 1–31 and 91–116.
3. John Harvey-Jones, 1988, *Making It Happen*, London: Collins.
4. R. Meredith Belbin, 1981, *Management Teams—why they succeed or fail*, Oxford: Butterworth-Heinemann.
5. Elliott Jaques and Stephen Clement, 1994, *Executive Leadership*, Arlington, Virginia: Cason Hall & Co Publishers.
6. Elliott Jaques, 1996, *Requisite Organization: A Total System for Effective Managerial Organization and Managerial Leadership for the 21st Century*, Arlington, Virginia: Cason Hall & Co Publishers.
7. General Sir Peter de la Billière, 1994, *Looking For Trouble*, London: HarperCollins.

CHAPTER 10

BUILDING AND MAINTAINING THE TEAM

A friend of mine was describing work in her new advertising agency job. She outlined the similarities with a TV soap ad agency—mistrust, lack of clarity of purpose, ineffective communication, politicking, back-stabbing and insincerity. She was particularly unimpressed with 'nibbles and drinks' being the only way her manager tried to build any personal relationships. 'If only he could be decisive, consistent and display some moral courage and foresight he could do so much more to enthuse people and earn some respect', she mused.

The author

In Chapter 4 we discussed the characteristics of teams and groups, group dynamics, introduced the stages of team development, and the role of discipline in teams. In this chapter we continue the examination of teams and discuss the principles of building and maintaining effective teams.

BUILDING THE TEAM

Forming

At the 'forming' phase of team development the leader must define the task, role, values, method of working and lay the foundations of teamwork by creating an atmosphere of mutual trust, confidence, support and inter-group relations. (Relate this to the functional leadership check-list in Chapter 5.) In this first phase you, as a leader, must get to know everybody as well as possible—learn about their attitudes, beliefs, needs, and personality—what makes them 'tick'. You should be able to write a coat of arms as you did (Chapter 2) for yourself for each and every team member. As a leader maintain a notebook with a section for each team member, recording each person's date of birth to remember their birthday, their work experience and all qualifications, hobbies and interests, strengths and weaknesses, summary of all interviews, coaching, and discussions, hopes and aspirations, spouse and children's names, and so on. It is useful and it can be handed on to your successor who will find it invaluable in his or her early days.

The team operates as a collection of individuals, and team members need to get to know each other. It is quite likely that some individuals try to impress others with their knowledge or experience and they may be rather more assertive, dominant or exuberant than is usual for them. This often passes when they settle in.

Competition and cooperation

We live in a competitive age and it is competition that drives us to improve standards. Leaders need to ensure, therefore, that teams understand and identify with the aim or mission of the team that inevitably will be to make more and better from less. Through this understanding, the internal informal groups will cooperate to get the task in hand completed. Competition is natural among teams and groups, so harness this to drive results even higher. Remember, too, the need to maintain a healthy rivalry, rather than a destructive competitive attitude internally. The leader of any team, while promoting internal competition to exceed targets set, must not allow his or her team to focus on beating their other colleagues at all costs. Ideas need to be shared and all the team's energy ultimately directed at competing with external enterprises.

Recruitment

Recruiting team members from either internal or external sources may form part of this task. The recruitment is a subject in its own right and beyond the scope of this book; however, it is essential that a candidate will 'fit' into the team and add value by nature of his or her personality, knowledge, and experience. A person's fundamental values and motivation guide that person's actions—his or her behaviour. Many organisations are now defining the values that will (when sound leadership exists at every level) define their organisational behaviour.

Assessing people's values is exceptionally difficult. Since their 'preferred behaviour' (the behaviour that is typically demonstrated) is a reflection of their values and is relatively easily assessed, recruitment should be, therefore, based upon this. Competence for a job may be defined as 'the required combination of skills, knowledge and a cluster of required behaviours in defined situations'. If a person is motivated to do a job, and naturally has the necessary preferred behaviour, it is usually not too hard to impart specific skills and knowledge to that person (assuming a base level exists). It is far more difficult to try to change someone's preferred behaviour and values, therefore, recruitment should be based primarily upon behavioural competence. Interviewing alone, even when based upon a highly structured behavioural competency methodology, has low predictive validity—an element of risk is attached. This is where assessment centres, although expensive in terms of time and demands on competent staff to run them, come into their own and are to be strongly recommended.

Belbin[1] has identified eight key roles that many teams need to undertake, especially in management teams; and this may be a factor included in recruitment. Team members do double up on notes. Belbin's titles and summary of each role follows:

- 'company worker'—reliable, practical, disciplined, possibly resistant to new ideas and inflexible;
- 'chairman'—fair, calm, and unbiased to all, objective and rational, confident and not insecure;
- 'shaper'—extrovert, energetic, hard-driving, challenges the status quo, and intolerant or impatient when facing inertia;
- 'plant'—intelligent, innovative, serious, unconventional, possibly lacking pragmatism and inclined to introversion;
- 'resource investigator'—outgoing, zealous, responsive, able to 'network' and requires stimulation to prevent boredom;
- 'monitor evaluator'—level-headed, careful decision maker, rational, possibly lacking emotion or affinity for 'people';
- 'team worker'—empathetic and responsive to people, promotes team spirit, but possibly oversensitive and indecisive;
- 'completer finisher'—conscientious, self-disciplined, an eye for detail, possibly prone to worry or anxiety.

Storming

In the 'storming' phase the leader may well be resolving conflict between individuals, sub-teams, or external teams, amending or changing rules, procedures and systems, and so on. The following are possible problem areas that the leader may need to address:

- **An atmosphere of tension, indifference or boredom.** The leader needs to cut through this early on, as he or she should with all problems, before it becomes a major issue. Everyone immediately recognises such an atmosphere, team members and visitors alike, and it will lead to a deterioration of the level of morale and *esprit de corps* within the team if it is not dealt with.
- **Unclear roles or objectives.** The need for clarity of duties and accountability in this regard was outlined in Chapter 9. Energy and resources are channelled into unnecessary diversions, and lead to a breakdown of unity and trust if there is a lack of clarity.
- **Overdominant individuals whose continued 'noise' disrupts other team members.** Leaders should present such people with 'behavioural evidence' (what they did or said and the reaction of others) and that requires confidence and moral courage. If such a situation is not sorted out, again stresses will be induced within the team and your credibility as a leader will be in doubt—trust will deteriorate.
- **Meetings that digress and do not remain focussed on the meeting's aim.** All of us would agree that far too much time is wasted in meetings that have no clear agenda or reason, and that degenerate into discussion of a multitude of trivial issues. Meetings need to be planned in advance with the aim and objectives of the meeting and an agenda forwarded so that all parties can prepare for it. Only those people who are essential to the meeting should be there. Too frequently managers invite the world when often the world only needs to know the result. Timings need to be indicated and should usually be adhered to. The leader, or chairman, if the leader has abdicated this responsibility, must keep the meeting on track and interrupt those who digress unnecessarily. Simple, accurate and clear expression is called for with the aim of the meeting always kept in mind. Normally Minutes should be kept and these are distributed to all attendees and stakeholders.
- **Disagreement and dissent.** This may be based on differing perceptions about the importance of issues, inflexibility or plain 'bloody-mindedness'. Perception can be overcome by effective two-way communication in which the reasons why are made clear in language that is understood and any doubts or concerns (whether expressed openly or not) are addressed.

- **Unclear reasons for decisions** etc. As above, communication is the key and for communication to be effective the leader needs to understand the nature of perception and the people who he or she is dealing with.
- **Disagreement expressed after the event, not during discussion.** This sort of 'noise' serves no purpose. The level of trust has to be built so that people feel free to express their concerns at the appropriate time. Just asking people is often not enough—they have an in-built mistrust and cynicism towards 'management', based on years of down-sizing, right-sizing and management fads failing! If the leader truly knows his or her people he or she can anticipate their reactions and allow for those in the initial stages, thus preventing problems from occurring.
- **Criticism, sarcasm and sniping at people.** This is based on mistrust, lack of mutual respect and/or confidence, and probably an inclination towards cynicism, 'playing' politics, back-stabbing and the lack of courage to speak directly to the 'target'. This has to be addressed by the leader and, if continued, despite 'an inter-view without coffee' and the example of others, may be a reflection of the basic signs of the malcontent. Their continued presence in the team must, therefore, be questioned.
- **Lack of awareness of the current situation and progress made.** The leader needs to constantly update everyone on the situation and plans. Remember that 'informing' was the fifth of the six key functions of a leader in our check-list in Chapter 5.

In Table 10.1, a table of trust-inducing practices identified by Jaques[2] is reproduced.

Norming

In the 'norming' phase, the settling-in period, trust starts to develop and the team identity starts to form. The identity is based on the norms established by the group that the leader should directly influence if unhealthy or undesirable characteristics start to emerge. These traits must be sorted out before they grow into larger problems.

Norms

The norms are the shared and accepted rules or standards that define what is and what is not acceptable in terms of the values, behaviour, attitudes and beliefs of the team members. Norms may be explicit when imposed on the team by the leader or the organisation. The

Table 10.1

Trust Inducing	Paranoiagenic
Equitable system of distribution of pay differentials related to differentials in levels of work.	Power bargaining over pay, or phoney output-related bonus 'incentive' systems.
Clear definition of accountabilities and authorities in lateral working relationships.	Leaving people to sort out their lateral working relationships by means of manipulation, personal networks, and power.
Managers one-stratum removed from immediate subordinates, in role and capability.	Managers more or less than one-stratum removed from subordinates and 'breathing down their necks,' or being 'pulled down into the weeds.'
Managers-once removed mentoring subordinates-once-removed on career development.	No mentoring, no career development, no real awareness of employee's potential capabilities.
Employees well informed on the context of their work, and on company vision.	Employees in the dark about what is likely to happen and why they are doing what they are doing.
Authority in line with accountability.	Accountability without equivalent authority.
Level of work in line with a person's level of potential capability.	Under-recognition and under-utilisation of capability.
Regular feedback on manager's judgement of your personal effectiveness.	Absence of feedback from manager, leaving you in the dark about how well you are doing.
Authority as required by the work in the role.	'Empowerment' as a phoney gimmick.
Team working a matter of individuals with individual accountability and recognition working together under an accountable managerial or project team leader.	Mish mash of obscure accountability and authority in 'self-managed' or in 'internally accountable cross-functional' teams with 'sponsors,' 'coaches,' 'champions,' etc.
Appointments and promotions based upon potential capability, commitment and knowledge.	

Source: Elliott Jaques.[2]

implicit and unwritten norms are determined by the behaviour of established team members who ensure they are complied with by new members and also by outsiders working with the team.

The factors that make a norm important to a group can be illustrated as in Figure 10.1.

Argyle[3] and Anantaraman[4] and Robbins[5] suggest that there are different kinds of norms that have different functions.

Figure 10.1

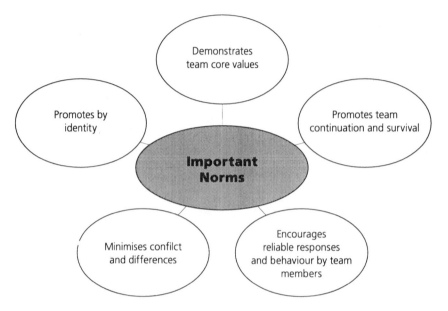

Work norms or performance-related norms

There are norms about the most efficient, simplest or easiest (but not necessarily the best) method of working. These represent the team's solutions to problems encountered or their attitude to work and when leadership is lacking can often differ from those preferred by more senior managers. This may be the front-line solution to inflexible or unnecessary bureaucracy, a better practice that has not been recognised by superiors whose finger is not on the pulse, or in badly led companies a lazy way of getting the job done with little attention to detail and lip-service paid to quality.

There are norms about the time and effort that people put into their jobs, the quality and quantity of work produced, their speed of operating, their personal standards, attitudes to matters like absenteeism and sick leave and company standards, safety and organisational values. The leadership provided directly influences the level to which these norms exist. In badly led companies these norms are kept to the maximum level that is possible and that makes life comfortable without incurring any penalty.

Undesirable norms reflect the quality of leadership provided and it is unlikely that the leader who has allowed this to happen can sort it out. It, therefore, poses a challenge for the next leader, particularly, if the team is cohesive. Sometimes efforts to overcome these norms can lead, albeit temporarily, to disruptive action from the team. The leader will need the unfailing support of the superior if he or she is to restore a healthy state of affairs.

Norms are not, however, necessarily negative. Many teams sustain a high level of output to satisfy their own needs. It is the leader's job to see to it that the team links its needs to those of the company. This is often the case for both groups of professionals and production teams, who may identify with, and firmly believe in, their work and company values, and display certain standards of behaviour.

Attitudinal and belief norms

The individuals who make up a team often develop common thoughts and feelings—attitudes—about their working environment and conditions of employment. This includes company policy, procedure, economic and technical matters, and even views about other parallel teams in the same organisation. For example, a sales team that spends its life on the road feeling possible rejection by customers might feel that the marketers have an easy job.

Some of these beliefs are based on inaccurate information and are, therefore, untrue. Leaders need to see that rumours are squashed immediately and that only accurate information is circulated. In this way leaders can influence beliefs and, therefore, behaviour.

Interpersonal behaviour norms

Personal conduct and social behaviour are usually more restrained at work than at home. Work becomes easier and energy is better used if team members agree to act in a predictable and reliable way—to adhere to their company or work team values or code of behaviour. For example, the members of a team may decide to share the workload of a sick team member. There may also be norms that relate only to social activity such as celebrating certain events, like birthdays, or milestones in the team's own development. These norms contribute to satisfaction, harmony, and the avoidance of conflicts, by making the behaviour of others more predictable.

Appearance norms

Teams or whole companies may develop norms about physical appearance that can result in both the style of fashion 'encouraged', physique and personality, or style of everyone in the enterprise. This can result in a personality cult in which actual competence and relevant experience of candidates during recruitment is overlooked in the search for a like-minded person to join the cult.

Language norms

Many teams or organisations often develop their own language that is difficult for outsiders to understand. It may include 'jargon' related to their tasks, abbreviations for processes and equipment, nicknames for people and the use of slang. This private language certainly eases communication, and serves to reinforce the team identity—the negative aspect is that outsiders are excluded.

We tend to conform to established 'norms' for several reasons:

- Because we agree with the norms, believe them to be valid. Beliefs are not easily challenged.
- Because team membership is valuable to us, it confers 'status' and satisfies affiliation needs. (See Maslow's hierarchy of needs, Chapter 12.)
- To avoid being 'different' and being singled out for attention.
- To 'fit in' and gain the cooperation and support of our team mates.
- To strengthen our beliefs and attitudes that make us feel less vulnerable.

Many of these reasons may be attributed to a lack of self-confidence, lack of self-esteem and/or lack of moral courage in the individual. This is why personal growth and maturity is so important in maintaining a healthy team.

An effective team satisfies both the needs of the task (and, there-fore, the organisation of which it is part) and the needs of the individual (the Adair three circles model). This is teamwork. Unlike morale that cannot be measured with accuracy, there are some measurable indi-cators of team performance:

- Output and/or productivity versus set targets and time scales
- Quality/standards maintained
- Absenteeism and staff turnover
- Interruptions to work flow.

In the performing stage the team has resolved any disruptive issues, ensured clarity of role and purpose, and can channel all its energies into achieving the task.

Performing—influences on team effectiveness

When groups or teams are compared, consider how much or how little a team achieves, how cohesive or how fragmented their members are, and how friendly or hostile they are towards outsiders.

What are the influences in team effectiveness? If we want our teams to be successful, leaders need to understand how these elements combine. We must, therefore, plan the elements shown in:

Figure 10.2

The team norms have been covered here already, organisation is covered in Chapter 9, problem solving and decision making in Chapter 7, and planning and briefing in Chapter 8.

The composition of the team

Teams are made up of individuals, each with his or her own personality, characteristics, attitudes, values, aspirations, and perceptions (see Chapters 2, 3), so difference is the common denominator in a team.

The differences among team members may include:

- Age
- Gender
- Race or ethnic origin

- Religion
- Previous experience and training
- Education and professional qualifications
- Family background and situation
- Motivation to work and aspirations—behaviour to satisfy needs (see Chapter 12).

Such differences can aid or detract in teamwork, depending upon the extent to which they complement or conflict with one another. Personality clashes or conflict between sub-teams are a common problem. When there is conflict other team members are likely to be drawn into it. Distractions, interruptions, poor working relationships, reduced morale and, possibly, the voluntary or forcible departure of some individuals could result.

The response to conflict falls into five categories according to Thomas:[6]

- Avoidance, when it is ignored in the hope that it will go away, is postponed when people do not 'grip' the situation, or isolated by keeping conflicting parties apart. It can also be withheld when feelings and thoughts are hidden because reconciliation is not possible.
- Accommodation. This is satisfying someone else's needs by neglecting your own. Noble self-sacrifice that will level to resentment.
- Competition. Forcing a solution on someone else, which is not likely to gain full commitment.
- Compromise in which arbitration and negotiation replace genuine problem solving by the leader.
- Collaboration in which open and effective communication and assertion promote consensus to a solution.

Although team stability can be desirable if all that is needed is the continued production of a standard product or service, it often leads to complacency and stagnation. A degree of variety, or diversity, in the team composition can stimulate innovation and creativity, as long as the differences of perspective and opinion are respected and managed. While personality and perspective can vary, there should be commitment to organisational values to ensure the efficient achievement of objectives.

Team size

A critical aspect of team composition is the size of the team. 'Management' usually decides this in organisations, influenced by the nature of the work, current 'fads' and financial considerations. These considerations often do not permit leadership and teamwork to flourish. Study principles of organisation in Chapter 9 again.

While it is desirable to have enough people with the knowledge, skills and experience necessary to perform the required tasks, motivated people lacking direct experience, but with the requisite behavioural tendencies and sufficient intellect frequently rise to the occasion when presented with a challenge. Team size presents two conflicting tendencies:

- The larger the team, the greater the range of knowledge, skills and experience.
- The larger the team, the more difficult communication becomes.

The latter point inevitably leads to potentially overlooking valuable contributions from some members or them not being put forward. The size of the team is a trade-off. My experience is that, for the highest degree of participation and involvement, a team should have about eight members or fewer, and more than 12 severely reduces interpersonal contact. 'True democracy' in teams is not possible with more than four and even then competence and motivation need to be similar—but a casting vote may still be needed.

A common trait of larger teams is their tendency to fragment into smaller units naturally. People often find it more satisfying to work in smaller teams where they can relate to others on a more personal basis. It is usually the case that morale is higher and absenteeism lower in small teams compared with larger ones.

Team role and tasks

Some tasks are very well defined in terms of process and standards and have limited scope or latitude for the display of individual initiative. Other tasks require a more flexible and/or creative approach with greater reliance on team members using their initiative and judgement in deciding what course of action is necessary to achieve a particular objective (Chapter 7).

Other factors that can vary, according to the type of task, are the time scale within which it has to be completed, the quality and quantity of the output. All these influence the level of team performance.

Team environment

Few teams perform their tasks in isolation, they are usually part of a much larger organisation, a team of teams. The company's objectives, policies and procedures, structure, culture, technology and physical surroundings, all ultimately determined by the CEO's leadership (and through him or her, by the example of all other leaders) very strongly influence team behaviour.

These organisational factors cannot be considered separately since they are interdependent and inter-related. In industry where there is commercial pressure to operate at the lowest possible costs and at maximum productivity, rigid and inflexible jobs to meet specified targets performed by semi-skilled people were (and still are) common. Organisational systems have imposed tight constraints that have limited the freedom of action, use of initiative, and have limited the personal communication among people. Teamwork has been stifled and the contribution that individuals can make has been restricted.

These factors are generally under the control of 'senior management', a term I personally detest since it is vague, promotes anonymity, and does nothing to project leadership—who or what is 'senior management', if it is a person let us see him! The factors have a direct influence on the way in which the team functions and, in turn, lead to the results achieved and the degree of satisfaction of members. Job rotation, participation and multi-skilling are possible, but leaders need to stretch out of their familiar comfort zone and initiate change if they are to lead change, rather than follow it.

Communication

Effective communication is vital to leadership to the success of any organisation and formal communication channels are an integral part of the organisation's structure. Restricting information flow is often an oversight on the part of a leader who simply overlooks the fact that something he or she knows directly affects, or has serious implications for, someone else—whether in the leader's immediate team or not. If it is not an oversight, it is a serious failure of leadership because knowledge is power, someone is feeling threatened, political advantage can be maintained by not passing information on.

Leavitt[7] and Shaw's[8] research studies have examined the communication channels in small groups and their effectiveness in work situations and the satisfaction of team members produced. The typical networks that are identified are shown in graphic form in Figure 10.3. The research shows:

- Centralised networks are most efficient in solving simple problems.
- Decentralised networks are more effective in solving complex problems.

Figure 10.3

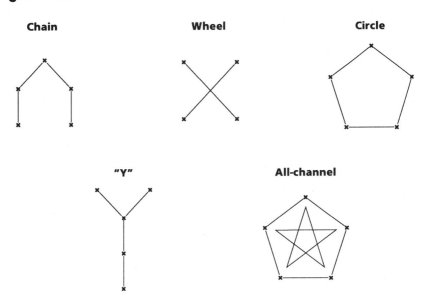

- Having access to communication with more people leads to a higher general level of satisfaction within the team.
- The more central an individual's position is in the network, the higher the general level of satisfaction felt by that person.

Ineffective communication patterns are typical of a rigid flow of organisational communication, and are often based upon unsuitable organisational structures. People in different parts of the organisation are in touch with one another only indirectly. All too often there is little to no face-to-face contact to convey important (clarifying) messages, instead impersonal methods such as memos, e-mail and the telephone, the easy options, are used. Effective communication is vital and it takes concerted effort on behalf of the leader to reach every person in his or her team.

The patterns of communication that develop are affected by the environment such as the physical setting in which work is done, work flow patterns, and the location of individuals. The physical distance or proximity of team members to each other influences the formation and development of team relationships. For example, seating arrangements in an office determine the ease and opportunity with which communication can occur.

It is very useful for a leader to note the dynamics, levels of participation, and the flow of communication within his or her team at meetings. A chart can be drawn from this illustrating the participation pattern and relationships within the group that can be used at a later date when messages are passed through the informal communications network.

Coaching

Coaching is a process by which a leader assists subordinates to understand their role fully, and highlights the subordinates' strengths and weaknesses. While the leader should try to develop both if possible, the leader must at least teach the protégé to play on his or her strengths and keep his or her weaknesses under control.

Coaching is an ordinary part of a leader's daily activities (review the functional leadership check-list in Chapter 5). Successful coaching depends as much on the personality or character of the leader as on a set of 'coaching skills'. The purposes of coaching are as follows:

- To help subordinates to comprehend the scope of their role and the opportunities that can be expected fully; and by explaining the role in context, indicating how the incumbent can take advantage of such opportunities.
- To assist subordinates in learning and in applying knowledge and skills to their roles; and to close any gap between required and actual performance and personal effectiveness.
- To ensure subordinates understand the importance of corporate values and philosophy, and to align subordinates with them.
- To feedback to subordinates the behavioural evidence that will assist in fully integrating the subordinates into the team and making each of them a valued and effective team member.
- To assist the growth of self-confidence and self-esteem.
- To develop personal accountability and commitment.
- To encourage the participation and interaction of all team members.

The essential ingredients of coaching, individually or collectively focussed, are:

- Clarification of tasks and objectives.
- Repeated questioning, effective listening, and support (moral and physical)—building confidence and the will to win.
- Knowledge of the task and of the person being coached.
- Wisdom, experience and judgement.

- Learning and applying the lessons from past experience. Encouraging continuous learning as learning is best achieved from analysis of mistakes, whether the protégé's or someone else's.
- Encouraging and introducing continuous improvement in product or service quality and promoting innovative thought.
- Demonstrating commitment and loyalty to corporate values and ways, as well as empathy and sensitivity to subordinates.

Leaders need to provide the environment and opportunities within subordinates' roles that enables them to apply, with clarity and understanding, their competence (competence being the combination of skills, knowledge and behaviour).

Clarity can be developed through clear planning and briefing (see Chapters 7 and 8) and the principles of organisation (see Chapter 9). There are some additional measures that can be taken and these are discussed below.

- Subordinates' personal objectives and performance measures. These form part of a role or job description and the incumbent has to be quite clear on what is expected of him or her.
- Appraisal interviews and feedback. Constructive criticism, recognition, and praise, where relevant, delivered with confidence, tact, empathy, moral courage, accuracy, and without any insult.

This results in a clear understanding of what will ensure high performance. An effective coach needs to display:

- A relentless pursuit of excellence.
- Wisdom and judgement.
- Sensitivity, understanding and empathy to each individual.
- Confidence in the protégés' ability and potential.

There is a difference between the coach and the critic; the coach and the instructor:

- The coach focus is on the problem; the critic on the person
- The coach is specific; the critic is general
- The coach emphasises change; the critic emphasises blame
- The coach meets the learner's needs; the critic meets the critic's needs
- The coach questions; the instructor advises
- The coach generates options; the instructor gives solutions
- The coach suits experienced students; the instructor suits the inexperienced.

Mentoring

Mentoring is the process by which a leader, ideally the LOR, helps an SOR, to understand his or her potential and how that potential might be applied to achieve a full career development within the organisation.[6] Mentoring helps subordinates to become 'street-wise' in the culture and organisational way of doing things and to develop sound judgement and wisdom.

Websters' Dictionary defines a 'mentor' as a 'wise, loyal adviser and teacher'. The implication for a mentor is that experience, wisdom and good counsel, are transferred through advisory means. The objective of mentoring in a career sense is to assist in propelling the protégés to a higher plane and/or to transfer experience that broadens the protégés' field of expertise. Mentoring is an important process that allows an organisation to:

- Maximise the use of its experienced leaders and technical experts.
- Assist in transferring knowledge gained in training to its application on the job.
- Form part of the management development and succession plan.
- Enhance individual protégé's motivation and thirst for knowledge.

Mentoring should be viewed as a contract between the mentor and the protégé, and requires effort from both parties to be successful. Remember that mentors exist to polish a protégé's expertise; he or she is not there to teach fundamental skills and knowledge needed for the job— that is for the direct superior leader and the training wing to do. Mentoring takes time and may need to be specified as part of leaders' job descriptions.

Mentors need to remember that they do not directly control their protégés, but that they have an advisory role that requires their interest, enthusiasm, and constructive criticism, to be successful.

Appraising performance and effectiveness

It is a fundamental responsibility of leaders to provide continuous feedback on a subordinate's performance and effectiveness at work. There is a difference between performance and effectiveness appraisal[10]. Performance is a measurement of actual achievement versus planned target output. It is, therefore, something that can be accounted for numerically. Effectiveness is a discretionary judgement made by a leader about how well his or her subordinate has gone about his or her work, taking into account any factors or circumstances that might affect the work environment.

The quantitative assessment of performance is straightforward, the qualitative assessment of effectiveness is far more difficult because it requires a deep understanding of the personal qualities and behaviours being assessed and requires the moral courage to feed them back to the subject honestly. Overgrading in these aspects is extremely common because either managers do not know the real meaning of qualities like 'flexibility' that they are assessing or because they do not realise the damage they are doing to the organisation and the assessed person by wishing to be nice and to avoid the unpleasantness of pointing out deficiencies and solutions, or they lack the moral courage, confidence, and tact, to be honest.

When anyone receives honest and frank feedback after a career noticeable only for overgrading by superior managers it can be a shattering blow to their self-worth and self-esteem.

For feedback to be effective, the receiver has to understand, accept and act on what has been said.

- To be understood it has to be clear, specific and indisputable, rather than general and vague.
- To be accepted it has to be constructive, to demonstrate respect and sensitivity, and be given in a climate of trust.
- To be acted upon, opportunities and support have to be provided.

Remember that part of a LOR's role (Chapter 9) is the application of quality control to assessments made by a subordinate leader to his or her immediate team. There should never be any surprises in an annual appraisal of effectiveness or performance since these should have already been discussed on several occasions.

Overview of the stages of team development

Figure 10.4 illustrates the stages of team development by relating behaviour and its objectives.

In Chapter 4 the fact that the stages of team development are cyclical and, having reached the performing stage, re-forming might take place, followed by re-storming, and so on, is discussed think of this as continuous evolution not in a circular or cyclical fashion, but following an Archimedes' spiral with time as the axis along which these processes are taking place. The team is a living organism that is constantly evolving and none of these processes are static for long.

Figure 10.4

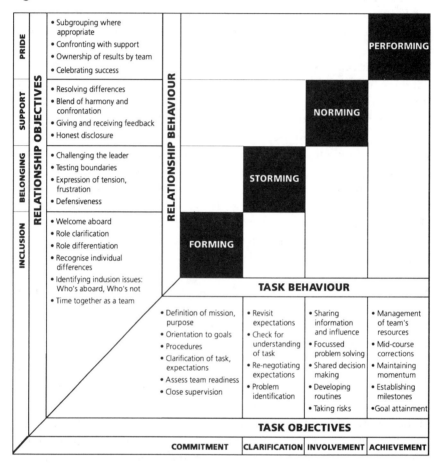

Original source unknown

Establishing development objectives

To further develop the team objectives must be set. This involves:

1. Identifying the strengths and weaknesses of the whole team and its members in relation to the tasks it must achieve and the overall goals of the organisation.
2. Establishing long- and short-term development objectives in order of priority that address the identified weaknesses.

    Good development objectives, like other objectives, are CARSMART.[9]

- Challenging
- Achievable
- Relevant
- Specific
- Measurable
- Agreed
- Realistic
- Time constrained.

In most teams the team members can contribute to defining these objectives and a plan to achieve them. Within a dysfunctional team, the leader may need to speak to people individually, consider all the differing advice and come to his or her own conclusions, sometimes having to be fairly authoritarian to initiate development. The leader's style will ease as momentum increases.

MAINTAINING THE TEAM

It is not so easy to discuss the leader's role in maintaining the team as it is not nearly so clear-cut as the steps a leader takes to either achieve the task or to satisfy individual needs. Adair[11] suggests that it is easier to think about teams that are threatened:

- From without by forces aimed at the team's disintegration such as internal political 'empire building' or external competition.
- From within by disruptive individuals or ideas.

The leader may then observe how the team allocates priority to maintaining itself and resisting these pressures to break up. For instance, one way is to use competition and identify an external opponent to cement relationships within the team. The common expression 'united we stand—divided we fall' feeling is applicable to all teams. For the leader the task is to build on this phenomenon of the team 'personality'.

It is universally accepted that nothing succeeds like success, or, conversely fails like failure. A team that has tasted success is likely to have generated the morale and confidence that will carry it to further success. Ideally, this means giving a new team the early taste of success by giving them a relatively simple task to start with—one at which their chances of success are high—so that confidence and high morale enables them to succeed at the more difficult tasks that they meet later. But watch out for failure: once the team has failed it must be given a chance to redeem itself, or it may collapse. Giving a team a task that it feels is beyond its capabilities is likely to so demoralise it that it will disintegrate from being a team to merely a collection of individuals.

Identification is another important element in building up *esprit de corps* and generating success. Everyone likes to be associated with success. Armies, football teams and clubs all have identifying emblems and colours. Wearing some form of uniform or team identifier may appear to the 'politically correct' view to be futile and irrelevant gestures, but they can touch some of the most primeval chords in the human mind.

Conflict between Teams

Inevitably there are times when differences in perception, poor communication, or some other failure of leadership, allows conflict to arise, between groups, between the subgroups within a team or between teams themselves. This conflict can be heightened through excessive competition among teams and a breakdown of trust. Such a breakdown can be catastrophic because mistrust leads to poor communication that, in turn, produces greater mistrust and so a vicious cycle has been established.

Within a team that is in conflict with another Adair[11] and Argyle[3] suggest the following characteristics may be observed:

- **Cohesiveness**. Conflict increases the degree of cohesion and loyalty once an outside 'enemy' has been identified.
- **Perceptions**. Perception of other teams become distorted as the team tends to see only its own strengths and the faults in others.
- **Security needs**. When a threat is perceived the team wishes to guard its own existence and space—it becomes territorial. It may cut itself off from communication with other groups.
- **Adherence to 'norms'**. Under threat, a team tends to demand more conformity from its members than the established norms and may accept more control from its leaders. There is a greater emphasis upon unity.
- **Change in priorities**. The team is likely to devote more effort to maintaining its own existence at the expense of directing its energy to the task.

In essence then, a team closes ranks and places more value on itself than other groups—it pursues win/lose resolutions to situations.

When competing 'teams' pursue the win/lose route the following will result. Winners become more cohesive, may experience a release of tension, and may become complacent and, therefore, less productive. At the same time the losing team may fragment and reorganise, experience a rise in tension as people prepare for the worst, see a deterioration in morale and may blame the organisation or its leaders.

Leader/member Relationships

Position power. Leadership implies control of, and influence over, other people. This influence and control is, naturally, greater if the leader has the support, confidence and the trust of the team members. If you are accepted by your team as its leader you obviously have considerable control. As a leader you have only authority by virtue of your appointment and your position. Power is derived from the willingness of your subordinates to accept you, when your leadership is accepted they give you power.

Sometimes it is difficult to tell just how much support and backing a group is giving you. We tend to be unrealistic—often believing that our relationships are better than they are. Be aware of this trend and beware of it.

Pointers to the existence of good relations with your team include:

- Do members of your team try to keep you out of trouble?
- Do they warn you of potential difficulties?
- Are they conscientious about tasks that you have allotted them?
- Do they do what you want, rather than just what you ask them to?
- Do they include you in 'small talk'?
- Do they seem genuinely friendly and eager to please you?

If you can honestly answer 'yes' to these questions then your relations with your team are probably good. The ideal leader, at any level, achieves the loyalty and affection of his or her team by inspiration, rather than by coercion and through wielding his or her authority.

It is of great importance to your team that you are seen to be getting on with your superior. When your superior supports you and works with you, you are held in esteem by your team members. If it can be seen that your suggestions and recommendations are accepted by the superior then the team grows in trust and confidence in your ability to lead them successfully.

Team Maintenance Functions

Lastly we review the list of things a leader should do to promote the solidarity of the team. These are discussed in Chapter 5 and are illustrated in Figure 10.5.

Figure 10.5

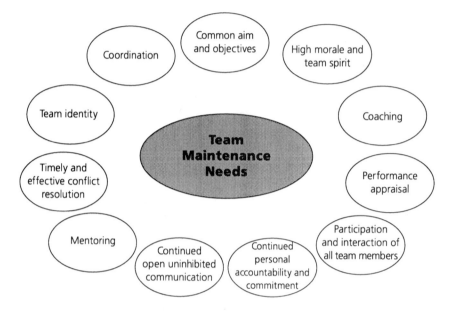

© Leading Initiatives (Australia) Pty Limited 1996

References

1. R. Meredith Belbin, 1981, *Management Teams—why they succeed or fail*, Oxford: Butterworth-Heinemann.
2. Elliott Jaques, 1996, *Requisite Organization: A Total System for Effective Managerial Organization and Managerial Leadership for the 21st Century*, Arlington, Virginia: Cason Hall & Co Publishers.
3. M. Argyle, 1974, *The Social Psychology Of Work*, Harmondsworth, UK: Penguin.
4. V. Anantaraman, 1984, 'Group Dynamics and the human relations organisation model', in V. Anantaraman, C. Chong, S. Richardson & C. Tan (eds) *Human Resource Management: Concepts and Perspectives*, Singapore: Singapore University Press.
5. S. Robbins, 1991, *Organizational Behavior: Concepts, Controversies and Applications*, Englewood Cliffs, New Jersey: Prentice-Hall Inc.
6. K. Thomas, 1976, 'Conflict and Conflict Management', in M. Dunnette (ed.) *The Handbook of Industrial and Organizational Psychology*, Chicago: Rand McNally.
7. H. J. Leavitt, 'Effects Of Communication Patterns On Group Performance', *Journal of Abnormal and Social Psychiatry*, 1951, 46.
8. M. E. Shaw, 'A Comparison Of Two Types Of Leadership In Various Communication Nets', *Journal of Abnormal and Social Psychiatry*, 1955, 50.

9. Larrie A. Roullard, 1993, *Goals and goalsetting*, Menlo Park, California: Crisp Publications Inc.

10. Elliott Jaques and Stephen Clement, 1991, *Executive Leadership: A Practical Guide to Managing Complexity*, Arlington, Virginia: Cason Hall & Co Publishers.

11. John Adair, 1986, *Effective Teambuilding*, Aldershot: Gower.

Note:

The leader's notebook containing information on individual team members should be divided into three sections.

1. Factual data–name, address, date of birth, spouse's details, previous employment, education, and courses attended.
2. Performance management and coaching information and evidence of 'preferred behaviour'.
3. Assessment of potential, strengths, weaknesses and motivators.

Section 3 should be kept secure at all times and not passed on to other leaders. Be aware of laws relating to data protection.

CHAPTER 11

DIRECTION, COORDINATION, CONTROL AND EVALUATION

Refer to the Glossary for definitions of Directing, Coordination, Control, and Evaluation before you read this chapter.

DIRECTION

Direction is establishing, through effective communication, what needs to be done, and giving any guidelines. The skill is in doing the minimum of thinking for the subordinate and in using the subordinate's initiative. This aids growth, development, and motivation, of the subordinate.

Except in emergencies when the occasion demands or in circumstances when there is a significant resistance to change and inertia to overcome, autocratic leaders probably do not achieve long-term results. We all naturally resent being pushed around, so such techniques cannot guarantee subordinates' effective cooperation.

The direct 'order' that something be done by someone in a certain way by a certain time is certainly not the best method of operation. Better results can be obtained by asking or suggesting that something be done—always explaining the reason why. Subordinates then have the leeway to use their own initiative and that gains their commitment.

Subordinates must clearly understand what is to be done, so leaders should try to use language that is understood by subordinates and the leaders' wishes explained clearly and concisely. Many terms and situations that are clear to leaders could convey a different meaning to their subordinates. At the end of a briefing leaders should always ask

170

questions to ensure that everything has been completely understood and that the messages that leaders intended to be received has been without 'corruption' by perceptual filters.

As a general rule written instructions are best when: it is desirable to make them a matter of record; precise figures or complicated details are involved; a particular subordinate or team has to be made especially accountable. A bulletin board can be used for general direction or work assignments.

Verbal requests are always best for giving simple instructions affecting routine tasks and for clarifying the details of a written order. Communication face to face allows leaders to inject their personality and inspiration into the request or direction, to clarify their meaning, and to identify any assistance subordinates may need.

In directing, leaders are charting a delicate course between too little supervision and too much. If it is insisted that all instructions are written down, the enterprise becomes bogged down with administration, and operations slow down. If subordinates feel their supervisors are always overseeing them, their initiative and interest is stifled. The amount of direction given to subordinates should always be the minimum necessary to allow each individual or team to ensure efficient completion of their tasks. Direction, as a function of leadership, is the heart of the problem of ensuring that people complete the job. Even the best of planning and organising fails if the direction given is unsuitable.

Effective direction of subordinates is only possible when the leaders ensure that the principles in Figure 11.1 are applied.

LEADERSHIP AND THE COORDINATING ACTIVITY

Leaders' responsibilities extend in three directions; upwards to their superiors, downwards to their subordinates, and sideways to teams or one person, not reporting direct, but that may be involved in, or affected by, their work. The coordinating function of leadership is about leaders' lateral relations within organisations.

The aim of coordination is to seek the cooperation of people not in leaders' own teams, or to link actions between the groups and leaders' teams. No team in an enterprise is so independent or self-contained that it does not rely on other teams for help in accomplishing its mission. Leaders need to work out joint problems with other groups, by person-to-person contact, by planned effective meetings and liaison visits.

Effective coordination is best achieved through foresight, anticipation and by advising those involved well in advance of what help is

Figure 11.1

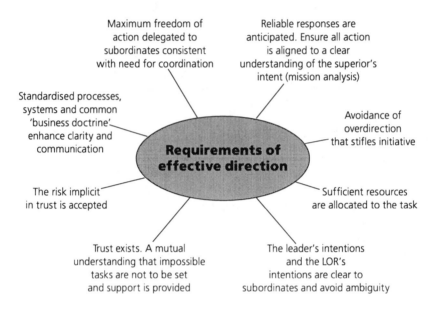

Maximum freedom of action delegated to subordinates consistent with need for coordination

Reliable responses are anticipated. Ensure all action is aligned to a clear understanding of the superior's intent (mission analysis)

Standardised processes, systems and common 'business doctrine' enhance clarity and communication

Avoidance of overdirection that stifles initiative

Requirements of effective direction

The risk implicit in trust is accepted

Sufficient resources are allocated to the task

Trust exists. A mutual understanding that impossible tasks are not to be set and support is provided

The leader's intentions and the LOR's intentions are clear to subordinates and avoid ambiguity

required. Leaders, though having control over their own activities necessary to achieve their plans, cannot control to the same extent the work of others whose help they seek. Therefore, leaders must give supporting teams and individuals as much time as possible to organise the assistance needed, appreciating that others have their own work priorities to fulfil, that because of pressure of work they might be unable to help, especially when help is requested at short notice.

Leaders wishing to seek the willing cooperation of the work of other departments, must make requests in a personable way. Express gratitude for help given, and help is usually given willingly in return when it is requested by those who have assisted you. Such cooperation secures good relations for the future, since few people are prepared to help the type of leader who consistently refuses, or fails, to help them when they, in their turn, seek the leaders' assistance with their own tasks.

CONTROL

The word 'control' has been given an unpleasant meaning to some in the 1990s, but it must be emphasised that control in the sense defined here is essential. Let us be quite clear that I mean 'control' not in the interfering and domineering sense, but in being able to influence events and outcomes. The most effective planning and preparation is to no avail unless it can be translated into action and unless that activity accurately reflects the original objectives of the plan. This is where the requirement for control and evaluation arises; in other words the control and evaluation functions exist to ensure that what ought to be done is done—that all activity is directed towards achieving the aim and to ensure that, if this is not the case, a change in plan or performance is implemented.

Perhaps one of the greatest fears new or inexperienced leaders have is that they cannot control a subordinate leader, perhaps a 'traditional' foreman or supervisor who may be a lot older and probably far more worldly wise. The leader's concern is 'how will I get him to do what I want him to do willingly?'

Providing that you are sensible in your approach and follow this advice those fears have little or no substance and you will soon become comfortable in your leadership role. Nevertheless, there are some techniques you can use to help you keep ahead of events, rather than merely reacting to them.

Timely, effective control and prompt evaluation by you, as a leader, helps to maintain momentum in an activity. The skill is in recognising that any given task or activity could be improved and implementing effective control measures in good time to ensure that it is. The development of this skill will assist you in becoming an effective leader.

Several conditions must exist before effective control can take place:

- **Plan.** A good plan that expresses clear objectives to be achieved within a precise framework is critical. Include detailed tasks, or what is expected of subordinates and how their part fits into the overall plan.
- **Standards or objectives.** These should be CARSMART (see Chapter 10). The reasons for such objectives are:
    People understand and meet business objectives
    People develop foresight and vision
    People's participation enhances their commitment
    People's effectiveness is more easily assessed
    People appreciate the work of both other teams and individuals.

- **Information.** Maintain a constant two-way flow of information. It can take many forms:
     Personal observation
     Face-to-face communication
     Verbal and written reports, both qualitative and quantitative. Keep these to the minimum and simple.
- **Influence.** The way to effective control lies in having the ability or means to exert influence on the course of events to be controlled—in other words, being able to affect things when the occasion demands.

THE MEANS OF CONTROL AND INFLUENCE

As a leader there are various means to assist you control and influence events.

- **Formal authority or position.** Your position gives you, as a leader, the authority to make decisions, but it does not mean that you have power. Power is given to you by those you lead when you have won your subordinates' acceptance, trust, and confidence.
- **Expertise.** Having recognised expertise and competence in your field.
- **Communication.** The ability to argue, persuade, or inspire, convincingly and change the attitude of others.
- **Obligation.** By building up your reputation for being caring, helpful and cooperative you could establish a credit balance of obligation with others, that is, when you need goodwill or assistance it is more likely to be offered if you have given the same in the past.
- **Qualities of leadership.** By behaving in a manner that accords with the highest standards of the team, in team members a tendency is generated to listen to leaders and to respect leaders' judgement. Leaders alone set the standards that teams conform to—high or low. Review the qualities discussed in Chapter 6.

TIMING OF CONTROL

Control is an ongoing function, but it is possible to identify particular types of control according to when it is exerted:

- **Before the event.** Obviously the best form of control is that anticipation prevents problems.

- **During the event.** Dealing with problems as they arise. Clearly this reduces efficiency and can be disruptive, however, it can prevent disasters.
- **After the event.** While control at this stage cannot prevent or deal with problems it can ensure that the same mistake is not repeated.

EVALUATION

The earlier that problems can be identified, the quicker that they can be resolved. Under ideal conditions this should be unnecessary because everyone should know their job and do it as best they can. Mistakes are made, standards slip, and the unexpected can occur and stop everything, therefore, leaders must keep a constant check on progress to ensure the achievement of the tasks.

Having set objectives it is necessary to ensure that they are met.

Figure 11.2 Components of Effective Evaluation

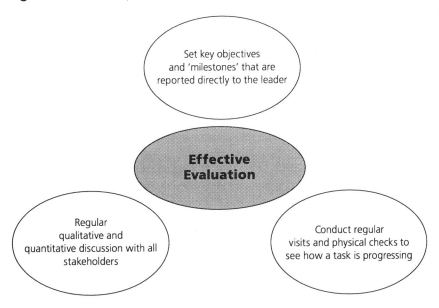

Evaluation should be an ongoing and progressive process. It depends on the task and overall plan, but whatever the case, progressive evaluation allows you the flexibility to alter a plan or the approach to ensure efficient completion of a given task. It is not usually as effective to wait until the end of a task to evaluate.

You can achieve this in a number of ways (see Figure 11.2).

The key is to ask yourself:

- Can the task be done any better?
- Can anything else be done at the same time?

Your answers indicate to you the control measures or changes of plan that need to be effected.

FAILURE TO MEET OBJECTIVES

When you see that an individual is failing to meet set objectives it is necessary to find out why and then perhaps set new objectives. You can do this by:

- Establishing that the individual understands the objectives.
- Ensuring that the subordinate is aware of the gap between performance and objectives.
- Exploring ways in which that gap can be closed.
- Ensuring that any external factors that may be influencing his or her performance are explored and dealt with.

It sometimes takes a great deal of moral courage, confidence, and initiative, to arrest a problem and to take what might appear to be an unpopular or awkward decision in order to rectify a problem. That is why you are there as a leader, and that is when you earn your pay.

CHAPTER 12

MOTIVATING THE INDIVIDUAL

> Man is not a finite resource. When motivated he can achieve a great deal, but when badly motivated he'll achieve nothing
>
> *Anon*
>
> When you have people who enjoy what they are doing and they have pride in doing it then they will be far more productive. You cannot measure that, we just know it is there. It is exactly the same in sport—you cannot underestimate the power of motivation and morale.
>
> *John Quinn, Managing Director, Thorn Lighting Pty Ltd*

MOTIVATION

In the 1960s motivation was thought of as 'an inner state that energises, activates, directs and channels behaviour towards "goals".' The level of motivation in a team can be sensed and felt by everyone around that group—including people who come into contact with the team such as the customer. Everyone is touched by the aura—the energy, sense of urgency, enthusiasm and sense of purpose that a well-motivated team produces. Whether they know it or not, leaders who have built companies like this are true to the Latin origins from which the word 'company' is derived. It comes from *companis*—'with bread'. In Roman times, 'company' described a group of associates who 'broke bread together', it is also the source of our word 'companion'.

Equally well, the lack of care and attention demonstrated by people who are less motivated is even more apparent to everyone, including the customer with corresponding bottom line performance!

If you were to ask your colleagues how many believe that they could be more effective at work, you might be surprised at the result. Many people only work as hard as they have to to keep their jobs, many are not working at full capacity, and most could be more effective or could contribute more if they were encouraged.

Symptoms of poor motivation include absenteeism, poor quality work, sick days, lateness, poor customer service, and high staff turnover. Motivation is the crucial difference between winners and losers whether on the sporting field, the battlefield, or in the ruthless warfare of modern business that sometimes is masked by a thin veneer of respectability. Motivated companies are not just pleasant to work for and deal with, they are almost always the most profitable in their industries.

We are demanding, we want things, we want to be loved, we want to be happy, we want our rights, we want food, or sex or air, we want to belong: everywhere you go you find that we humans are demanding things.

If you think about it you will see that it is the non-fulfilment of our demands that channels our behaviour and forms our attitude. In this chapter we consider the 'individual needs' of the three circles functional leadership model.

Superficially motivation is simple—but like the iceberg there is more depth beneath; it requires careful thought if it is to be effective, for if ill-considered attempts are made leaders could look foolish and incompetent and that does not build confidence.

Successful motivation includes attributes that may be classified as 'interpersonal skills', such as knowledge of individuals and basic psychology, empathy, listening and other communication skills, judgement, and so on. Like leadership generally, the study of motivation can be a science, but its practice is an art developed by experience and testing situations.

In considering the science of motivation a pool of knowledge is there to be used by all leaders. Successful approaches can, therefore, be built by studying the most successful motivators and modelling their planning and actions.

All human behaviour is governed by unfulfilled needs as shown in Figure 12.1. It is the presence of these unfulfilled needs that is known as motivation.

Figure 12.1

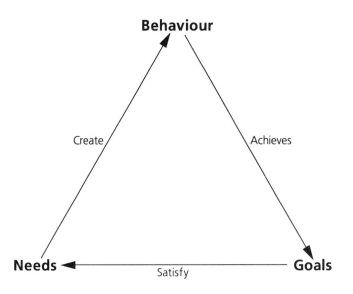

Individual motivation is best explained by an American professor named Abraham Maslow.[1] He suggests that our needs are organised in a series of levels—a hierarchy of importance, in an ascending order (Figure 12.2). When one level of need is satisfied, the next level is of importance. More modern research suggests that this hierarchy of needs does have some cultural variations. A full appreciation and knowledge of each individual team member, however, in addition to the application of the individual needs circle of the functional check-list, combined with empathy, awareness and sensitivity should overcome most discrepancies.

MASLOW'S HIERARCHY OF NEEDS

According to Maslow, five needs (see Figure 12.2) are related to one another as a hierarchy. The satisfaction of a lower need results in greater concern with a higher one. We are motivated by unsatisfied needs, rather than those that have been gratified. Maslow, in fact, contends that the 'average person' is most often partially satisfied and partially unsatisfied in all of their wants.

Subsequent research suggests that different kinds of motive may be important at different levels and with different people in an

Figure 12.2

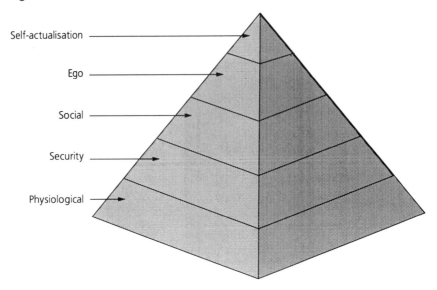

organisation's hierarchy. For instance, high needs for achievement seem to be particularly important for success in junior and middle management jobs. Those high in achievement motivation appear to be stimulated to greater efforts by both success and failure.

The key point here is that it helps to understand what factors in the work environment are likely to be important for most employees. While pay and conditions are important they do not make up the whole picture. Maslow points out that employees' commitment would increase if they received positive feedback, the opportunity to work where they could develop friendships and be developed to realise their full potential.

Physiological needs. At the lowest level, but of enormous importance when they demand satisfaction, are the physiological needs. Indeed the way to a man's heart is through his stomach, when he is hungry. For, except in exceptional circumstances, man's need for security, love, even status count for nothing if he has been without food for a while. The picture and stories that came out of Africa in the 1980s and 1990s of families trekking hundreds of kilometres to find food, of turning up at camps even if there were no accommodation or shelter just to get food demonstrates clearly the strength of this drive. On the other hand, when we eat regularly, hunger is no longer an important need driving us on to satisfy it.

Remember, 'A satisfied need is no longer a motivator of behaviour.' This simple statement is of profound importance, but it is often forgotten or ignored by conventional approaches to leadership. Think about your own need for air. It is only if you are deprived of it that the need for it has any motivating effect on your behaviour. One cannot wilfully commit suicide by holding one's breath.

Security needs. Once physiological needs are reasonably satisfied, needs at the next higher level come into play and start to dominate our behaviour. These Maslow calls 'safety needs'. These are needs for protection against physical danger, threat, and deprivation. Not, as many have tried to interpret Maslow, the need for feeling secure in a financial sense. The need is for 'the fairest possible break'. When a person is confident of this he or she is more than willing to take risks. But when someone feels threatened or dependent on someone or something else the need is for guarantees, for protection and for physical security. Another example of this can be seen in the ways that some people reacted after the Chernobyl nuclear accident. The demands that all nuclear programmes be halted, that power stations be closed down, and the constant demands for more and more information; demands for guarantees, for physical security from danger of radiation.

Social needs. Once a person's physiological needs have been satisfied and that person is no longer fearful for his or her safety then the needs for social intercourse come into play. We need to belong, to be accepted by our fellows, to give and receive love and friendship. These are many of the factors that are discussed in group behaviour. Leaders should harness these forces for the development of teams. Thwarting social needs can lead to individuals becoming resistant, antagonistic, and uncooperative. Be sure to remember though that exhibited behaviour by any members of the team is the result, not the cause. Think for a moment about the most 'difficult' person in your team, and consider, is he or she really well integrated into the group? Has that person had difficulty in being accepted by others?

Ego needs. These can be classified into two groups.

1. Those that relate to a person's self-esteem, the need for independence, for achievement, for skill and competence.
2. Those that relate to recognition by others, the need for status, for application, for the respect of our fellows.

Unlike lower needs these are rarely satisfied and they continually drive

181

us on to strive to 'make it', but when we get there there is always another mountain to climb.

Self-actualisation needs. Finally, at the top of the pyramid, is the need for self-actualisation or self-fulfilment; the requirement to realise our own potential, for continued development of our own creative ability.

Understand that the operation of the hierarchy is not a rigid stepping up and down the pyramid as life progresses. There is, in fact, a constant moving up and down the hierarchy as an individual's situations and circumstances alter.

HERZBERG'S TWO-FACTOR THEORY

Another American, Herzberg,[2] conducted a study in the late 1950s on the workers in a town in the USA to try to discover more about why they worked. He found that there were really two sets of factors, and he calls them:

1. Motivators or Satisfiers, because they actively worked towards satisfying a worker's motivational needs.
2. Hygiene and Maintenance factors. He called them hygiene factors because he said they were in the same relationship to Satisfiers as Hygiene is to Health, that is it is useful to have hygiene, but it is not crucial for good health. When present they were unimportant it is when they are absent that they are the cause of dissatisfaction.

Herzberg discovered that Satisfiers, the things that really drive workers are, responsibility, achievement, opportunities to exercise their skills, variety, the possibilities for promotion, growth and recognition. The Hygiene factors turn out to be things like pay, conditions of work, the quality of supervision, company policy, and administration, interpersonal relations.

Compare the two. There is a degree of similarity between Maslow's bottom two layers and Herzberg's Hygiene factors while Satisfiers can be equated with the top three layers of Maslow's hierarchy. Indeed, it is sometimes said that Maslow's top three layers are 'Brain Needs' and the bottom two are 'Belly Needs'.

If we consider that it is rewarding to a person to satisfy a need then we can be said to be offering 'carrots' to induce the behaviour wanted. But, beware of imagining that the same carrot works with everyone. It is the individual's perception of the value of the reward that induces the behaviour. For example, where the offer of an afternoon off may induce many people to work more quickly, there may be those with domestic problems to whom the extra time at home is no reward.

BEHAVIOUR AND MOTIVATION AT WORK

These theories enable the leader to understand the different human responses and behaviours demonstrated at work.

- Offering people more money as an incentive does not necessarily motivate them to work harder. If the current salary is enough for their lifestyle they may not want the extra responsibility and workload that accompanies the higher salary. Most people gain job satisfaction from success, teamwork, and a sense of purpose or direction. Money is no substitute for these. Complimenting and congratulating people continually devalues compliments for real achievements from leaders and lowers the respect in which they are held.
- If the lower needs are not satisfied then motivating people by addressing higher level needs does not work, for example, if people expect to be made redundant (security needs) then appealing to their self-actualisation needs is unlikely to be very successful.
- The needs can vary as people change. Young people with families and mortgages may be motivated by money in their early years, but in middle age, with independent children and no mortgage, needs may change and higher level needs become more effective motivators.
- Meeting the higher level of Maslow's needs is hard compared to those of the lower order because it depends on effective working relationships—good leadership.
- Obvious status symbols such as large desks, higher chairs, ensuring that the occupant is higher than the person to whom the leader is speaking, that is, the trappings of success, frequently affect the flow of communication by intimidating the subordinate.
- Social events after hours can contribute to building personal relationships and understanding but fail to build motivation where basic leadership is lacking. Too many coffee breaks during the working day disrupt well-motivated people who wish to get on with the job. Extra breaks in the day do not help build morale or motivation since they erode efficiency.

- Job rotation does not necessarily raise motivation. It always does this initially when there is something new to learn, but if frequent rotation means that all jobs are kept simple then all jobs can become boring and that is the cause of lack of interest and demotivation.

Team spirit satisfies a security need, and people are rejected by the team when they let the team down by failing. Building team spirit, therefore, assists motivation.

COMMUNICATION AND MOTIVATION

Perhaps the single most important factor in motivating a person is in building their belief in themselves, in bolstering self-esteem and in helping to create strong personal standards to which they feel bound to adhere. Leaders must convince people of their worth and the value of what they do. This is taken for granted by all army officers whose entire training and 'corporate culture' is geared towards leadership, teamwork and promoting trust and confidence. To do this leaders not only need awareness, sensitivity and communication skills, but need a genuine interest in, and knowledge of, the people with whom they deal—especially an understanding of those individuals' perception. When communicating to anyone, especially when resolving 'motivational problems', always ask yourself:

- What do I mean to say?
- Have I said what I meant?
- How was it interpreted?
- What does the respondent mean to say?
- Has he or she said what he or she meant?
- Is my interpretation of what I have heard what was intended?

Garry Morton[3] offers this advice:

When dealing with well-balanced people, a broad view of the situation and rationale, logic, and some mention of personal development helps effective communication. Self-centred types and opportunists are more interested in personal gain and advantage and require detail since they tend to distort things to suit their own ends. Optimists need to be shown particular enthusiasm and emotion, while pessimists like to offer critical examination of proposals at the same time as being praised to boost their self-esteem and self-confidence. Shy, retiring types need to feel protected and do not like to be publicly pointed out; the detail-minded like precision, logic, and opportunities to display their attention to detail.

THE LEADER'S PERSONALITY AND TRUST

Motivation is about answering a need a person has, to find out what the person really wants open communication is necessary—that requires total trust if the main causes of frustration are to be discussed. Trust and leadership qualities are discussed in Chapter 6. The 'leader' who maintains an aggressive posture, and fails to listen to people or to encourage the flow of conversation and ideas will prevent any form of effective communication taking place. Simple, clear language with sensitivity in relation to tone, combined with questions to ask for feedback and to ensure clarity of understanding are, as ever, the key to communicating.

MOTIVATION IN PRACTICE

The most effective efforts to motivate people are those that work from a genuine knowledge and understanding of the people that you are dealing with and a clear plan. Ask yourself the following series of key questions. They will assist in developing your approach.

1. **Who** is lacking motivation? Give consideration to each person that you are trying to motivate. They are all individuals with a unique mix of family background, life and work experiences, cultural values and training. In many people the effect of all these factors is a deeply ingrained mode of perception that frequently perpetuates a 'them and us' mentality.

   It is very hard to overcome lack of motivation and trust is not built easily. It is important to consider this from the recruitment stage. 'Who' works for you in the first place is one ingredient over which leaders should have a lot of control.

   Never assume that what motivates one person motivates another.

2. **What** precisely is it that needs to be done? It is vital to define clear goals that are real and achievable, based on organisational objectives. When 'coaching' individuals, discuss recent performance, clarify roles and expectations, and follow up specific requests for action or improvement.

3. **Why** is it necessary? Explain the reasons why something has to be achieved, and where it fits into the 'big picture'. People can relate to the need when it is explained clearly.

4. **How** is it to be done? Give clear guidelines that leave people in no doubt about their constraints or the parameters within which they must operate, or the freedom of action that they might employ. Relate the 'what' and the 'how' to their own personal development needs and desires; motivation is always greater when the needs of the person and the needs of the organisation coincide.

5. **When** do you want it to happen? Proper planning furnishes both objectives and a realistic time scale. Also consider the timing of your motivating meeting with individuals. During staff drinks or the evening before someone goes on leave is hardly going to inspire anyone.

6. **Where** will the work be done? This could be simply environmental—such as improving the office furnishings and facilities. Geographical location is also important as cultural norms come into play. Motivating people in New York is very different from motivating people in Papua–New Guinea. Differences between people in Sydney and those in Darwin might be less obvious, but just as important. Individual 'counselling sessions', a euphemism for a 'rocket', should always be conducted in private as no public 'roasting' ever works, it breeds mistrust, disrespect, and bitterness.

The detailed answers to these questions are in Chapters 3, 7, 8, 11, and 15.

HINTS FOR DELEGATING

Delegation is a powerful motivator for many people since it demonstrates trust, helps growth or development in the person to whom a task is delegated, and requires participation from people. It, thus, addresses social and ego needs. A good sign of a healthy organisation is the way authority is delegated within it. The larger the organisation, the greater is the need to set up a clear and efficient delegation system that enables the leader to exercise his or her influence overall.

Remember that authority can be delegated, responsibility cannot. The responsibility for the successful completion of a task always rests with the leader, irrespective of whether he or she has delegated authority to a subordinate to carry it out on his or her behalf. It is for this reason that a general manager should be responsible for everything that goes on in that organisation. By force of circumstances the general manager has to delegate authority to selected people to organise that unit's resources, accounts, sales and administration, and so on, and plan the training of its personnel, but overall if anything goes wrong, as the leader, the general manager should accept full responsibility.

Delegation is considered in detail in Chapter 9 under the headings of:

- Reasons for delegation
- What and what not to delegate
- Principles of delegating
- To whom to delegate
- Why leaders do not delegate.

References

1. A. Maslow, 1954, *Motivation and Personality*, New York: Harper.
2. F. Herzberg, 1959, *The Motivation to Work*, New York: John Wiley & Sons.
3. Garry Morton, 1990, *The Australian Motivation Handbook*, Sydney: The McGraw-Hill Book Company Australia Pty Limited.

CHAPTER 13

MORALE

After a merger there is a real rollercoaster of emotion that happens when two organisations have to come together and this really reflects the fact that there is a lot of anxiety about who is going to be promoted, who is going to be retrenched, how the balance of power is going to shift, how customer relationships are going to change. You can map the shift of morale from initial concern to the promises made of high expectations. In the consistently better performing companies these expectations are met and morale is high.

There are a lot of intangibles, such as morale, that lead to performance. Whilst this cannot be quantified on the balance sheet it is reflected in the market capitalisation of stocks.

Robert McLean, formerly Managing Director,
McKinsey & Co Australia

'Morale is to the material as three is to one', said Napoleon Bonaparte. By this he means that high morale counts for much more than simply having enough physical resources for a task. The *Concise Oxford Dictionary* defines 'morale' as 'the mental attitude or bearing of a person or group as regards confidence, discipline etc'. It is defined in *Websters' Dictionary* as 'A confident, resolute, willing and often self sacrificing and courageous attitude.'

Morale is vital to us because if it starts to wane it becomes very apparent to our customers and is reflected in our customer loyalty. A person on our front line talking to a customer on the telephone is leading our relationship with that customer, so making sure that their frame of mind and approach is positive and that they are able to mould a solution are vital. If morale is low people will seek to undermine a process. If people have a belief in success, even though it may be in a bleak situation you can feel quite positive about the outcome. Building morale takes time—it has to filter through the organisation.

Malcolm Jones, CEO, NRMA Limited

Morale is critical; it leads to high motivation and stems from a shared sense of purpose. It definitely produces results although morale is something difficult to measure. Low morale is observed by all sorts of 'misfit' behaviour such as lethargy, apathy, absenteeism and illness. In terms of the effect of morale on the bottom line, high morale has always coincided with high profits in my division. To sustain high morale the leader has to be genuinely interested in people, seeking their views and gaining their participation. Discipline is a part of morale because it ensures that the team adheres to expectations, standards and values.

Robyn Fitzroy, Division Director, Macquarie Bank

Morale cannot be built by a quick fix or bought with parties and presents. It is the result of good leadership: people enjoying their work, being satisfied by it, being involved, feeling important, developing new skills, etc. Superficial attempts to build it breed cynicism and mistrust.

Karen Lonergan, Education & Development,
Manager, Castrol Australia

People in business often refer to the level of morale in organisations and departments within them; but morale is rarely defined or analysed. There is little that has been written on the subject by business leaders and we need to look at the writings of military leaders to gain a deeper understanding of the subject. Armies worldwide realise the value of high morale and its absolute necessity for success. It is true that 'battles are won in the hearts and minds of men' and there are many examples of engagements in which numerically superior, better equipped forces have failed in the face of determined action by small, poorly equipped groups of soldiers, but whose leaders maintained high morale.

Morale is based upon leadership, teamwork, and giving people pride, satisfaction and enjoyment in what they do. Every winning team and every successful organisation has high morale; the power of morale is underestimated and that is shown in short term expedient decisions and cost-cutting measures. Morale has to be sustained and that needs longer term thinking in companies and their shareholders. That is why the Asian competition is so strong—they are looking for performance in the long term.

*John Quinn, Managing Director Thorn Lighting Pty Ltd and
Sydney–Hobart Ocean Racing Skipper*

In this company people are in love with the product and this stimulates the high level of morale. My challenge as a Management Development Manager is to ensure that all our 'leaders' understand how to sustain morale in all our international markets which all have differing conditions.

*Kathy Rozmeta, Learning & Development Manager,
Coca-Cola Amatil Limited*

Soldiers, like their civilian counterparts, are in many ways a reflection of the society that they come from. The soldier comes from the same background as the person in industry—people are people whatever their jobs, and they respond in similar ways to the same stimuli. The understanding that armies have of morale stems from hard and bloody experience, and armies have to sustain morale for longer periods in more extreme conditions of stress and discomfort. It is, therefore, not surprising that business can improve its understanding of the nature of morale from studying the profession of arms.

Morale is certainly not contentment or satisfaction evolving out of good material conditions and an easy job. Morale is essentially a state of mind. To quote Slim:[1] 'It is that intangible force which will move a whole group of men to give their last ounce to achieve something, without counting the cost to themselves; that makes them feel they are part of something greater than themselves.' Morale is the ability to rise to challenges and to overcome them, to carry on with the job with confidence and determination. It is the product of a mind with a conscience. It contributes to the motivation of the individual and a team's *esprit de corps*, and it is a reflection of the leadership of that group.

Implicit in high morale is a motivated and cheerful workforce. Not only does this produce the climate that encourages innovation, cooperation, productivity and efficiency; it reduces staff turnover ('knowledge' loss), boosts customer loyalty (a reflection of your sales force and customer service team's loyalty) and, therefore, raises profitability.

Morale. This might be described as a 'feel good' factor. It is achieved when people feel confident and happy about their work or task within a team or individually. The confidence that high morale brings helps to keep a team trying whatever the difficulties. It cannot be measured but it can be observed. Take two people, ships, crews, teams, whatever; the one with the high morale shows in its performance.

Sir Robin Knox-Johnston

At this point it is appropriate to review one of the most incisive studies of morale that has been written in my opinion.

Field Marshal Slim took command of 14th Army in Burma in 1943, an army shattered by continuous defeat, exhausted by a relentless 800 mile (1300km) retreat, convinced of the supremacy of an invincible enemy. In the list of global priorities, 14th Army was at the bottom after the armies in Europe and North Africa, it was thus deficient in the most basic necessities.

Slim[1] considered his first essential task was 'for us to convince ourselves that we could beat the Jap at his own game'. This is how he approached the problem:

Morale must, if it is to endure—and the essence of morale is that it should endure—have certain foundations. These foundations are spiritual, intellectual, and material, and that is the order of their importance. Spiritual first, because only spiritual foundations can stand real strain. Next intellectual, because men are swayed by reason as well as feeling. Material last—important but last—because the very highest kinds of morale are often met when material conditions are lowest.

I remember sitting in my office and tabulating these foundations of morale something like this:

1. Spiritual

a) There must be a great and noble object.

b) Its achievement must be vital.

c) The method of achievement must be active, aggressive.

d) The man must feel that what he is and what he does matters directly towards the attainment of the object.

2. Intellectual

a) He must be convinced that the object can be attained; that it is not out of reach.

b) He must see, too, that the organisation to which he belongs and which is striving to attain the object is an efficient one.

c) He must have confidence in his leaders and know that whatever dangers and hardships he is called to suffer, his life will not be lightly flung away.

3. Material

a) The man must feel that he will get a fair deal from his commanders and from the army generally.

b) He must, as far as humanly possible, be given the best weapons and equipment for his task.

c) His living and working conditions must be made as good as they can be.

It was one thing thus neatly to marshal my principles but quite another to develop them, apply them, and get them recognised by the whole army.

At any rate our spiritual foundation was a firm one. I use the word spiritual, not in its strictly religious meaning, but as a belief in a cause. . .

The fighting soldier facing the enemy can see that what he does. . .matters to his comrades and directly influences the result of the battle. It is harder for the man working on the road far behind, the clerk checking stores in a dump, the headquarters' telephone operator monotonously plugging through his calls—it is hard for these and a thousand others to see that they too matter. Yet everyone had to be made to see where his task fitted into the whole, to realise what depended on it, and to feel pride and satisfaction in doing it well.

Now these things, while the very basis of morale because they were purely matters of feeling and emotion, were the most difficult to put over. . .I felt there was only one way to do it, by a direct approach to the men themselves. Not by written exhortations, by wireless speeches, but by informal talks and contacts between troops and commanders. There was nothing new in this; my Corps and Divisional commanders and others right down the scale were already doing it. . .And we all talked the same stuff with the same object. . .

I learnt, too, that one did not need to be an orator to be effective. Two things only were necessary: first to know what you were talking about, and, second and most important, to believe it yourself. I found that if one kept the bulk of one's talk to the material things the men were interested in, food, pay, leave, beer, mail, and the progress of operations, it was safe to end on a higher note—the spiritual foundations—and I always did. . .

It was in these ways we laid the spiritual foundations, but that was not enough; they would have crumbled without others, the intellectual and the material. Here we had first to convince the doubters that our object. . .was practicable. . .A victory in a large scale battle was, in our present state of training, organisation, and confidence, not to be attempted. . .

All commanders therefore directed their attention to patrolling. In jungle warfare this is the basis of success. It not only gives eyes to the side that excels at it, and blinds its opponent, but through it the soldier learns to move confidently in the elements in which he works. Every forward unit. . .chose its best men, formed patrols, trained and practised them, and then sent them out on business. These patrols came back to their regiments with stories of success.

Having developed the confidence of the individual man in his superiority over the enemy, we had now to extend that to the corporate confidence of units and formations in themselves. This was done in a series of carefully planned minor offensive operations. These were carefully staged, ably led, and, as I was always careful to ensure, in great strength. . .we could not at this stage risk even small failures. . .the individual superiority built up by more successful patrolling grew into a feeling of superiority within units and formations. We were then ready to undertake larger operations. We had laid the first of our intellectual foundations of morale; everyone knew. . .our object was attainable.

The next foundation, that the men should feel that they belonged to an efficient organisation, that Fourteenth Army was well run and would get somewhere, followed partly from these minor successes.

A most potent factor in spreading this belief in the efficiency of an organisation is a sense of discipline. In effect, discipline means that every man, when things pass beyond his own authority or initiative, knows to whom to turn for further direction. If it is the right kind of discipline he turns in the confidence that he will get sensible and effective direction. Every step must be taken to build up this confidence of the soldier in his leaders. For instance, it is not enough to be efficient; the organisation must look efficient. . .

Thus the intellectual foundations of morale were laid. There remained the material. . .Material conditions, though lamentably low by the standards of any other British army, were improving. Yet I knew that whatever had been promised...from home, it would be six months at least before it reached my troops. We would remain, for a long time yet, desperately short. . .

These things were frankly put to the men by their commanders at all levels and, whatever their race, they responded. In my experience it is not so much asking men to fight or work with inadequate or obsolete equipment that lowers morale but the belief that those responsible are accepting such a state of affairs. If men realise that everyone above them and behind them is flat out to get the things required for them, they will do wonders, as my men did, with the meagre resources they have instead of sitting down moaning for better.

I do not say that the men of the Fourteenth Army welcomed difficulties, but they grew to take a fierce pride in overcoming them by determination and ingenuity. From start to finish they had only two items of equipment that were never in short supply; their brains and their courage. They lived up to the unofficial motto I gave them, 'God helps those who help themselves'.

In these and many other ways we translated my rough notes on the foundations of morale, spiritual, intellectual, and material, into a fighting spirit for our men and a confidence in themselves and their leaders that was to impress our friends and surprise our enemies.

Here is a recent example of false economy, accounting parsimony, and the need to maintain morale:

> . . .to maintain morale. . .I had two principal weapons. . .a fortnightly paper. . .The other was the radio station. . .something on which I insisted in the face of determined opposition from civil servants. . .who maintained it was not worth the £750,000. . .It proved a major success.
>
> *General Sir Peter de la Billière commanding British Forces in the*
> *Gulf War 1990/91*[2]

But what is the link between motivation and morale? Remember that morale is the mental attitude of a team, and motivation is that which stimulates interest in a job and induces a person to act in a particular way (behaviour that satisfies a personal need). Slim's analysis places the 'spiritual' over the 'intellectual' that is superior to the 'material'. There is an apparent paradox when this is compared with Maslow's hierarchy of needs that places basic physiological needs (the material) first then security, affiliation, self-esteem and self-actualisation needs.

Perhaps the answer lies in the following. Physiological needs are all relative, and people want more than is necessary for survival—people can change their perspective. A cohesive team, unified around a common challenge or task, satisfies the security and affiliation needs. Leadership may persuade people that their physiological needs have been satisfied (to a minimum acceptable level that permits human endeavour), that their security needs can best be met by achieving the aim or the vision that ensures survival in whatever form, and that each person is vital to the success of the plan (self-esteem is satisfied). Self-discipline and a sense of duty reinforce acceptance of what needs to be done to ensure success. Thus, for a relatively short time, self-actualisation is achieved by making the supreme efforts illustrated in Slim's analysis given earlier.

In the packaged goods company that I joined as a salesman on leaving the army, there was a general malaise and lack of interest in boosting sales and distribution of our products among the state sales force. People were often bored, disinterested and took no pride in their work. One day a competition was started, the scene was set, its importance communicated and the sales force issued cameras and asked to take photographs of displays of their products that they had built in their stores.

While the prizes were insignificant, this sudden apparent surge of interest in the humble sales rep, briefings on the importance of us building brand presence in store, and the issue of a camera in a parsimonious company had a very positive effect on morale and hence, sales. Unfortunately the interest that was taken in each sales rep's work, display of leadership and emphasis on teamwork was short-lived and a couple of months later the malaise had returned. Twenty per cent of the state sales force found jobs elsewhere within the year.

The author

Field Marshal Montgomery expresses his view of morale in a different way.[3] He identifies four basic factors that are essential:

- leadership
- discipline

- comradeship
- self-respect.

He also believes that devotion to a cause would influence some people, but not everyone and that there are numerous other contributing factors to morale, but that they are not essential.

LEADERSHIP

'Morale is, in the first place, based on leadership. Good morale is impossible without good leaders. Human beings are fundamentally alike in that certain common characteristics apply to all people in varying degrees.'[3]

It is when times are hard or confusion abounds and uncertainty is rife that people cry out for leadership. 'The leader himself accepts the burdens of others and by doing so earns their gratitude and the right to lead them. The men recognise in their leader some quality which they themselves do not possess; that quality is "decision".'[3] Change, uncertainty and confusion and the fear this induces in people breeds inertia, indecision and lethargy. Leaders' power is given by the acceptance of the followers and they accept the leader who can cut through the 'fear paralysis' allowing them to escape from confusion and give them a sense of direction.

> The two vital attributes of a leader are: (a) decision in action, and (b) calmness in crisis. Given these two attributes he will succeed; without them he will fail.[3]

Soon after I was commissioned in 1984, I joined my battalion in Londonderry, Northern Ireland. The city was very 'busy' we were coming towards the end of a two-year round of patrolling, cordons and clearances of improvised explosive devices—bombs, searches and sniper shoots. We'd had a week full of incidents and not much sleep; it was winter, cold and wet.

My platoon deployed as the cordon around a bomb in the Bogside area of the city late one afternoon—too late to start a clearance operation for which we needed daylight. We knew that we would be out all night while we waited for the air photo recce at first light, and we'd stay out most of the following day while the bomb disposal team did their stuff. I gave a quick brief and the platoon deployed; as soon

---

as possible I went around the location and gave each person a confirmatory brief and a pep talk.

As the night wore on, I knew we would become easy targets—I ensured that I toured the position (at some risk to myself) every hour-and-a-half or so to speak to every soldier. There was no detail to update them on, just idle gossip about leave, family and friends, and a reminder of the need to keep vigilant and their importance to the whole platoon's security and well-being. Every three hours or so my Platoon Sergeant was able to deliver a hot drink and a sandwich—every delivery a risk in itself, but worth it.

Back in camp, others noticed that instead of the long drawn faces and robotic movement that were usual after a long, cold wet period without sleep, my platoon was chirpy, banter was freely exchanged and energy was obviously present. My Company Commander was staggered to learn that there had been no whining or complaining on the ground by my platoon. Instead—morale was high, and tangibly so. So different from the usual after cordon feeling. I don't think that I did anything special. I just told everyone as much as I could, took an interest in them as I always had, maintained our high standards, and ensured that the admin did not fail.

The author

DISCIPLINE

The aim of discipline is to instil the self-discipline in people that guarantees their self-control and sense of duty in whatever task they are doing. It ensures a team's efficiency, contributes to team spirit, and develops a corporate identity that satisfies members' affiliation needs. Corporate identity can make a person feel that he or she is part of something more powerful than the individual. It is here that discipline shows its value, for it can help a person to become a part of a larger and stronger unit. It is in this way that discipline helps to overcome confusion and fear of the unknown.

The method by which the conquest of doubt and fear and group cohesion is achieved is by the unifying people into a team so that they give of their best. People 'learn to gain confidence and encouragement from doing the same thing' or working closely with their peers; they 'derive strength and satisfaction from their company; their own identities become merged into the larger and stronger identity'[3] of their team.

> Discipline implies a conception of duty. Nothing will be accomplished in the crisis by the man without a sense of duty.
>
> *Field Marshal Montgomery*

This sense of duty is developed by discipline in the team that reinforces a sense of duty because people learn what is expected of them, what their responsibilities are and that it is wrong not to live up to these expectations. It is the job of the leader to encourage this sense of duty. 'Discipline aims to create a body strong enough to carry each of its members through the difficulties that they alone could not face. In this way it promotes comradeship', the third factor of morale.

COMRADESHIP

> Morale cannot be good unless men come to have affection for each other; a fellow-feeling must grow up which will result in a spirit of comradeship.
>
> *Field Marshal Montgomery*

All organisations are composed of people and however inspiring a leader is or however perfect the cohesion and discipline in the team the morale will be 'cold' and 'harsh' if the warmth of comradeship is lacking.

> Comradeship is based on affection and trust, which between them produce an atmosphere of mutual good will and a feeling of interdependence.
>
> *Field Marshal Montgomery*

The comradeship of true teamwork teaches people how to depend on each other's strengths, how to develop trust, confidence and faith in each other. Teamwork and the spirit it generates induces people to do their best not to let the team down. Comradeship provides the support needed when people are at a low point and feel weak and vulnerable. Comradeship challenges and draws out a person's best features that contribute to self-respect.

SELF-RESPECT

No man can be said to possess high morale if the quality of self-respect is lacking. . . Self-respect implies a determination to maintain personal standards of behaviour.

Field Marshal Montgomery

A person with self-respect will not allow the quality of work, attention to detail, customer service, or standards of dress to drop. It is the function of the leader to encourage and instil self-respect.

Efficiency is inseparable from self-respect.

Field Marshal Montgomery

To make people feel that they are valued and capable employees trust is vital.

A man who feels he is trusted will feel that he is efficient, and he will at once begin to respect himself. He will have confidence in his own ability. . .Men who are trusted gain self-confidence.

Field Marshal Montgomery

It is the job of the leader to help team members become more effective and to do that they must be convinced that their leader trusts them. Leaders must develop pride in individuals' ability to do what is asked of them.

As Montgomery has said cause (or purpose) does not influence everyone, but it does affect enough people to be an important factor in the maintenance of morale.

DEVOTION TO A CAUSE

> It is impossible to make devotion to a cause either a basic or a contributory factor to good morale. . .I do not believe that soldiers are greatly influenced by 'cause'. . .
>
> *Field Marshal Montgomery*

CONTRIBUTORY FACTORS

Montgomery also refers to the contributory factors to morale. It is possible to have high morale without them, but that demands the highest quality of leadership and discipline throughout an organisation.

> The exhilaration of operating successfully in this tough environment had our own morale soaring.
>
> *General Sir Peter de la Billière as a young officer with the SAS fighting rebels in Oman in 1958/59*[2]

Success. High morale is possible in failure but not during a long and sustained period of failure. In such situations confidence in the leaders is eroded and without confidence in leaders, nothing can be achieved. Success reinforces good morale by building confidence in leaders and in organisations.

Team spirit. The team spirit can be a powerful factor in making for good morale. The more a person feels himself or herself to be identified with the organisation the higher will be his or her morale if the four essential conditions have been fulfilled. There is a difference between comradeship and team spirit. Comradeship is the spirit of fellow-feeling that grows up between a small group of men or women who live and work together. Team spirit or *esprit de corps* is the employee's pride in the organisation and his or her determination to be worthy of it. In armies regimental tradition and customs do much to build pride and loyalty. It is hard for organisations to develop this pride and loyalty since so often the employees would say that loyalty is a one-way street in the days of down-sizing.

Personal happiness and welfare. Trouble in private life leads to trouble at work. The person is preoccupied and this erodes teamwork and efficiency.

Administration. People lose confidence in their organisation when pay is late, expenses are not paid promptly, reviews and counselling fail to happen when scheduled, and what is absolutely necessary to do the job is not provided. They quite understandably cease to think that they belong to an efficient enterprise.

Many people, especially those with limited experience or understanding of morale, have the belief that high morale is found only in a successful organisation—or that high morale is directly the result of success. It is clear that while success helps to build morale to a higher level, the foundations of morale can be firmly established in very adverse conditions. That is the challenge for the leader.

So how can you recognise that morale is low? Below is a list of tell-tale signs that should trigger concern in the leader.

- **High staff turnover**. While some staff turnover can be healthy and people may need to leave to satisfy personal needs that an organisation, or their leader, cannot meet; an abnormally high turnover of staff is indicative of poor morale and, therefore, poor leadership. This is obviously very costly to organisations in terms of lost expertise, costs of hiring and retraining, lost accounts, and lost opportunities that are not quantifiable.

- **Uncooperative, unhelpful attitudes, lack of commitment and lack of enthusiasm**. This all contributes to 'atmosphere' and is noticeable by anyone with any sensitivity walking into the environment, even for the first time. Do people go out of their way to assist you, or do things grudgingly? Does routine bore them and would they rather do something more stimulating? Has their leader kept them informed of the reasons behind major decisions, have they been involved in low level decisions, do they know that they play an important role in the organisation? Has communication and the passage of information failed? If the answer to any or all of these is 'yes', leadership is lacking.

- **Is cynicism, doubt, complaining and finding fault with everything on the increase?** Is negativity pervading the air? Again, these are more signs of poor morale.

- **Falling standards**. In product quality, work area cleanliness, personal appearance, or timeliness, punctuality, and so on. These all result from a lack of self-respect, itself a part of morale. While some people may be habitually untidy—any change from the norm should be noticed.

You know things are really bad when people openly talk about how bad things are—you then have a major problem to sort out. The causes of low morale are all the result of leadership failing to 'grip':

- Clarity of purpose and role
- Unrealistic and constantly moving goal posts
- Inconsistency in discipline, standards, priorities and ever-changing decisions
- Poor communication and feedback
- Failure to meet expectations, or giving rise to false expectations
- Failure by leaders to keep promises or meet commitments
- Unworkable organisational structure
- Lack of effective performance management
- Lack of organisational pride and *esprit de corps*
- Poor administration
- Indecision.

All these statements relate to the functional leadership check-list and Slim's analysis above. This reinforces the adoption of this check-list as the cornerstone of leadership development and the teamwork, morale, and motivation that is a natural follow-on.

There are some conscious steps that you can take to promote and improve morale among your team members:

- **Objectives.** It is important to set clear objectives and probably the ones you, as a subordinate leader, give your team will be passed to you. But, nevertheless, it is your responsibility to give clear objectives to your team.
  - A team that sees itself succeeding in achieving objectives grows in confidence. Set progressively more difficult goals. Morale grows as the team finds itself tackling ever-more challenging tasks, and succeeding. Such progressive proficiency in difficulty builds resolution. Success breeds success.
  - When failure occurs, avoid repeated failure since this can erode the level of confidence and hence, morale. This may mean reducing targets while confidence levels are rebuilt.
- **Recognising and satisfying individual needs.** People have their individual strengths and skills, and want them to be used. They also want to grow and develop and the leader must enable them to do this. You, as a leader, must keep people interested.

- **Building *esprit de corps*.** Promote team spirit, team identity and, therefore, a sense of belonging.
- **Communication.** Hold frequent team briefings (keep them brief and to the point) and individual feedback and catch-up sessions to reinforce your message constantly.
- **Taking an interest and recognising and rewarding effort.** Perhaps the greatest boost to morale is the interest that the leader takes in the success of individuals and—the team in attaining the set goals. Generation of 'esteem' needs and their satisfaction are powerful motivators for any group as Maslow and Herzberg demonstrate. Remember then to 'praise where praise is due'.

It is clear that leadership is vital in building morale. Through communication, the team understands the vision and mission, realises that their role is important, knows that the objective is attainable, and knows that people matter. Good planning and swift and successful execution of plans convince people that they belong to an efficient organisation, and allows them to have the resources necessary to do the job in good working conditions. Leadership by example (displaying leadership qualities) builds the trust and confidence that is needed to see things through in tough times. Setting clear objectives, making them progressively more difficult while still ensuring, so far as you, as a leader, are able, success; and making sure that you are on the spot to offer praise and encouragement, contributes to building morale. Finally, lead with conviction and enthusiasm; leadership that has the ring of true conviction always inspires.

References:

1. Field Marshal Sir William Slim, 1957, *Defeat Into Victory*, London: Cassell.
2. General Sir Peter de la Billière, 1994, *Looking For Trouble*, London: HarperCollins.
3. Field Marshal The Viscount Montgomery of Alamein, Believed to be from Forward From Victory—Speeches and Addresses, reproduced in *Serve to Lead*, compiled at the Royal Military Academy Sandburst and printed by Her Majesty's Stationery Office.

CHAPTER 14

STYLES OF LEADERSHIP, LEVELS OF LEADERSHIP

There are two main strands that run throughout this book:

- there is leading, and taking charge of, or responsibility, for the team and using leadership 'tools' such as the functional check-list, mission analysis and the appreciation.
- and there is being recognised as a leader, that is behaving in such a way that you are clearly seen to be the leader—displaying the necessary qualities.

So far, most of this book has been largely about providing you with the skills and knowledge that is needed to lead: to plan, make an appreciation, to organise, and to motivate and build your team. It is now time to broaden the horizon and start to look more closely at the manner in which leadership is exercised.

THE LEADERSHIP ENVIRONMENT

Within every organisation there is a leadership environment that tends to vary with the organisation. Levels have been identified and are illustrated in Figure 14.1. The organisational strategy leaders (directors) lay down policies, and represent the organisation externally. Their views set the tone and direction for others to follow and influence all, especially middle (line) managers and their staff by their decisions and actions. For example, remuneration policies can develop a self-centred streak in individuals and can prevent teamwork flourishing if they are wrongly structured. Training policy, or the lack of it, sends the message

Figure 14.1 Levels of leadership

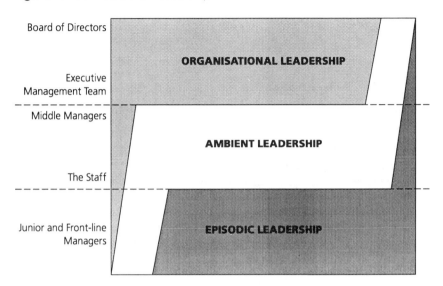

Source: Adapted with permission from a model at The Royal Military Academy
Sandhurst

that people have to go elsewhere for further growth and personal development. Gaps between organisational values espoused by senior executives and the senior executives' actual behaviour lead either at best to confusion as to what is necessary for success within the organisation, and at worst to the reproduction of that behaviour. Performance management policies not linked to leadership, teamwork, values and the desired culture tell people that the rhetoric is just that, it does not really matter if leadership is displayed and values actually 'lived'.

The staff in head offices and middle managers provide the 'ambient' leadership; they should generate a climate in which good leadership is taken for granted. Too many readers can think back to other places where the leadership ambience was different. Perhaps to a company where initiative was stifled by fear, intolerance of mistakes, or lack of trust; or teamwork was hindered by ill-defined roles or plans lacking the necessary clarity and detail.

Finally, there is episodic leadership: this is the level at which junior and front-line managers and supervisors operate. They exercise leadership to solve a series of 'local problems' that require relatively quick solutions—the leadership episodes. It is these episodes that allow the leader to build the respect, confidence and trust that the team has to have in him or her.

These three areas of leadership within the organisation are obviously not discrete entities, which is why, 'organisational' leadership has a 'point' reaching down to the episodic level. After all directors and senior managers can and do lead others in accomplishing short-term tasks and usually have a team of direct reporting subordinates to build and maintain. They also have a contribution to make to the ambient leadership climate even if their main energies are focussed on the organisational leadership that includes:[1]

- Firstly ensuring that the organisational values defined by the CEOs are adhered to and demonstrated in everyday behaviour.
- Second, responsibility for formulating the policies and procedures within the company that provides the environment, or culture that allows leadership and teamwork to flourish.
- Third, responsibility for developing a long-term view and direction for the organisation to which all energy and resources can be directed by others further down the hierarchy structure.

Leaders at the episodic level where energies are concentrated on solving short-term problems do occasionally have contributions to make to the organisational level, possibly from research and development findings or to the success of newly tried techniques and processes. The ambient level has considerable contributions to make in both directions by interpreting policy and providing the day-to-day framework for episodic leadership to occur—following the practices of a requisite organisation—while keeping the organisational leaders informed of developments, issues, areas of concern, actual progress, and so on. Although organisational leaders should not rely purely on such reports fed upwards—they need to 'get out onto the ground' and talk to front-line employees to form an appreciation of how information or plans have really been interpreted and executed. They also demonstrate their concern for people by such visits, providing they show a genuine interest in their conversation.

While the hierarchical pyramid works effectively at every level it is usual in many organisations, whether the public service, government, business, or armed forces, to form a collegiate view. This can be seen in the Cabinet of Government, the Army Board, or the Board of Directors in business. At this level there is a distinct difference in the level of work undertaken and the level of abstract thought required. Often implicit in this type of structure is the acceptance of collective responsibility, and/or collective support for decisions made. It is interesting that at this level consensus is more often sought than at other levels within the hierarchy. This is probably because it is understood that as things cascade downwards, any slight incongruence or difference of opinion is noticed, magnified, and echoed, in the actions of those at lower levels.

Style of Leadership

Style is a very difficult thing to discuss since there are at least two views of what 'style' is. Do we mean the manner in which we choose to handle a specific situation or our general approach to leadership, based on the extension or projection of personality—our own personal style that Slim described (Chapter 1). We cannot change our personality easily and to try a chameleon approach to interpersonal dealings reeks of insincerity and that leads to a breakdown of trust and confidence. Consider the first definition of style, the manner in which we exercise episodic leadership.

A number of researchers, including Fiedler, Taylor, and Likert since the 1930s have tried to identify what it is that decides the style of leadership that a leader displays. One school of thought believes it is a leader's view of his or her subordinates and team members that influences 'style'. The American Douglas McGregor is famous for his 'Theory X' versus 'Theory Y' (*The Human Side of Enterprise* © 1960, reproduced with permission of The McGraw-Hill Companies). McGregor[2] suggests that we should look to the two extremes that he called X & Y.

McGregor's proposition is summarised as:

Theory X

Man is:

    a. Lazy
    b. Unambitious
    c. Self-centred
    d. Resistant to change
    e. Gullible

Theory Y

    a. Man is not by nature:
        i) Passive
        ii) Resistant to change
    b. Men all possess the potential for:
        i) Development
        ii) Accepting responsibility
        iii) Identify with the organisation's goals.

The first proposition, Theory X, suggests that the organisation through its leaders, has to direct, control and modify the behaviour of subordinates because inherently there is a belief that:

a. We are naturally indolent—we work as little as possible.
b. We lack ambition, dislike responsibility, prefer to be led.
c. We are self-centred, indifferent to organisational needs.
d. We are by nature resistant to change.
e. We are gullible, not very bright, the ready dupe of the charlatan and the demagogue.

This extreme view does not fit in well with Maslow's theory of the growth and satisfaction of higher level needs (Chapter 12). This view McGregor proposes, seems to deny the very existence of the ego and self-fulfilment needs. Any leader accepting this view of the world would have to be a man or woman with a strong sense of the 'Task' and little faith in people. He or she would, because their belief in people is so low, have to adopt a style of leadership that is strongly authoritarian: a style that involves the leader in making all decisions, taking little or no advice. A leader that relies on fear or giving out punishment.

At the other extreme McGregor sets up his second proposition, Theory Y.

a. People are not by nature passive or resistant to organisational needs. (Although they may have become so through experience.)
b. People all possess the potential for development, the capacity for assuming responsibility, and the readiness to identify with organisations' goals.

At this extreme a leader would have little to do since people would be self-motivated achievers. McGregor suggests that this should be the goal for organisations, but in reality this *laissez-faire* style would be a complete abdication of responsibility by the leader. Real life shows us that Theory Y does not work either. People, particularly those in companies that have not developed a culture based upon teamwork, innovation and continuous improvement and learning (a culture derived from good leadership) can be resistant to change such as the introduction of new methods and technologies that, they feel, threaten their familiar patterns of behaviour. Human nature, being as it is, will ensure that some people lack the self-discipline to be self-motivated, or lack the intellect to see what needs to be done or the initiative to do something about it.

Leadership is necessary if things are to get done. The leader's perception of subordinates must lie between McGregor's extremes, since it is a 'perception' that is coloured by the leader's personality, maturity, and experience, the main modifiers of the leader's style of leadership (see Chapters 2 and 3).

An important influence on the perception of a leader's subordinates is their 'style and expectations'. Several researchers, including Vroom,[3] have shown that if you

> Place a group with strong independence drives under a supervisor who needs to keep his men under his thumb the result is very likely to be trouble. Similarly, if you take docile men, who are accustomed to obedience and respect for their supervisors and place them under a supervisor who tries to make them manage their own work, they are likely to wonder uneasily whether he really knows what he is doing.

A leader can permit subordinates greater 'freedom' when the following conditions apply. How much freedom does depend on the conditions being met or exceeded. Finer judgement is required of the leader.

a. Subordinates have a relatively high need for independence.
b. Subordinates have a readiness to accept accountability for their actions.
c. Subordinates are able to display initiative—they do not need tasks to be 'spelt out' stage by stage.
d. Subordinates are interested in the task or problem and believe it to be important to their own success as well as that of the organisation.
e. Subordinates understand and identify with the organisation's objectives and values.
f. Subordinates have been sufficiently well trained to cope with the problem faced or the type of task undertaken; their likely reactions are then reliable.
g. Subordinates understand their tasks in context—they understand both their leader's and LOR's intentions.

In other words, team morale and individual motivation are high and the functional check-list has been applied. This is the sort of leadership climate that we should all seek to promote.

Situation

Another way to look at 'style of leadership' is to consider how the situation surrounding the task might influence the style of leadership the leader displays. For example, in a crisis, the leader needs to give orders that will be instantly obeyed, adopting an authoritarian style while, in a more relaxed atmosphere with a less important task the leader can ask for, and accept, advice from his or her subordinates (though maintaining direction and ultimate control) adopting a more *laissez-faire* style. Also the level of ability of subordinates is taken into account when considering the 'style' to be adopted.

Two American behavioural scientists, Paul Hersey and Kenneth Blanchard, have produced an interesting and useful way of looking at the relationship of style and situation called 'Situational Leadership®'.[4] The Adair two circles of team maintenance and individual needs are combined in this picture into the dimension of relationship behaviour (emotional support), combined with the level of direction or control given by the leader (task behaviour) displayed during the completion of a task.[4] 'Relationship behaviour' is defined as 'the degree to which the leader listens, displays empathy, gives support and encouragement, coaches and involves team members or followers in decision making, etc.' 'Task behaviour' is 'the degree of control or delegation of authority exercised by the leader: the extent to which guidance is given and initiative expected from followers or close supervision is exercised and no latitude given.' Figure 14.2 illustrates the various combinations of task and relationship behaviour.

The styles of leadership Hersey and Blanchard describe can be termed:

S1—telling. The leader focusses on the task and bothers little with personal relationships between himself or herself and group members, or support/coaching—an authoritarian style.

S2—selling. The leader gives a high priority to both the TASK and to the relationship with his or her subordinates, demanding compliance to get the job completed, but he or she tries to get the group to want to achieve the task itself at the same time and coaches and supports it. The leader tries to 'sell' the task to the group.

S3—participating. Here the leader with lower focus of attention on the TASK is prepared to spend more energy on the establishment of good relations with his or her subordinates. He or she is prepared to accept suggestions from group members.

S4—delegating. The leader is so much confident in subordinates that he or she can reduce focus on the task and can relax efforts at maintaining the team's cohesiveness and satisfying its needs. The leader can set it the task and let it get on with achieving it.

The key to which style to adopt is based on the level of 'readiness' of the followers, derived from their level of demonstrated ability (skill and knowledge), willingness, commitment, confidence and motivation. Four levels of development were identified (see Figure 14.3). These levels determine the situation on which the model described is overlaid as shown in Figure 14.4.

Figure 14.2

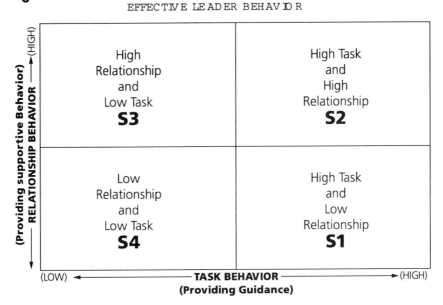

EFFECTIVE LEADER BEHAVIOR

| High Relationship and Low Task **S3** | High Task and High Relationship **S2** |
| Low Relationship and Low Task **S4** | High Task and Low Relationship **S1** |

(Providing supportive Behavior) ——→ (HIGH)
RELATIONSHIP BEHAVIOR

(LOW) ◄——— TASK BEHAVIOR ———► (HIGH)
(Providing Guidance)

Figure 14.3 Continuum of follower readiness

HIGH	MODERATE		LOW
R4	R3	R2	R1
Able and Willing or Confident	Able but Unwilling or Insecure	Unable but Willing or Confident	Unable and Unwilling or Insecure

Source: Paul Hersey & Kenneth Blanchard, 1993, *Management of Organizational Behavior* (6th edn), Englewood Cliffs, New Jersey: Prentice Hall Inc.

Figure 14.4 Situational Leadership®

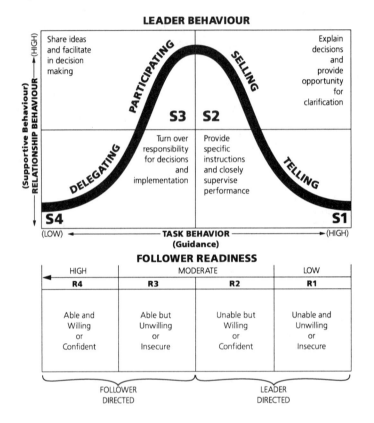

LEADER BEHAVIOUR

(Supportive Behaviour)
RELATIONSHIP BEHAVIOUR

(HIGH)

Share ideas and facilitate in decision making

PARTICIPATING

SELLING

Explain decisions and provide opportunity for clarification

S3 **S2**

DELEGATING

Turn over responsibility for decisions and implementation

Provide specific instructions and closely supervise performance

TELLING

S4

S1

(LOW) ◄──── TASK BEHAVIOR ────► (HIGH)
(Guidance)

FOLLOWER READINESS

HIGH	MODERATE		LOW
R4	**R3**	**R2**	**R1**
Able and Willing or Confident	Able but Unwilling or Insecure	Unable but Willing or Confident	Unable and Unwilling or Insecure

FOLLOWER DIRECTED

LEADER DIRECTED

Source: Paul Hersey & Kenneth Blanchard, 1993, *Management of Organizational Behavior* (6th edn), Englewood Cliffs, New Jersey: Prentice Hall Inc.

This is a fairly simple concept showing four 'pigeon-holes', but they do clearly indicate the interconnection of the two relationships with the leader's style (in the sense of manner, not personality).

Think of styles in straightforward terms of the situation when a new leader takes over a team. Now think of the situational model. To start with he or she is unknown to the team members and does not know much of them, the leader can offer little support and needs to give plenty of clear instructions to get things done. The leader starts telling. As he or she gets to know the team, the leader can offer more support while slowly gaining confidence in the team members' abilities and hence, needs to give them less guidance than earlier. The leader starts selling.

As time progresses team members begin to feel that they can rely on the leaders who gain confidence in their ability and so are able to give them more 'rope', permitting them greater freedom of action under guidance. This stage is participating and delegating.

The path through the four styles is not just one way. At times a leader may find he or she has to backtrack when situations change. For instance, although an experienced leader may have been operating by delegating most of the time, in the heat of a crisis he or she is likely to revert to telling. Leaders must be flexible with a style to meet the needs of the situation. Now relate these styles to the stages of team development in Figure 14.5.

To show you that these ideas are compatible with, and have a relationship to, the Maslow and Herzberg motivational theories: consider the paths of 'effective leadership style', and review the section on motivation (Chapter 12). We can see that 'telling' and 'selling' relate to the lower order of Maslow's hierarchy of needs where the leader provides clear-cut decisions that insist on satisfying physiological and security needs. As you move to participating, social needs are being satisfied as more effort is put into relationship behaviour and less into task behaviour.

As the leader comes to accept the abilities of the team to take responsibility, so their esteem and self-fulfilment needs are catered for. In Herzberg's terms the Hygiene factors are operating for the team by telling, selling, and participating while the real motivating factors, the motivators, are at work in delegation.

THE LEADER, POWER AND AUTHORITY

I shall desire every Officer by love and affable courage to command his soldiers, since what is done by fear is done unwillingly and what is unwillingly attempted can never prosper.

The Earl of Essex addressing the Parliamentary Army in 1642[6]

In Chapter 1, I put forward the notion that the leader has authority by virtue of appointment and that power comes from acceptance by the subordinates. We explore that notion a little further. There are three types of authority that the leader can use at work.

213

Figure 14.5

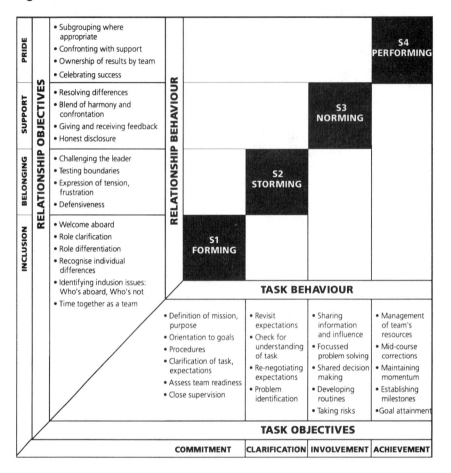

- **The authority of appointment.** That is the leader uses his or her position, status or title in ordering people to do what he or she wants, or tightly controlling resources (people, money, and so on) to ensure that his or her objectives are achieved in his or her way. This does little to generate mutual trust and respect.
- **The authority of personality.** That is the leader using strength of character to influence people to do what he or she would like done. The leader's personal values largely dictate his or her behaviour and the way in which character strength is employed. Organisations that rely solely on leaders' personality to provide leadership find it hard to replace these people.

- **The authority of knowledge and skills.** It is often said that knowledge is power, and having an intellectual advantage, whether professional or technical, over other people may confer some authority. If this type of authority alone is used the perception of others is likely to be negative since they will view the leader as an arrogant know-all. Too many people in business are promoted to leadership roles based solely on technical expertise, there is no one who has not witnessed the damage that they can cause.

The authority of position enables leaders to get the job done, but only just. It does not inspire people to innovate or improve. Leaders' real power comes from their acceptance by their teams and that is based on track record, respect, confidence and trust. The more competent leaders are seen to be, the less people question their actions or decisions, and the less **some** people need to be involved or consulted. They have faith in their leaders and do not want to waste time. Leaders, however, must be aware that some people will want to be involved and if leaders assume too much their acceptance and power base falls away.

THE LEADER–FOLLOWER RELATIONSHIP

The leader–follower relationship is characterised by trust and respect both ways. It is easily built by making clear, fair decisions on the part of the leader, and by the followers' willingness to carry them out. It is very easily lost by one bad decision.

Sir Robin Knox-Johnston

Within my division, both leader and the individual team members gain a lot of emotional sustenance from each other and are almost as close as family. We treat each other as equal beings and value each other. If I am not present, I have no hesitation in trusting them to do the right thing and this is reflected in what they achieve. We have great loyalty within the team and their level of morale and approach to teamwork is reflected in a lower turnover rate of staff and greater stabil;.y than in other divisions within the enterprise. My team know that they can depend on me to go into bat for them.

Bank Director

215

In one sense we are all leaders and we are all followers. What differs is the conscious decision to exercise leadership, whether it is to influence a social group in the choice of 'which pub to visit next', or to influence the activities of entire organisations. To lead you not only need the skills and qualities already discussed, but also the desire to lead. In many organisations with a 'flat' structure peers frequently pass from a leadership role to a follower role, depending on the nature of the project. But who is accepting all the responsibilities of the functional check-list? So what is the nature of the relationship between leader and follower?

> If you are going to get something out of people they have to at least respect you, they may not necessarily like you but they must respect you. It is critical that you are perceived to be working with them and recognised as a person who would not ask someone to do a job that you are not prepared to do yourself.
>
> *John Quinn, Managing Director, Thorn Lighting Pty Ltd*
>
> People hate being told what to do. The beauty of Clean Up Australia is that people own the idea and the results.
>
> *Ian Kiernan, sailor and founder of Clean Up Australia*

General Sir John Hackett had this to say on the subject[7]:

For the discharge of the function of leadership the establishment of a dominant position for the leader over the led is indispensable. How does this come about?

In the archetypal leader/follower relationship it happens of its own accord. I do not mean here the establishment of dominance by brute force and fear. In all I have to say here I am concerned exclusively with subordination by consent.

The leader has something the others want and that only he can provide. The man who can show the tribesmen where the water hole is has a special knowledge: he can direct those in need to a place where their need can be satisfied. But you would call him no more than a guide and not a leader unless something else was present. *This something is partly the ability to find an answer to a problem which the others cannot solve. But there is also the power, when difficulties have to be overcome, to help people over them. A capacity to help people in the overcoming of the difficulties which face them in a joint enterprise is one of those things which distinguish the person who is a leader from the person who is no more than a guide.*

In the more complex leader/follower relationship which you find in a modern army the leader is still giving something which the led require. All are bound together in a common undertaking whose success is of common concern. . .What the leader has to give is the direction of a joint effort which will bring success. That is what he is there for, and he must have sufficient mastery of the techniques involved to do what is demanded of him by those he leads. *Very early on in the inquiry, you will notice, there emerges the suggestion that the function of leadership cannot be discharged on the one side without a requirement to be led on the other.*

To make a commanding position over other men acceptable to them it is also necessary for the man holding it to possess in a higher degree than they do qualities which they respect. . .

You have in fact, as it seems to me, to be good at what is done by professionals under your management if you are to exercise effective leadership over them, especially where the leader/follower relationship comes under considerable strain. It is not good enough any longer to be able simply to coordinate, in military affairs any more than in industrial enterprises, and the heavier the stresses the more clearly this emerges. . .

But in my own submission the leader, besides being a competent manager, must be known to possess a high degree of competence in some specific skill or skills closely relevant to the discharge of his organisation's primary task. . .

Of course people set in authority at all levels in an army can be carried along by the machine itself, caught up in its rank structure. But when this happens the relationship between leaders and led may be too weak to withstand strain. It is very likely to break down when stress is heavy. . .

Can we distinguish between the qualities required in any leadership situation and the qualities required in specific situations, between main qualities and ancillary? I believe there is such a distinction, but it is not easy to draw. Knowing what it is best to do is important but knowing how to get things done seem to me clearly more so. . .

In fact, the heavier the stress on a group the higher the importance of what I might call personal qualities as distinct from professional competence. The relationship between these two areas is very complex and in the structure of a hierarchy organisation. . .it must be approached with care. Selection of personnel, training methods, the system of appointment and promotion—all these are matters in which this relationship is closely concerned. They need the most careful handling and deep and sympathetic attention.

The essential leadership situation does not arise unless there is a recognised requirement by someone to be led. Leadership is, in fact, a response on one side to an awareness of need on the other.

It is just worthwhile, perhaps, pointing out here that the relationship between a leader and those led is essentially different in one important respect when looked at from different ends of the nexus. The leader leads a group. However much he seeks to bind the members together in it by individual treatment his responsibility is over the group and to them as a whole. The member of the group, on the other hand, however much he may be bound together with the other members, responds to the leader essentially as an individual. . .

The power of example is very important to people under stress. For one thing it affords an outlet for hero worship, to which there seems to be an important and deep-rooted inclination in men. The person under stress is aware of inadequacies. He sees someone else apparently less burdened in this way. To some extent he identifies with that other person. This gives him some release. He is then likely to be grateful and become even more biddable. He will be even more open to the influence of suggestion and example than he was before.

. . .the example of officers is the keystone of morale. Lord Moran, in that wise and compassionate book The Anatomy of Courage, *refers to 'the electrifying effect of any act of coolness and courage on the part of an officer'.*

A great part of this effect is, I believe, due to a sudden surge of relief in those who are witnesses. They are helped to shed a part at least of the intolerable burden of inadequacy under which they labour. They see another man doing what they long to do and cannot, someone being what they long to be and are not. Hope and purpose are shown to them where they labour in futility and despair and a rush of gratitude and humility and love can be the result.

Effective leadership. . .depends more on knowing how to get things done than on being good at knowing what it would be best to do. Nonetheless, a group of people can often be dominated by the one person who sees most clearly, and can best explain, the issue. Bewildered men turn towards anyone who can help to clear the confusion in their minds. Even to create in confused men the illusion that their minds have been cleared can have a similar effect. When effectively done, the clarification of an issue can act upon people under pressure like a magnet. . .

One important thing in the leader/follower relationship, it has always seemed to me, is that you get what you give, and no more. You are only really entitled to ask from below what you are prepared to give to those above. Beginners in this game have sometimes thought to acquire prestige with their subordinates by affecting a fine disregard of their superiors. But buying compliance by disloyalty is a short-term expedient which is in the highest degree dangerous [my italics].

ADVICE TO LEADERS

Mutual trust, confidence and respect should exist among leaders and followers—essential for effective teamwork. The relationship must be close and friendly, but professional leaders cannot seek popularity. This is difficult in flat-structured teams when considerable moral courage may be needed to keep friends or close colleagues on track to meet agreed commitments. You, as a leader, need to be efficient and competent because unless you are good at your job you will not have the team's respect or its confidence that you will succeed.

As a leader, you and your followers are all part of the same team; their successes and failures are yours; when you speak or write never say 'you'—always say 'we'. Put the team's interests first, and your interest in them as individuals must be sincere. Never think of taking an interest as an unwanted distraction. You must be your team's champion and, at the same time, their chief critic. Your loyalty to them must be unquestionable, and in tough times the team will remain in good spirits if it knows you are trying to do the best for it.

As a leader, you may hold a superior position within the structure of the organisation, you may be the superior manager to a team of subordinates, but that does not make you a 'superior' being. This difference in interpretation of the word 'superior' is vital if you are to understand the nature of the leader–follower relationship. To make the false assumption that as a 'superior manager' you are 'superior' in all things leads to arrogance and prevents leaders from winning over teams.

If you really look after people—which does not mean being soft with them, but taking more trouble about them than you take about yourself—they quickly appreciate your efforts on their behalf. You win their respect, and a special relationship develops.

General Sir Peter de la Billière[8]

Your administration should be faultless. Division of work, rosters, training course allocation, and other details must be scrupulously fair.

Performance reviews must happen when they are expected to happen, and pay/reward matters promptly attended to as these are close to everyone's heart.

Be accessible at all times to discuss problems or concerns, never 'brush people off' or 'fob them off' with lame excuses. Expect 'normal' minor complaints, but watch for signs of morale slipping.

Be careful with your choice of words, say what you mean and mean what you say. Do not give rise to false expectations or make promises that you cannot keep.

Understand your people. You cannot deal with material that you do not know. Your people are your material—you must know all there is to know about them. If you are to lead their hearts and minds you must know how each person responds under a wide variety of conditions.

In a formal structure team members will not see things, or perceive things, in the same way as people above them in the hierarchy. You need to know how each person perceives matters if you are to communicate effectively with them as individuals.

If you find fault with a person, discuss performance not personality in private. Criticise constructively. Do not be sarcastic and do not embarrass or criticise people publicly. Give praise, publicly, when it is due.

As a leader, you should keep a notebook about each person in your team; in it record all that you know about an individual—education, courses taken, qualifications, background, ambitions, interests, hobbies, family, children, birthdays (including the team member's spouse and children), spouse's occupation, the results of interviews, coaching and the like, etc. If a team member moves to another team, his or her new leader will benefit from a copy of your records, making the new leader's job much easier.

Take every chance to talk to your team, at work, at social or sporting events, in interviews—wherever and whenever you can. To have effective leader–follower relationships you must spend time getting to know your team and you must establish mutual confidence, trust and respect. It takes a lot of hard work, but if you do not do this, you will fail.

Sometimes it is difficult to tell just how much support and backing a group is giving its leader. We all tend to resort to wishful thinking in this area—often believing that our relationships are better than they actually are. It is important to be aware of this trend and **beware** of it. Re-read the section on leader–team relations in Chapter 10.

If you can honestly answer yes to the questions posed there then your relations with your team are probably good. The ideal leader at any level, achieves the loyalty and affection of his or her team by inspiration, rather than through coercion and wielding of their authority. The relationship is also enhanced by the leader's recommendations being accepted and supported by his or her superior. It is a demonstration of confidence in the leader and recognition of the leader and that team, thus managing upwards is also vital to ensuring good relationships with followers.

References

1. Elliott Jaques, 1996, *Requisite Organization: A Total System for Effective Managerial Organization and Managerial Leadership for the 21st Century*, Arlington, Virginia: Cason Hall & Co Publishers
2. Douglas McGregor, 1960, *The Human Side Of Enterprise*, New York: McGraw-Hill.
3. V. H. Vroom, 'Some personality determinants of the effects of participation', *Journal of Abnormal and Social Psychology*, 1959, pp. 322–327; also published under the same title, 1960, Englewood Cliffs, New Jersey: Prentice Hall Inc.
4. Paul Hersey and Kenneth Blanchard, 1993, *Management of Organizational Behavior* (6th edn), Englewood Cliffs, New Jersey: Prentice Hall Inc. The Situational Leadership® model is the registered trade mark of The Center for Leadership Studies, Escondido, CA. All rights reserved.
5. Kenneth Blanchard, 1986, *Leadership and The One Minute Manager*, London: Collins.
6. E. S. Turner, 1956, *Gallant Gentlemen*, London: Michael Joseph Ltd.
7. General Sir John Hackett, 1983, *The Profession Of Arms*, London: Sidgwick & Jackson.
8. General Sir Peter de la Billière, 1994, *Looking For Trouble*, London: HarperCollins.

CHAPTER 15

LEADERSHIP ACROSS CULTURES

> Our values' include flexibility, teamwork and responsibility. Because of the national culture in each market, we have to blend in our corporate culture with sensitivity and awareness. We cannot impose our culture, but rather ensure that we can develop the local subsidiary.
>
> *Kathy Rozmeta, Learning & Development Manager,*
> *Coca-Cola Amatil Limited*
>
> Every man takes the limits of his own field of vision for the limits of the world.
>
> *Schopenhauer*

At the opening to this book I introduced the notion to you that the globalisation of business and the global paradox are some of the factors driving change. When enterprises post expatriate executives to overseas subsidiaries, particularly those in senior roles, they place a large burden on these individuals who have little margin for error in their endeavours. These executives rapidly have to learn how to integrate a foreign subsidiary whose personnel may come from a very different cultural and economic background into the organisation's own 'corporate culture'.

In addition to these 'overseas postings', people from most countries are far more mobile than in years gone by. Within countries that are members of the European Union whose borders have all but disappeared, and countries such as Australia that have high immigration numbers, the need to lead diverse people from a variety of cultural backgrounds becomes imperative. Besides understanding this 'ethnic diversity' is the need to improve the still lamentable record of most organisations in their acceptance (and hence, identified career paths) of female managers, and especially senior women. As this book is about the skills and knowledge of leadership, and not the rights and wrongs of corporate culture or policy, the women in management debate will not be argued here.

Without being trite, the Adair three circles model of leadership presented in Chapter 5, will stand leaders in good stead. This is because the functions of the leader—what a leader has to do—varies little from job to job or culture to culture. The essential difference is the need for leaders across cultures to develop an appreciation and sensitivity towards the cultural heritage of employees and tread lightly on first assuming such appointments while 'learning the ropes' of the local environment.

> The allies of Rome (as the provincials were called) were little interfered with: They continued to lead the life to which they were accustomed and to manage their own affairs. The system of administration was adapted to the conditions of each province and the Roman government respected the liberty of its subjects.[1]
>
> . . .Nor did Rome block its subjects from participation in government or the military, even at the highest levels. This may have been Rome's greatest innovation.[2]

LEADERSHIP AND CULTURE

Having made the point that the leadership discussed so far is applicable to all environments you need to temper that with local understanding, sensitivity, and awareness of both people and markets. Here we examine some of the most important aspects of cross-cultural leadership, much of which are based on perception and communication (Chapter 3).

By considering leadership and business strategy from the perspective of culture, we can analyse the influences of different national cultures on the way in which an organisation functions. This enables a multinational company to gain acceptance in the community within which it operates. As an accepted 'local company', a flow of relevant local information and opportunities is maximised and influence in local policy-making bodies may be exercised.

I define 'cross-cultural leadership' as 'the reconciliation of the parent enterprise organisational culture with that of a local host nation'.

Multiculturalism and its implications for managing diversity poses additional complexities for global organisations by increasing the variety of perspectives and approaches that need to be considered in developing and executing the plans. While the global village has reduced the barriers and access to markets, people generally wish to have their own identity and customs recognised and, therefore, wish to be treated specially.

What is 'Culture'?

'Culture' can be defined as 'the combined atmosphere and environment of an organisation or people characterised by values and beliefs, knowledge, historical experience, heroes, rituals, symbols, art, political systems and law—it is a way of life for the people within that grouping'. Culture consists of patterns that describe and dictate behavioural norms. The core of culture consists of traditional ways and values that both define future action and are produced by past action.

Culture is, therefore:

- An environment shared and maintained by the members of an organisation or social group.
- A way of life and set of beliefs and values that the 'elders' wish the younger members to inherit.
- A major influence on the perception and behaviour of everyone living within that culture.

What are 'Values'?

People demonstrate or express the 'norms' of their culture through the values that they hold which dictates their attitudes and behaviours in particular situations.

A 'value' is 'something that is desirable to an individual or a group and which influences their choice of behaviour'. It is arguable whether values determine beliefs, or whether beliefs determine values—the two are inextricably linked. Beliefs and values are those things that shape a people's attitudes and, therefore, the way they act in specific situations.

HOW DO CULTURES VARY?

Nancy Adler,[3,†] Susan Schneider,[4] and Geert Hofstede[5] have suggested that several dimensions describe the major differences in culture among people. They are:

- How people see themselves
- How they relate to their world
- How they relate to other people
- Primary activity
- How they relate to time
- How they relate to space
- How they relate to authority—power distance
- Masculinity versus femininity
- Uncertainty avoidance.

How We See Ourselves

The two extremes of culture in this context is whether people consider others as 'good' or 'bad'.

Societies that have a positive view of people are inclined to place more trust and confidence in others initially and have a similar expectation of the way that they should be viewed. The opposite view is to consider people as inherently 'weak' which results in a low attribution of trust.

Apart from this negative view of people, there are those societies that believe people can change and in an organisational sense emphasis is placed on training to bring this about. The opposite view is that people are incapable of changing themselves and organisations taking this approach place greater emphasis on their selection processes to ensure that they have the right people in the right job. They rely on other companies to provide the training grounds. If they offer little or no development then they must expect a high turnover with associated costs of recruitment, both apparent and hidden.

How We Relate to Our World

Fundamentally this is the relationship that we have, individually, to the world and nature. It can be contrasted by considering the Western approach to dominating the environment and the Eastern philosophies

---

† Much of this chapter is drawn from *International Dimensions of Organizational Behavior* (2nd edn), Nancy Adler, Wadsworth Publishing Company, Belmont, USA: 1991. ISBN 0-534-92274-0.

that emphasise living in harmony with the environment. The Chinese approach to interior design of Feng Shui demonstrates this. In a business sense this can be viewed as a controlling win/lose approach or a partnership win/win approach to developing business and relationships.

How We Relate to Other People: Individualism versus Collectivism

The major differences here are the focus on individuals and personal characteristics in contrast with societies that focus upon the community or collective group. Many Western cultures emphasise the liberty, rights and achievement of the individual and recognise individual excellence and opportunity. The policies of Western organisations recognise and follow similar practices. In those countries which have a more collective orientation the personnel policies of companies reflect collective achievement, loyalty and compatibility with the team.

This aspect of cultural difference is frequently reflected in the participation sought by leaders in their decision making, and the status symbols maintained or discarded by the leaders within the hierarchy.

Activity versus Passivity

Many Western ways of life emphasise 'doing'—what you do, action. Measurable achievements are emphasised and compared with external standards. The opposite to this is the idea of 'being' in which views, events, and ideas, flow spontaneously. Those people working in this sort of environment expect to enjoy the company of their colleagues and the nature of their work or they are likely to leave.

In the 'being' orientation, common in Eastern philosophy, people expect planning to be linked to time that is viewed in the context of generations. Major projects and change will, therefore, take a long time in Western terms to occur. In the action-based culture people believe that the implementation of plans can be accelerated through careful planning and objective-setting. People of the 'being' orientation believe that accelerated change is unwise since it rarely works immediately and is not sustainable over time.

The Concept of Time

Some societies rely on the traditions of the past and view innovation and change in relation to past experience. Those groups that focus on the future consider the implications of plans for long-term benefit and generally display less concern for long-established customs than others.

Different cultures also view time in a different context. What is considered late and, therefore, discourteous for an appointment in one culture may not be considered late or rude in another. This notion of time may also be reflected in the length of time a person may spend in a particular role before moving on and the sense of urgency with which problems and planning are approached. Eastern cultures frequently think in terms of generations and the unwary Westerner is frustrated by the apparent lack of progress in negotiations.

The Sense of Space

Some cultures prefer privacy and hence, allow senior executives to occupy private offices, other cultures take the opposite view and encourage large partition-free open-plan offices. This attitude is reflected in the way that people discipline themselves so as not to give offence to others—the sense of order, uniformity, consideration and quiet courtesy often found in the Far East.

It is usual for both Middle and Far Eastern cultures to have more people present at important meetings than would be the case in the West and this reflects their public orientation.

How Different Cultures Relate to Authority— Power Distance

Different cultures view leadership and organisation structure in different lights. Some cultures view the reason for a hierarchy in the sense that it defines who has control over whom, whereas others believe hierarchy exists purely to ease problem solving, decision making and planning, and that hierarchical structure makes it possible for the organisation to function and for tasks to be completed.

This is reflected in whether a company starts a project by defining the aim, objectives, and phases involved in a plan, or whether the emphasis is on the individuals leading the project. While both need to be understood irrespective of culture, the emphasis differs.

Some cultures view leaders as the source of all knowledge, expertise and answers, whereas others believe that leaders should assist subordinates to solve problems for themselves and develop personally, rather than rely totally on the leader.

This different view of leaders' roles could create the perception in other cultures of over-dominant or incompetent leaders, despite the fact that leaders are viewed as perfectly capable in their own countries.

Another important consideration is the inherent respect for authority that exists in some cultures. In many Eastern cultures junior employees have a natural respect for authority and rarely question the decision of their leaders. Many Western leaders operating in this environment try to encourage participation in various activities and seek to build personal relationships and find it difficult to break through a wall, based on this respect and possibly class status. In such environments leaders may need to be rather more directive that they would prefer if they are to keep things happening. (Re-read Vroom's comment in Chapter 14, 'Styles of Leadership'.)

This respect for authority or power could mean that in negotiations it is important to have people of the right level of seniority or with the requisite status, present to ensure mutual respect without which no progress can be made.

We should consider to what extent the imposition of an organisational culture reduces the effect of national culture in its employees. Given people's lifetime exposure to their own national culture, it is unlikely that an organisational culture will rapidly, or easily dominate, and, therefore, organisations need to blend what is acceptable to both company and country if they are going to be able to operate in another nation with maximum efficiency and minimum disruption.

The British Army excelled in this with the way that Indian Army regiments were officered by Britons who carefully produced an amalgam of British operating procedures and local customs, traditions, and celebrated events. That is continued today in the Gurkha Rifle Battalions serving in the British Army. They share British Army tactical doctrine and systems, but they have their own 'pundit' or holy man, have their own 'scale of rations' and cooks, and have basic training tailored to their needs. They celebrate their own religious festivals, blend the caste system with meritocracy and have both Gurkha and British officers. Significantly the British officers serving with Gurkha battalions spend at least six of their first months learning the language and going 'on trek' in Nepal to visit the hill villages, pay pensions to retired soldiers, and learn about the culture that their soldiers come from. Some Korean companies are now sending managers to live in Australia for long periods, not to work, but to learn about the culture before taking on a role. By contrast, more than one inflexible major corporation has been slow to recognise the need for sensitivity and tried to stamp their corporate culture on a new overseas venture with unpleasant results that have surprised them! I have experienced that with the imposition of a stereotypical mid-west USA attitude onto an Australian sales force. Needless to say the two did not mix!

Masculinity versus Femininity

The variance in roles and attitudes held by members of both sexes varies considerably. Male values are often competitive, assertive or aggressive while female values are more caring and modest. This difference can also be seen among entire societies, although at present there still tends to be a difference between men and women in any one society.

In many countries companies do not capitalise on the talent and potential of their women, although many of whom are far more capable than their male counterparts. Despite promises to the contrary, the 'glass ceiling' is maintained and opportunities for senior appointments restricted. The embracing of merit, not bias, has to be inculcated, certainly in Western companies whose primary religion is unlikely to pose the cultural bar seen in some countries.

Uncertainty Avoidance

This is the degree to which a cultural grouping feels comfortable or uncomfortable in unstructured situations. Peoples that avoid uncertainty have more rules and regulations than others to minimise the effects of unknown or uncertain situations. They are also prone to greater displays of emotion and higher levels of internal nervous energy.

COMMUNICATING ACROSS CULTURES

We have already established and discussed elsewhere that communication, whether verbal or non-verbal, is vital to organisational effectiveness. The factors that affect perception are discussed in detail in Chapter 3 and the influences on perception can only be magnified with the addition of a cultural context.

Remember that our perceptual filter is selective, based on learned and culturally determined experiences and the way in which we perceive things tends to remain constant. It is, therefore, very easy for us to chose the message that we understand and act on from what we have seen or heard. In a cross-cultural context it is very easy for us to extrapolate stereotypical characteristics and attribute those to a person with whom we are communicating.

There are some particular factors that lead us to misinterpret or misperceive events in a cross-cultural context.

- **Subconscious false assumptions and beliefs.** Through our own background and life experiences we have developed beliefs that we take for granted and that we do not challenge. When working with people who are less similar to those with whom we normally work this will lead inevitably to problems in communication and understanding.

- **Cultural self-awareness.** If we misinterpret people from other cultures and think of them in stereotypical terms, they are probably doing the same about us. We should, therefore, understand the impact of our own culture on our way of doing things and how this might be perceived by others. Remember never to assume that people have similar values or assumptions as we do; to do that is to invite misunderstandings. The golden rule should be to assume difference until similarity is proven.

If we are to work at ease with people from other cultures then it is essential that we develop a sincere appreciation of how that culture has developed, and the values and beliefs within that society.

Leaders operating in overseas subsidiaries need, in particular, to develop sensitivity to both people and their environment and to expect to face unclear or ambiguous situations that will remain not fully understood until the relevant cultural considerations have been made. Communication frequently fails among people of one culture, and communication can only be more difficult in a cross-cultural situation. Remember that if a message is not understood, rather than repeating the message, the message should be changed or reworded and, if possible, as many delivery channels as possible are used. This means that oral communication may need to be accompanied by rehearsed physical gestures or pictorial representations.

Remember in the discussion about teamwork that diversity of cultural background can assist in situations in which creativity or different ways of thinking are required, or new approaches, products, and operations, are desirable. In organisations in which processes require people to think and act in similar ways, or organisations in which absolute clarity is required, however, cultural diversity within the same team can hinder progress.

It is possible, sometimes probable (but not certain) that levels of frustration and stress increase in culturally diverse teams because differences in perception and poor communication lead to greater disagreement and unclear expectations. Leaders of such teams have greater challenges in reconciling differences in attitude, understanding, and lower levels of trust.

Because other cultures are unfamiliar, they can often be seen as a threat by leaders lacking understanding or self-confidence. Leaders can become parochial, making the assumption that their way is the only way of doing things and that other cultures have nothing to offer, other than posing problems. Leaders need to rise above their own ethnocentric view and approach cross-cultural relations in the belief that neither culture is superior.

MOTIVATION

While motivation has been examined, it now needs to be thought of in a cross-cultural context. Hofstede[5] has suggested, for example, that Maslow's theory does not hold good in many countries other than in the USA. Hofstede intimates that countries with high uncertainty avoidance (such as Greece and Japan) are motivated more by security needs than by higher order needs when compared to a country such as the USA. In other countries social needs may be predominant among employees who place a high value on their quality of life (such as Scandinavian countries). In more collectivist-orientated countries, the social needs of the whole group are considered more important than the ego and self-actualisation of the individual. It is, therefore, likely that the rank order of Maslow's needs may vary across different cultures. This is why leaders need to fully appreciate the culture in which they are working.

The manner in which leadership is exercised also varies among cultures. People living in cultures in which unequal distribution of power is accepted are less comfortable with delegated authority and the need to use initiative and to make discretionary decisions. This can be linked to Vroom's statement (in Chapter 14) that subservient people used to respect for authority cannot work effectively for a leader who tries to involve them and who expects initiative to be displayed, and vice versa.

DECISION MAKING ACROSS CULTURES

In making decisions the cultural perception of a problem needs to be considered.[3] Is the issue actually considered a problem or is it not? In one culture a problem may pose a situation to be changed, while in another it is viewed as a situation to be accepted. One culture may emphasise collecting information and analysing facts, applying a scientific and logical approach, while another may prefer to generate ideas. One culture may consider that people are willing to learn and are able to change, while maybe another may view people as unable to change. Decision making can be delegated and speedy decisions encouraged in one culture, while in another only senior executives are able to make a decision that is done slowly.

From the preceding paragraphs you can be seen how the complexity of leadership increases in a global context. It is impossible within the scope of this book to provide an insight into leadership and teamwork within every culture on the planet. The considerations highlighted should assist leaders in making their choices, however, when exercising their responsibilities, and should provide the first principles on which to base decisions and actions.

References

1. G. H. Stevenson, 1939, *Roman Provincial Administration*, Oxford: Basil Blackwell.
2. Richard Luecke, 1994, *Scuttle Your Ships Before Advancing And Other Lessons from History on Leadership and Change for Today's Managers*, New York: Oxford University Press.
3. Nancy Adler, 1991, *International Dimensions of Organizational Behavior*, Belmont, Ca: Wadsworth Publishing.
4. Susan Schneider in Vladimir Pucik, Noel Tichy, & Carole Barnett, 1992, *Globalizing Management: Creating and Leading the Competitive Organization*, New York: John Wiley & Sons.
5. Geert Hofstede, 'Motivation, Leadership And Organization: Do American Theories Apply Abroad?', *Organizational Dynamics Journal*, 1980.

CHAPTER 16

DISCIPLINE

True discipline is not someone shouting orders at others. That is dictatorship, not discipline. The voluntary, reasoned discipline accepted by free, intelligent men and women is another thing. To begin with, it is binding on all, from top to bottom.

Field Marshal Sir William Slim[1]

Without discipline, either collective or self, there will be no success.

Sir Robin Knox-Johnston

Discipline is a state of mind that produces a readiness for willing, intelligent and appropriate conduct. It is essential to distinguish between discipline and punishment. They are not the same, and punishment or disciplinary sanctions are means that can be used to influence the action of people—their discipline. Resorting to punishment is a negative approach to developing discipline, but there are occasions when it needs to be used without hesitance. For example, gross breaches of integrity and dishonesty; acts that can and should not be tolerated (despite the appalling 'example' set for us by some of our political leaders).

In Chapter 4 I introduced discipline as a necessary part of effective teamwork and morale because an efficient organisation needs to know the likely actions of the people within it. This organisational stability

can only be achieved by a high degree of self-discipline. Discipline
has already been briefly discussed as a factor affecting morale and
coherent and coordinated teamwork, and in conditions of adversity
particularly, the penalty for a lack of discipline is disorganisation and
low morale.

We can consider discipline under three headings:

- **Imposed discipline.** This is a type of discipline that armies apply
  to recruits and it is a popular civilian conception of discipline in
  the armed forces. It is simply the first step in developing self-
  discipline within the recruit. It is through the imposition of discipline that they learn basic standards of behaviour that are
  expected in army life and they learn to maintain mental alertness
  and perseverance in adversity through demanding training. This
  requires a very authoritarian approach to leadership, and as training
  progresses the recruit can meet both the physical and mental
  challenges set and gains satisfaction and a sense of achievement.
  Soldiers will now start to carry out their tasks because they want
  to—their own self-discipline is asserting itself. Thus imposition by
  others gives way to imposition by self.
- **Self-discipline.** The basis of all order and efficiency is self-
  discipline. People need to have an inbuilt set of standards that
  governs their behaviour and conduct. This varies from person to
  person and its level depends on the number of factors, including
  the influences on people in early life. When people see the need
  to maintain certain standards and adhere to them, self-discipline
  has been achieved and its essence is mental self-control and
  restraint, and awareness of the need for a sense of duty towards
  others.
- **Collective discipline.** This is a discipline within a group or team
  and is founded upon the self-discipline of individuals. This is
  the discipline that ensures stability under stress and consistency
  in performance. Such discipline only develops under positive leadership and from the individuals within the team accepting and
  aligning themselves to team objectives. This inevitably requires
  a degree of self-sacrifice of personal interests in favour of the
  group, and that is why self-centred people never really become full
  members of any team to which they belong; they are members on
  paper only.

If you ask clients why they think it is effective to have McKinsey assisting them it is because we bring to them discipline and rigour. Unfortunately our (Australian) culture has valued the individual and the 'doing your own thing' attitude. This has prevented emphasis in many companies on managing through processes and all the other elements of organisational discipline that lead to high performance.

Robert McLean, formerly Managing Director,
McKinsey & Co Australia

Consider these views of discipline:

'The best form of discipline is the subordination of self for the benefit of the community' (Field Marshal Montgomery[4]) and

'Discipline is teaching which makes a man do something which he would not, unless he had learned that it was the right, the proper, and the expedient thing to do. At its best, it is instilled and maintained by pride in oneself, in one's unit, and in one's profession; only at its worst by a fear of punishment. Discipline is a vital component of high morale, and it is required to some degree in all but an anarchic community' (Field Marshal Wavell[2]).

It is unfortunate that the word 'discipline' is frequently used as a substitute for the word 'punish' (to discipline a person). This creates inaccurate perceptions of the subject and inclines people to not discuss it. It is particularly distasteful to those who grew up in the 'hippy era' and have promoted their perception of the word in the education of their own offspring and taken it into their own place of work.

In this chapter discipline is presented as a constructive force for the promotion of teamwork and morale, and advice is given to assist in developing self-discipline—the foundation of discipline.

If you think hard, discipline can be linked to Maslow's theory of motivation. Security as we have seen is one of our basic needs, as is 'belonging' to a group. Knowing the rules, the norms, of the group can further add to the sense of satisfaction of that need when people realise that the 'rules' exist purely to ensure an environment of mutual support and act as an aid to effectiveness.

Furthermore, consideration of another person's need for acceptance and support—team spirit—provides any individual with a sense of duty with the motivation and self-discipline of standing by and assisting team members. This is the subordination of self for the benefit of the group.

Self-control. To be disciplined we strengthen our minds so that we can overcome any negative influences that may surround us. Through it, people learn to restrict their thoughts or behaviour within definite limits and through discipline the habit of self-control is instilled, thus enabling us to display fortitude in the face of fatigue, stress, or discomfort.

> Unless the lesson of duty be first well learned, the lesson of discipline can be but imperfectly understood.
>
> *Sir John Fortescue*[3]

Sense of duty. The fact that a psychologist like Maslow can offer a rational explanation for observed behaviour does not in any way diminish the behaviour or the person exhibiting it. Our needs are common to most, if not all, people and act as the 'goads' to behaviour. It is, therefore, extremely important that we understand that people under stress experience a heightened need for the support of others, and often they want to merge themselves into the corporate body of which they are a part. We learn to gain confidence and encouragement from working with our fellows; we can derive strength and satisfaction from their company; and our own identities merge into the larger corporate identity. There is, however, a price to be paid for this sense of 'belonging'. To be a member you have to accept that you have a 'duty' towards the organisation and its other members.

Discipline implies a concept of duty. Nothing would be accomplished in any crisis by a person without a sense of duty. This sense is instilled through our discipline because through it we are taught to do what is right as a matter of course, and to know that it is wrong not to do so. This knowledge is self-discipline, and with it we have a set of standards that we impose on ourselves. The best form of leadership is that which encourages and expects people to have self-discipline. Trust, is therefore, linked to self-discipline, for trust is only given to us when there is confidence in our reliability and consistency; self-discipline is implicit in trustworthiness.

THE LEADER AND DISCIPLINE

Retailing is about providing customers with a consistent experience over time and a wide geographical area. You cannot provide this without having a disciplined organisation. Discipline ensures success by minimising and hopefully eliminating unpleasant surprises for the customer.

For discipline to be effective, you need to work out exactly what has to be 'tight' and what can be left 'loose'—what has to be controlled and what can be left to initiative and originality.

Chris Walsh, Operations Director, David Jones Limited

A sense of insecurity is often the reason that young or inexperienced leaders exhibit inappropriate behaviour when they first take over a group. The greater the sense of insecurity the more likely it is that the 'leader' will try to dominate the group that can, in its turn, generate conflict with individual members; not in a physical sense, but in the sense that members withdraw their cooperation and, thus, interrupt the ability of the team to work effectively together. This must be seen as a partial failure of discipline, especially the self-discipline of those involved.

Psychologically, once positions have been taken up it is very difficult to get the principals to relent because each is frightened of being perceived by others as weakening and, in the case of leaders, they feel they will be perceived as having had their authority weakened. Aggression and conflict must be avoided.

Look now at Figure 16.1. It compares the characteristics of 'assertiveness', essential in a leader for the maintenance of discipline, versus 'non-assertiveness'. Notice that the characteristics of assertiveness that assist the leader to build discipline are very closely linked to the factors that we have considered as part of trust and 'the character that inspires confidence and trust'. Again consider and re-read the proposition that 'Liberty Implies Discipline'[1] (Chapter 4). Recall that in the road safety analogy you keep to the correct side of the road when driving because:

1. It is to your own advantage.
2. Of consideration for others.

Figure 16.1

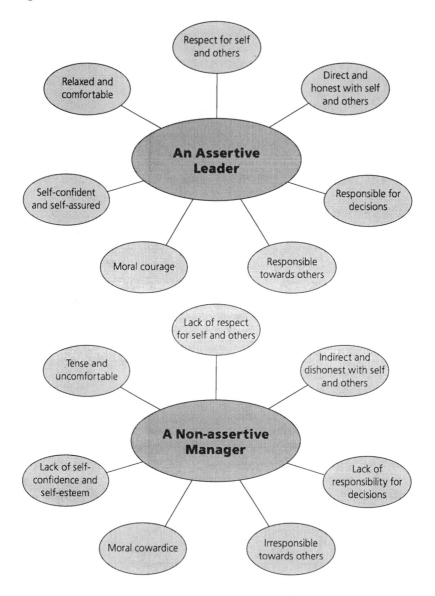

3. You have confidence in your fellows.
4. Of fear of punishment.

Whenever we put a curb on our natural desire to do as we like, whenever we temper liberty with discipline, we do so for one or more of those reasons. It is the relative weight we give to each of these reasons that decides what sort of discipline we have.

Here are some more of Field Marshal Montgomery's thoughts on discipline[4]

> . . .I would like to give you my general views on the subject of discipline. . .
>
> The word 'discipline' has a somewhat nasty smell to some people. I do not think that is right. Possibly many people do not understand what is meant by it. I believe that the idea of discipline, properly understood, underlies civilian life in the same way as it is the basis of military life. In other words, discipline is both a civilian and a military necessity.
>
> The basis of all discipline is self-discipline. This self-discipline may come from within a person, or it may be imposed upon him from without. Whatever its source, it involves the idea of self-control and self-restraint.
>
> . . .We all recognise that the interests of the community as a whole make demands on us. . .
>
> . . .we believe in a subordination of self for the benefit of the community. This involves a voluntary self-discipline which recognises and respects the rights of others, and, in so doing, enables us all to enjoy freedom of thought and speech. And at the same time we believe in a state which, recognising the importance of the individual, only imposes those restraints upon him which are necessary for the communal good. Therefore discipline has both a moral and a social foundation. There can be no doubt of its military significance. It is the backbone of an army, and no changes in methods of warfare, or in scientific developments, will affect this truth.
>
> . . .Training in self-discipline consists in analysing a man's character and then in developing the good points while teaching him to hold in subjection the bad points. This leads on, automatically, to collective discipline, in which the outstanding factor is the subordination of self for the benefit of the community. We must work on these lines. . .

Self-discipline also has a foundation in trust. If you have delegated a task and made someone accountable for it with an understanding of why it is important the chances are that they will live up to your expectations. Trust has thus contributed to their sense of duty and self-discipline, but requires the leader to take a risk. Sometimes, leaders are let down when something goes wrong. If you do not help people to learn from their mistakes and apportion blame, you will never gain subordinates' commitment and the mutual trust implicit in achieving self-discipline has been lost.

References

1. *Courage and other Broadcasts* (by Field Marshal Sir William Slim G.C.B., G.C.M.G., G.C.V.O., G.B.E., D.S.O., M.C.), 1957, London: Cassell.
2. Sir John Fortescue, n.d. *A Gallant Company*, England: Williams and Northgate.
3. Field Marshal Earl Wavell, 1948, *The Good Soldier*, London: Macmillan.
4. Field Marshal Viscount Montgomery of Alamein. Believed to be from *Forward from Victory—Speeches and Addresses*, Her Majesty's Stationery Office.

CHAPTER 17

LOYALTY

In Chapter 6 we considered loyalty as a part of integrity, an essential characteristic in leaders if they are going to gain the respect, trust and confidence of both their teams and their superiors. Remember that loyalty must be displayed upwards to support your superiors and your organisation, downwards to ensure that the interests of your team are addressed, and sideways among your peers.

Loyalty in the leaders at every level of organisational hierarchy develops loyalty within the remainder of the enterprise and this is reflected in loyal customers.

> Morale is vital to us because if it starts to wane it becomes very apparent to our customers and is reflected in our customer loyalty. A person on our front line talking to a customer on the telephone is leading our relationship with that customer, so making sure that their frame of mind and approach is positive and that they are able to mould a solution are vital. If morale is low people will seek to undermine a process. If people have a belief in success, even though it may be in a bleak situation you can feel quite positive about the outcome. Building morale takes time—it has to filter through the organisation.
>
> *Malcolm Jones, CEO, NRMA Limited*

Loyalty to Principles

Josiah Royce[1] suggests that loyalties arrange themselves in a hierarchical group. At the bottom of the pyramid is loyalty to individuals, above that loyalty to groups and at the top of the pyramid loyalty to principles. He maintains that loyalty *per se* could not be judged but that the principles that one is loyal to can be. He suggests that loyalty to those principles is what determines when a person should end his or her loyalty to an individual or a group.

The leadership practices that generate loyalty are not only about loyalty to individuals and groups, but about loyalty to a set of principles that enables an enterprise to sustain performance over time. Implicit in this is a preference for a partnership approach to business and careful selection of people, whether customers, employees or shareholders.

Here we look at 'The Loyalty Effect'[2,†] again and discuss how the concept of loyalty can affect the bottom line. Detailed research by the loyalty practice of management consultants Bain & Company International indicates that disloyalty at current rates stunts US corporate performance by 25% to 50% and that businesses that locate and retain loyal customers and investors continually display superior performance.

Where there is a high incidence of disloyalty within staff, teams are dysfunctional, leaders have been wrongly appointed, and staff turnover is high. This can occur whether the structure is hierarchical or flat.

It seems that many companies fail to analyse in detail the loss of their customers, and the rate at which they are lost. It is not unusual for some organisations to lose half of their current accounts every five years. In contrast, a high retention rate of customers (reflecting company success) assists in building company morale, reduces the cost of sales and operating and, therefore, generates greater competitive advantage. Companies that accept a high turnover in customers eventually have more dissatisfied customers than satisfied customers in the marketplace, and eventually their collective voice will severely damage potential customers' perception of the value that the company offers, increasing further the cost of sales while the level of company morale slips.

---

† This chapter is based on Frederick F. Reichheld, *The Loyalty Effect: The Hidden Force Behind Growth, Profits, and Lasting Values* © 1996 by Bain & Company, Inc. Boston: Harvard Business School Press, pp. 1–31, 91–116.

Sound, effective leadership generates innovation, a focus on customer needs and service, and loyalty within the company. This is reflected in creating value for the customer and hence, loyal accounts. Those companies that focus solely on the current year's profit are likely to do so to the detriment of loyalty. Short-term expedient decisions, particularly those that directly affect employees, assist in eroding loyalty and while short-term gains may be seen on the bottom line that year, performance is not sustainable over time. Then both employees and shareholders suffer. If the focus is on developing long-term sustainable performance and customer value, profit is a welcome byproduct that inevitably builds customer, employee, and shareholder loyalty. This means a paradigm shift from 'we exist to generate immediate profit and make short term decisions to 'we exist to create sustainable value for all stakeholders and as a result generate profit'. Ask yourself which paradigm your organisation reflects.

Obviously, two distinct paradigms have been suggested here: the leadership practices that generate employee loyalty, customer value and customer loyalty, and the financially driven approach which seeks short-term gain at the cost of long-term performance.

Few companies would deny that their people are their most important asset, and almost every chairman's opening address in a corporate annual report alludes to this. However, there are few accounting systems that take note of the assets created by loyal customers, loyal and experienced employees and loyal shareholders. To generate loyalty companies must view people as assets not expenses and must constantly strive to increase the value of these assets and their productive lifetime. Such human assets cannot be controlled so leaders have to earn their loyalty and to earn loyalty requires effort and effective leadership.

Reichheld and Teal[2] suggest that this approach makes loyalty 'a truer litmus test of corporate performance than profits ever were or could be. Profits alone are an unreliable measure because it is possible to raise reported short-term earnings by liquidating human capital.'

Bain's research quantifies how the policies, procedures and practices (including selection, training, career development, customer acquisition and marketing) that help to generate loyalty can put impressive and consistently high growth rates on the corporate bottom line. As an example the US State Farm Mutual Insurance Company that has built itself around loyalty has capital of in excess of \$US20 billion[3] that is greater than the capital commanded by AT & T or General Motors.

Building a base of loyal accounts has to be integral to any company's business strategy. For it to be successful, a company's leaders have to believe in, and display, the leadership practices consistent with loyalty-based management. Few senior executives will state that their primary aim is to create superior customer value for customers so that investors and employees alike can prosper in the long term. Rather, many instinctively say that they are there to maximise profit for shareholders.

Bain's loyalty model shows that loyalty sparks a series of economic effects that filter through the entire organisation and its systems.

- Loyal customers spend more rapidly and easily over time, generating repeat sales and referrals. This minimises a company's cost of sales and produces more profitable accounts.
- The sustainable growth that results from this permits an enterprise to recruit and retain the best talent available among the ranks of its employees. As employees become more knowledgeable about their company and their customers they are better able to exceed customer expectations and hence, add greater value. Their consistency and service delivery reinforces customer loyalty and helps to sustain growth.
- Customer-focussed, motivated and loyal staff is able to anticipate customer needs, challenge assumptions and innovate, thus reducing operating costs and improving customer service and value. This leads to better productivity and more loyal customers yet again. (But beware the loyalty of 'blind obedience and complacency').
- Spiralling productivity and the ease and efficiency of working as a partner with loyal customers generates both the cost and value advantage that is difficult for any competitor to match.
- The sustained performance of a company produced by the effects outlined above, attracts loyal shareholders, ready to invest in measures that will further sustain long-term performance and help to stabilise the company.

LOYALTY AND US

Despite what I have said about adding value to products and services everything is delivered by people, us. Therefore, motivation and behaviour are critical and the relevance of other chapters within this book may now become clearer to you.

Most of us do not work for money alone. We have other needs to be satisfied and it is usual for those of us who work in companies with a service attitude to display more energy and initiative than those in companies who simply exist for shareholder profit. We gain satisfaction from giving, from being of service. The pay-off is that we are then valued for what we do and receive (or should receive) recognition; the satisfaction of more of Maslow's needs.

This all seems to indicate that companies with leaders that abdicate their responsibility to their team members by asking employees to take full responsibility for their careers, expect a high turnover of staff and view long periods of service in one company as a practice long gone, will never enjoy the fruits of loyalty. Could the fads of re-engineering, down-sizing and lean companies (too lean to plan for the future where everyone works on crisis management) be understood for what they are?

THE SCIENCE OF LOYALTY

While various altruistic aspects to loyalty have been discussed, the processes and systems that generate it can be studied as a science,[1] but like leadership it will, at times, be an art to implement.

Why Loyal Customers Are More Profitable

Loyal customers have no cost of acquisition, provide greater revenue over time, and they generate cost savings as they become known and systems are tailored to their needs. They generate referrals and often pay a premium price for perceived value. As customers get to know a business, they learn to be efficient customers who understand exactly what you are able to supply and, therefore, require less time-intensive servicing.

Employees

Only loyal employees take the time and energy to build strong personal relationships with their customers. Only loyal employees have access to the knowledge and experience necessary to increase their efficiency and ability to exceed customer expectations. A tendency of companies to restructure and down-size constantly as executives follow management fads, rather than adhere to the fundamental principles of leadership and teamwork generate mistrust and anxiety over job security. This damages morale and are all reflected in a reduced ability to generate customer loyalty. The increasingly common practice of companies advising their staff to take complete charge of their own careers is doing little to develop loyalty through this fundamental application of leadership. In such a climate of mistrust and fear would any of us dare to take a risk to be creative or are we likely to keep our heads down and hope to avoid the next cut?

Despite the frequent claims that employees are a company's most important asset, there are still many organisations that fail to display this through their 'people policies'. An investment in effective recruiting and selection, training and development, and performance management is vital to develop maximum efficiency, customer retention and referral. The constant worry is that a company starts a programme of change and when no noticeable change is observed after six months or so the programme is aborted. Any programme that is designed to ensure long-term sustainable performance takes time and money to come to fruition and senior executives and their successors, if changes are made, have to remain committed to the programme that works, if properly planned and executed.

Fads often promise the benefits and culture that can only really be delivered by leadership and teamwork at every level (see Figure 1.2). Fads seem simple, relatively quick-acting (on paper) and 'look good'. They are all generally aimed at realising the benefits that can only be provided by a culture of leadership and teamwork, but that is much harder and more expensive to achieve, so the fad is chosen as the easy option.

Remuneration

Any system that pays us for the importance of our job, instead of the collective teams productivity, suggests that the only way to get ahead is to look after number one. Since all hierarchical pyramids reduce in numbers at each level, most people never make it to the top and so do not recruit a company of ambitious MBA qualified 'thrusters'. This can produce internal politicking and shattered self-esteem in those who 'fail'. A more useful method is to allow fairly autonomous small groups to share the benefits of their own productivity where the interests of the individual can be aligned with that of the company. Other useful benefits of organising work in relatively small teams is that it becomes much easier to identify where productivity and profitability exists. People prefer to work in smaller more intimate groups anyway (see Chapters 4 and 10).

MEASUREMENT OF THE VALUE OF LOYALTY

Bain[1] suggests that a hierarchy of measurement exists. At the top there is the customer-base net present value used in the sense of profit (net of acquisition investment). Beneath this are three key measures:

- Customer duration
- Life cycle profits
- New customer gain rate.

The first two measures relate to the net present value of your current customer accounts and the third to the capture of potential customers. The life cycle profits can be considered in two further levels. Firstly:

- The investment made by the company
- Volume
- Cost
- Price
- Referrals.

Beneath this level of consideration are those that drive the value you offer. While the value of anticipated customers needs to be considered in the gain rate, new customers should also be assessed for their quality, whether they are enriching or diluting the customer base.

Summarising this, some of the economic realities of loyalty and a different paradigm of thinking are pinpointed. For this loyalty approach to work the three components of investor, employee and customer loyalty have to be maintained. If any one of these components is weak or absent there are serious consequences for the complete system.

It is, therefore, the role of leadership to generate loyalty in staff to retain loyal customers, and by their success to retain loyal investors and shareholders. Loyalty is a vital personal quality of leadership, and a way of successfully operating a sustainable business.

References

1. Professor Josiah Royce, Professor of Philosophy at Harvard, 1908, *The Philosophy of Loyalty*.
2. Frederick F. Reichheld *The Loyalty Effect: The Hidden Force Behind Growth, Profits, and Lasting Value*, © Bain & Company, Inc., Boston: Harvard Business School Press.
3. One US billion here equals 1,000 million.

CHAPTER 18

ORGANISATIONAL LEADERSHIP: VISION, MISSION AND THE LINK TO VALUES

> To make a great dream come true, you must first have a great dream.
>
> *Hans Selye*

There are three kinds of people and organisations: those who lead, those who follow, and those who keep their heads in the sand oblivious of everything. In today's competitive environment no company can afford the luxury of following others, let alone slumber in complacent and ignorant bliss. The time to think about meaning and direction is well in advance of change, not while others are changing, and any business that lacks a clear sense of purpose and direction is risking its own survival. Think of examples you have read of in the late 1980s and in the 1990s where major companies' recent history confirms this. Clarity of meaning and direction throughout the organisation can never exceed that level of clarity at the top of the organisation. In 1960 President Kennedy stated, 'I believe that this nation should commit itself to achieving the goal, before this decade is out, of landing a man on the moon and returning him safely to earth.' That speech electrified the Apollo team and the USA into action by giving them a compelling and achievable mission. It demonstrates that a vision and mission are the key to harnessing people's energies, and corporate values are vital in defining the atmosphere in which people work.

As a senior executive, as well as providing episodic leadership in relatively low level day-to-day episodes while working with your immediate subordinates, you also have three main tasks of organisational leadership. Jacques identifies these:[1]

- Firstly, you need to ensure that the organisational values defined by the CEO are adhered to and demonstrated in your everyday behaviour. So many senior executives fail to understand the power of example, yet if they are alert and become aware of what is really going on they will see that their actions are copied. They are imitated because they have sent the message that 'I am a senior and by implication successful person in this company, I am therefore a role model, imitate me and you will succeed'. When example conflicts with 'the official' organisational values there is confusion. Cynicism and mistrust follow because reality does not match the rhetoric.
- Second, you are responsible for formulating the policies, procedures and systems within the company that provides the environment and allows leadership and teamwork to flourish. Such policies, procedures and systems have to be congruent with organisational values and have to be common to other departments. The principles of organisation in Chapter 9 give guidance on this.
- Third, you have responsibility for developing a long-term view and direction for the organisation to which all energy and resources can be directed by others further down the hierarchical structure. Without this, much energy and many resources are unnecessarily expended while subgroups work towards their own interests that may or may not be aligned to the organisation. This does lead to stress and disillusionment in your people.

While the hierarchical pyramid works effectively at every level (providing competent people are appointed) it is usual in most organisations, whether the public/civil service, business, or military, to form a collegiate view at the highest levels. This can be seen in the Government Cabinet of the Army Board or the Board of Directors in business. At this level there is a distinct difference in the level of work undertaken, characterised by the level of abstract thought required. Implicit in this structure is the acceptance of, and need for, collective support and usually collective responsibility.

VISION

My vision for Qantas is the development of a very positive and distinct way of behaving and working within our own structure and outwards towards customers which will create such a level of enthusiasm and personal participation that every one of our people will look forward to coming to work every day, anticipating playing their important individual part within a large and complex operation, and at the end of the day feel satisfaction, recognition and pride in the results provided for customers by their own contribution, and the group as a whole.

Creating that atmosphere depends on leadership, clear expectations of behaviour and conduct, constant communications, investment in training and resources for staff, involvement of people in changing the way things are done, looking outwards towards customers and knowing what they want and expect, constant monitoring of performance, celebrating success and recognising individual contributions, all with a sense of being cheeky, aggressive and using an innovative approach as an organisation—a leader, not a follower.

Most importantly it depends on the matching of everyday behaviour at every level of leadership with this vision or mission. Are people listened to, is interest taken in their work, are their contributions recognised, how often do you talk to them, listen to them, invest in them to make them more confident and proud of what they do and achieve?

Organisational culture cannot be created by mission or vision statements. It is literally the result of the reality of behaviour within the operation on a daily basis.

James Strong, Chief Executive, Qantas Airways[2]

The 'what'. A vision statement should be exactly that, a simple affirmation of what you, as an organisation, aspire to be. It is an image that can be kept in view with three key components, identified by Karl Albrecht[3] as:

- A focussed concept—an end-state that everyone can picture that avoids comfortable platitudes, ambiguity and vagueness.
- A sense of noble purpose—it has to be something that really is really worthwhile, possibly a purpose beyond profit that will satisfy

most people's desire to do something for the betterment of others (connect this with the components of morale in Slim's analysis).

- The end-state must be achievable—people can, therefore, strive for it knowing their efforts will not be in vain (again connect this with the components of morale that Slim identifies).

(Excerpted by permission of the publisher, from *THE NORTH-BOUND TRAIN* © 1994 Karl Albrecht. Published by AMACOM, a division of American Management Association. All rights reserved.)

The key is to keep a vision or mission statement clear, concise and unambiguous, so that it can be understood and remembered by everyone. For unless it is remembered it cannot be compelling, it will not act like a magnet to attract people's energy and efforts. Leaders should not be frightened of continuously promoting it and asking others to recite it. A vision or mission statement has to be reinforced.

Too many vision and mission statements are bland, uninspiring, vague, or simplistic. They state the obvious and are often plagiarised from other companies. Many companies are unclear about the meaning of 'vision' as opposed to 'mission' and thus, their statements are either wrongly labelled or easily confused with each other. Each should be different and should be kept as separate statements. Together with organisational values both should be the ultimate arbiter of decision making in an organisation.

When a CEO's vision is deficient or it is not fully understood because it has been badly articulated within the organisation then the following negative consequences are likely to be observed as Bennis, Parikh and Lessem identify:[4]

- **Lack of purpose.** When people are working without any clearly understood purpose, the nature of work itself seems to lose its value.
- **Lack of meaning.** When work has no meaning then one of the criteria for job satisfaction is missing. Work is not only not valued whether it is your own work or someone else's.
- **Lack of coordinated and coherent planning.** When there is no clear vision or direction it is impossible for planning to be integrated, and unnecessary confusion and stress follow.
- **Lack of motivation.** Individuals' drive is reduced when they do not know in what direction they are heading. Energy is wasted and lethargy starts to creep in.
- **Lack of priorities.** Without a clear understanding of the ultimate

aim it is impossible to allocate priority of one task over another and, again, unnecessary confusion, chaos and stress follow.

- **Lack of pride.** When people do not know what their ultimate purpose is, that is, the reason for which they are employed, it is hard for them to generate pride in their own work.
- **Lack of action.** Without an 'aim' or 'reason why', inactivity, lethargy, inertia, and indecision multiply. This leads to paralysis of the organisation.

The erosion of morale and ultimate self-destruction of the cohesion or unity that all organisations need to ensure sustainable success ensues.

MISSION

The 'how'. Much of what has been said about the drafting of vision statements is applicable here. Following on from what you want to be—the vision, the mission statement should indicate how you get there or how you achieve the vision. It is a template for your approach to doing business. According to Karl Albrecht, mission statements must include:

- A focus on the customers and their needs and, therefore, their reason to do business with you.
- The value that only you can offer in meeting customer needs.
- Your 'differentiators', what makes you special and, therefore, why you will win and retain the account.

For maximum effect, mission statements should be:

- **Definitive.** It defines the customer or the market, and the product or service value to be offered. It is not driven by what you wish to sell, be it product or service, rather it is focussed wholly on the customer and the customer's needs.
- **Identifying.** The mission statement has to at least identify the organisation's industry, if not the company itself. Without this the statement could apply to anyone, anywhere.
- **Clear, concise and unambiguous.** Be careful in the choice of words, they must convey impact. It must be understood by all and be brief enough to be remembered.
- **Action descriptive.** The reader, who may well be a customer or potential customer as well as your own staff, needs to be able to

imagine how the mission is actually carried out, the approach to doing business.

- **Consistent with organisation values.** If this is not the case, another conflicting message has been sent and the question is what should people believe and follow?

Although several senior executives may collectively draft these statements, they must not read as though they have been 'written by committee' and, therefore, full of compromise, ambiguity and ill-defined suggestions. Before going to print it is a worthwhile exercise to test them on a sample of employees, shareholders, customers, and suppliers—the key stakeholders.

VALUES

John Harvey-Jones[5] wrote an excellent piece on 'values' which is abridged here:

> . . .The value system is one of the prime means of transferring the ownership of problems to your people. The integrity of the system will then be enforced by the people themselves. Values are also an invisible recruiting sergeant. . .likely to attract people who share your basic values. . .A value statement is. . .a personality profile of the company, and hence of the people in it.
>
> . . .values are. . .codes of belief and behaviour and involve making hard choices clearly and unambiguously. . .you need to check that you are prepared to reject the opposite of what you are selecting for the basis of your future business.

The essence of a values statement is that there can be no compromise, the values are the arbiter in all decision making. Leaders must live and work by their stated values 24 hours a day or they will give rise to cynicism and mistrust.

People decide what it is that they value greatly and from this they develop their beliefs, attitudes, and behaviours. In the ideal corporate situation all members share and agree to one code of behaviour. It is essential for you to understand the concept of values fully if you are to come to terms with, and understand, a corporate culture and develop 'shared meaning'. Since behaviours are the outward manifestation of values they can be viewed as the truth, as seen by a particular person.

Values or beliefs developed over a lifetime are among the most constant and enduring characteristics of any individual. Decision making has its base in values and beliefs as much as logic, even among those people with a scientific or engineering bent. Organisations, too, have their own value systems that define their corporate culture, and research supports the commonly held view that people whose values match those of their organisation are more productive and satisfied.

Alma Whiteley[6] writes that:

> values dictate standards. . .Next comes beliefs. These express what people know. . .This information is often acquired over a long period of socialisation. Information is the key to changing beliefs. Attitudes are. . .based on the way individuals see or perceive things and if an attitude is important and closely related to a value it will be difficult to change.

For an organisation to be truly effective its values as an organisation must represent those of its employees (both 'management' and 'front-line workers'), shareholders and investors, and the marketplace. Imagine that these as overlapping—like the earlier three circles model. Some writers view the values of management and those of employees as differing. This may be the case in practice when a 'them and us' syndrome exists, but is not something that a company should strive to achieve. Therefore, I present them as the same since achieving this is one of the tasks of organisational leadership.

I suggest that the values that most people are seeking in an organisation revolve around the following employee values:

- Honest and open communication, a climate of trust and confidence, that is, teamwork. The ability to participate and be listened to.
- The display of moral courage, doing the right thing not simply what is expedient.
- Clear, effective and sensitive leadership at all levels.
- Institutional intolerance of incompetence and dishonesty, that is, no carrying of 'dead weight' or untrustworthy people.
- Security, if not guaranteed employment, guaranteed employability from personal growth and development.
- Recognition and reward for contribution and effort.

To be successful in the marketplace, the commercial values below have to be addressed:

- Innovation and creativity.
- Continuous improvement and learning.
- Customer focus and service.

These last three values listed contribute largely to organisational agility and are underpinned by the employee values.

Shareholders and investors value profitability generally above all else.

It is common to see values statements on the walls in the reception area in any company office. Unfortunately many only give rise to cynicism among employees and suppliers and customers because the rhetoric internally does not match the reality. If these commercial values listed are not being adhered to, senior managers are simply deceiving themselves and self-deception ultimately leads to failure. Some of the strongest organisational cultures have no written set of values, but what is acceptable, and what is not, is very well understood. The British and US armies are good examples of this.

Another interesting set of values are those of the British SAS. Their founder, David Stirling, wrote these values in 1941 and they still form some of the key criteria in candidate selection and the basis of their approach to their business:

1. The relentless pursuit of excellence
2. Maintenance of the highest standards of discipline in all aspects of life
3. No sense of class
4. Humility.

They are remarkable because not only have they endured, but few people would associate these values with a rigid hierarchy and a tradition of 'officers being gentlemen' that was usually the case in 1941.

Just a comment for those of you who strive for perfection: it is unobtainable while excellence is obtainable.

Purpose. A company's purpose is its fundamental reason for existence and in the most successful companies it includes an altruistic reason for existence beyond simply making money. Collins and Porras give many examples.[7] Purpose, therefore, underpins 'vision' and may, or may not, be part of the vision statement. Do not mistake or confuse this purpose with particular business vision, strategies or objectives. The primary role of purpose is to inspire employees by giving it greater meaning to what to do and why, not necessarily to differentiate a company from its competitors as that is done by the mission statement.

> If an organisation is to meet the challenges of a changing world, it must be prepared to change everything about itself except its basic beliefs as it moves through corporate life. . .the only sacred cow in an organisation should be its basic philosophy of doing business.
>
> *Thomas J. Watson Jr, founder of IBM*

When this purpose is combined with an organisation's core values (that must remain a code of acceptable and defining behaviour, not a specific operating practice) then the resulting combination is a company's core ideology. James Collins and Jerry Porras[7] show admirably that companies that are built to last and have constantly out-performed their competitors over long periods do not compromise this ideology and they do not sway with the trends and fads of management gurus.

Figure 18.1

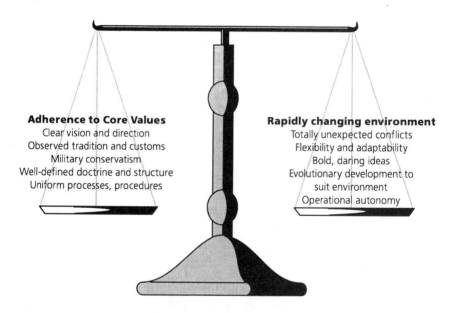

Adherence to Core Values
Clear vision and direction
Observed tradition and customs
Military conservatism
Well-defined doctrine and structure
Uniform processes, procedures

Rapidly changing environment
Totally unexpected conflicts
Flexibility and adaptability
Bold, daring ideas
Evolutionary development to
suit environment
Operational autonomy

It is vital not to confuse this core ideology with strategy, operational effectiveness, policies or procedures. As time goes on systems, policies and procedures will inevitably need to change as will strategy, people, and products. The competitive environment can require everything about a company to change—except its core ideology.

256

The British Army has an enviable and unparralleled record of success and achievement. It has a very strong 'core ideology' and culture.

The organisation's culture has enabled it to balance what to outsiders would seem paradoxical situations. See Figure 18.1.

Collins and Porras' research has shown that most enduring successful companies can balance similar paradoxes, rather than make an 'either' 'or' choice.

DEVELOPING CULTURE

In building a corporate culture in addition to the guidelines in the preceding paragraphs take the following factors into account, each of which is the subject of a book in its own right.

Current structure, policies, systems and practices. These factors reflect the reality of life in the organisation. Are they inflexible and rigid or adaptable to new situations? Do they encourage initiative and risk-taking or stifle action? Do your recruitment and selection systems identify the necessary raw human material? Do you train people in what you actually want them to do? Does your performance management system measure not just numerical outputs, but the way in which these outputs are gained? Is your remuneration and recognition policy aligned to the performance management system and corporate values? Is your organisational structure 'requisite'? Does it allow leadership and teamwork to flourish? Do people have clarity?

Traditions, customs, ceremonies and events. These factors all define an organisational identity. We like to feel part of a close-knit team and it is no accident that unlike many other armies that post individuals from unit to unit, and in which one infantry battalion looks and feels the same as any other, the British Army is very different.

The British Army is a collection of smaller regimental 'tribal groupings' that work very well together. Each regiment has its own unique customs such as the way in which the loyal toast is drunk, the celebration of specific battles and moments in history, regimental parades, family and sporting events. Each regiment has its own 'Stand Of Colours', the flags under which soldiers used to rally, emblazoned with the regiment's own and unique collection of battle honours that are viewed as the living embodiment of the regiment's spirit. Every regiment has its own badges and accoutrements, ways of adding difference to standard uniform. All this difference creates 'identity', inculcated in all new recruits and preserved at all costs. It is this identity and feeling of closeness to one's immediate colleagues that helps leadership to generate pride and self-respect, to reinforce morale, and to create cohesion and unity. All factors vital in effective teamwork.

References

1. Elliott Jaques, 1996, *The Requisite Organization: A Total System for Effective Managerial Organization and Managerial Leadership for the 21st Century*, Arlington, Virginia: Cason Hall & Co Publishers.
2. James Strong, *The Australian Way* (Qantas Airways Magazine), October 1994.
3. Karl Albrecht, 1994, *The Northbound Train: Finding the Purpose Setting the Direction Shaping the Destiny of Your Organization*, New York: AMACOM (a division of American Management Association).
4. Warren Bennis, Jagdish Parikh, & Ronnie Lessem, 1994, *Beyond Leadership*, Oxford: Blackwell Publishers.
5. John Harvey-Jones, 1994, *All Together Now*, London: William Heinemann Ltd.
6. Alma Whiteley, 1995, *Managing Change a Core Values Approach*, Sydney: Macmillan Education.
7. James Collins and Jerry Porras, 1994, *Built To Last*, Century Hutchinson Australia.

CHAPTER 19

LEADING CHANGE AND INNOVATION

> Change is as much an attitude of mind as it is a specific skill
>   The task of leadership is really to make the status quo more dangerous than launching into the unknown.
>
>   *John Harvey-Jones, formerly Chairman ICI[1]*
>
> The only living organism that survives is that which adapts to change
>   *Field Marshal Slim*

The words 'change management' have made many authors and consultants extremely rich, and this subject has been overcomplicated and made unnecessarily daunting to further the perception that a capability to lead 'change' is the preserve of outside experts and that change is a complex subject in its own right, divorced from day-to-day leadership. It is not.

Usually, a 'change management' expert is appointed for a specific exercise to assist an organisation move from one 'state' to another. Often, this is a move from one static state to another defined state, occasionally perceived to be static also. The notion of developing a way of working in which change is viewed as a challenge, not a threat, and continuous improvement, learning, and innovation become a way of life—a dynamic state—is sometimes overlooked.

Leadership has always been about change, it is, as John Harvey-Jones has repeatedly said: 'making more or better from less'.

Implicit in such improvement is change—in resources, practices, structure, product, delivery, and so on. Without change it is impossible to meet customers' requirements and needs—the market is dynamic and, therefore, companies need to be agile and flexible and that depends upon a culture of leadership and teamwork to make that possible.

If the fundamental functions of leadership are carried out, that is, the functional leadership check-list (Chapter 5), and applied with the personal qualities of leadership I have examined earlier, change will happen without unnecessary drama. Leadership is about—making things happen and building effective teams. 'Change management', in essence, is simply an appreciation of a situation and the implementation of a well-communicated plan. Developing leadership based on the premises of this book will produce the enduring effective organisation and no need will exist for 'change management' experts. The word 'change' will simply disappear because change will be part of everyday life.

> Dealing with change is all in the mind. Once you have people working in the same direction as real members of real teams then change becomes part of everyday life. Leaders need to start the process which ultimately the team will complete.
>
> *John Quinn, Managing Director, Thorn Lighting Pty Ltd*

The point is that the most natural and painless way to effect change is to develop leadership and teamwork. Here I identify the barriers to change, the components of change and transition, and highlight the importance of communication in order to ease the implementation of change.

Change may be incremental over time, or 'cataclysmic', occurring in a short-time frame. If change is to be steered and monitored then it must be planned. If unplanned change occurs as a result of external forces then you are not in control. You have to lead change or it will lead you. Most of us find change uncomfortable, threatening, or frightening, so ensuring that everyone understands 'the reason why' as well as 'the how' is imperative. It is, however, virtually impossible to change organisations that do not accept the dangers of their present way of doing things. Therefore, leaders need to make complacency of the present seem more dangerous than the unknown that change will bring.

John Harvey-Jones[1] identifies two major limitations on managing change. The first is that no one actually manages change, but rather releases and guides it.

Employee expectations of management are that direction is clear, accurate, farsighted, and provides attainable objectives. When change is unleashed people need to support it. To break free from bureaucratic authority, forms, and triplicates of procedural memoranda is to release people from paralysis, paranoia, and frustration. To take action about problems that are local to a section without the superior's say so when specific knowledge and skills are in that section is both appropriate and desirable. The superior is then able to plan ahead, without wasting time on matters that are not their problem, thereby preventing un-necessary crisis management. At the same time, the superior has sent an important message about trust.

The second limitation is that we do not accept change readily and until we change the organisation cannot change. Acceptance of change is crucial as time is of the essence and staff can cause loss of customers and credibility if they do not change quickly.

If you are instrumental in a rate of change that is greater than the organisation is used to, remember that change comes from dissatis-faction, and fear of change is from the unknown. Going slow might be the only way to gain acceptance and to instigate change. Your convic-tion, as a leader, must become your team members' conviction, through their trust in you. You need to lead the change to lead them, by confronting their fear of change.

When the climate is right and people are unhappy with the present then the ideas for future can be communicated. Symbolic acts from the top can be the catalyst that initiates change and sets the tone for the future. For instance, when a consumer goods manufacturer started to change its culture in a Sydney factory the director instigating change, ceremonially ripped the time-card clock from the wall—imagine the message of trust and change that was sent to a workforce who, until then, were not trusted to arrive on time and had to queue to get their cards stamped. Change needs to be seen from the top down, with leaders setting the example, by changing faster. They need to be seen as initiating and then accepting the change.

Inevitably, some people do not change or cope with retraining and separation is necessary. This must be handled sensitively and with dignity. If major change is necessary it is probably because superior 'leaders' failed to anticipate the future or to ensure an agile and flexible organisation was in place. When separation occurs the most important aspect is the preservation of individuals' self-esteem and dignity.

Firstly, an employer has a moral obligation to take care of those whose lives they are changing dramatically by throwing them into turmoil and uncertainty. Second, a mentally scarred group of former employees does nothing to give confidence to those that remain or to those you may wish to recruit. The self-confidence and self-esteem of those who leave, for whatever reason, must be maintained.

THE STAGES IN LEADING CHANGE

Look at this common sense cycle in Figure 19.1. It will help you identify where change is needed, plan its introduction, implement it, and review its success. Being a cycle it is continuous.

Figure 19.1

In planning change the 'appreciation process' should be used since everyone is familiar with this flexible and powerful tool, and the factors that should be considered include: corporate culture, tradition and values, communications strategy and channels, processes and systems that will be affected, and obstacles to be overcome (including the barriers to change). Considering these factors and the consequent deductions will lead to a plan and evaluation measures that will centre around communication—'the reasons why' and 'the how'.

CHANGING BEHAVIOUR

If a person's behaviour is to change, that person's leader must ensure that the following criteria are satisfied.

- **Clarity.** The person must understand what to change and why.
- **Self-awareness.** The person must understand the need to change and its benefits, how to change, and the person must have the will to change.
- **Opportunity.** The person must have opportunities in which behavioural change can and should occur.
- **Measures.** The benefits must be apparent and recognisable. Positive change must be recognised.

These criteria, combined with the assumption that role competence is a combination of skills, knowledge and required behaviour, form the basis of formal 'development centres'. This approach should really be adopted in daily leadership and the whole of life should be viewed as one big development centre.

When a stimulus is received, there is a response following 'a moment of choice' that depends upon the subject's self-awareness, conscience, will, imagination, values, and perception. It is only sound leadership that can help to shape some of those attributes.

RESISTANCE TO CHANGE

Maslow's hierarchy of needs indicates the need people have for security. Change threatens that. Change takes people out of their comfort zone that can induce 'defensive actions' from real or imagined threats. Below are the common barriers and hindrances to change.

Perceptual Blocks

For the problems caused by perception see Chapters 3 and 15. In relation to change people may be inclined to stereotype, encounter difficulty in defining the exact nature of a problem, limit the scope of a problem's examination and wallow in the excessive flow of information that hides the actual data that are needed. Hence, the need for the appreciation process described in Chapter 7.

Emotional Blocks

The emotional blocks to change include the fear of failure (largely based on low confidence and low self-esteem, and ineffective leadership), the inability to cope with apparently conflicting information, a predisposition to be judgemental and to reject ideas without consideration, and the inability to devote time to considering a problem.

Organisational Blocks

Cultural blocks to change may include taboo subjects that are never discussed, a conflict between reason based on logic and facts and intuition based on experience and feelings, and the effect of inflexible tradition. Environmental blocks to change include a lack of support for individuals within the organisation, the inability to cope with constructive criticism, and the inability of leaders to listen to the ideas of subordinates.

> Dealing with change is all in the mind. Once you have people working in the same direction as real members of real teams than change becomes part of everyday life. Leaders need to start the process which ultimately the team will complete.
>
> *John Quinn, Managing Director, Thorn Lighting Pty Ltd*

Cognitive Blocks

The cognitive blocks to change being implemented include use of inappropriate or imprecise language and terminology that is not commonly understood, mental inflexibility in the use of processes and procedures, and insufficient or inadequate information.

Figure 19.2 illustrates the main barriers to change.

Unless these barriers are removed by effective leadership and communication, programmes and priorities can easily become derailed without apparent cause. Attitudinal shifts in staff can only be created through a positive, consistent and frequent articulation of direction, values and benefits, by leaders in language and demonstrated behaviour, personal example, that is understood by all.

Achieving results is a matter of leadership—planning, commitment and tenacity—by all leaders in the enterprise, any other approach increases the risk and radically reduces the chances of success. By eliminating these barriers, integration of development programmes is less costly and considerably more effective.

Figure 19.2

LOSS AND THE GRIEF CYCLE

People fear change and that underlies their resistance and the difficulties 'change agents' experience. Looking deeper it is not really a fear of change, *per se*, but rather a fear of anticipated or potential loss associated with the change. This is easily demonstrated by considering the impact of the introduction of word processors in organisations. Some of the more typical types of loss people experience are the following:

- **Loss of security**. Previous certainties end and the future is perceived as uncertain.
- **Loss of competence**. In the face of change people are not confident that they can cope. They do not trust in their capacity to succeed and to learn new skills or ways. They may feel inadequate.
- **Loss of relationships**. Change often means restructuring and established work relationships are lost, this effect is emphasised when strong social relationships have developed from work relationships.

- **Loss of direction**. People customarily have a sense of purpose and direction. In the face of change there is suddenly a lack of clarity in their mission.
- **Loss of territory and/or status**. During major change people might not only lose physical space, for example, lose a separate office to join an open-plan one, but they may also lose psychological space, like status such as—a change in car policies.

What any leader of change must expect and must accept is that these are natural and common feelings and that there must be some plan in place to deal with them.

Leaders' need not only to recognise and acknowledge that there is loss, but to encourage bringing these feelings out into the open. Leaders should not pretend that it is 'business as usual'.

For most of us the difficult thing to accept is that for those undergoing change something familiar ends and something new begins. The most common error in change leadership is under-estimating the effects of change on staff. Organisations that recognise the sense of loss can move through the transition processes more quickly.

The grieving cycle that psychologists are so aware of, can be applied to the change process (see Figure 19.3). Like all cycles there are a number of stages. These include the following response.

1. Disbelief. When we are faced with trauma or bad news we often experience instant disbelief or denial. We think there must have been some mistake, for example, if a parent is visited by police and told that the son has been caught stealing there is disbelief. Similarly, in the work environment, when a major change is communicated there is a tendency to deny its existence. This is the **denial phase**. The underlying behaviour is that if we ignore it, it will go away.

2. Anger. Using the example above, once the parent finally accepts that the police have not made a mistake he or she experiences considerable anger. This gives vent to all sorts of emotions. In the workplace we begin the **resistance phase**. There is likely to be a lot of angry language used and, in some cases, acts of sabotage may be observed.

Bargaining. People then move through the bargaining stage. With the police the parent might try to obtain the child's release in exchange for the parent's own style of punishment. Similarly, at work there tends to be a bargaining element in the resistance stage with counter suggestions that often amount to leaving everything as it was.

Depression. The next stage in the grieving cycle is usually depression. We surrender, or give up, sometimes and become lethargic, disinterested and melancholy. A drop in morale and productivity often accompanies this stage.

3. Acceptance and hope. Eventually we do emerge from the depression. We accept the new order and begin to have some hope for the future, accepting that the change is inevitable and we begin to look positively at the future. Exploration of possibilities and options start to occur. In the change process we customarily refer to this as the **exploration phase**.

4. Positive activity. Ultimately everyone moves to a stage where once more there is positive, healthy activity. We become proficient at new skills and new relationships are formed. In the cycle of change this is the **commitment phase**.

Figure 19.3 Source unknown

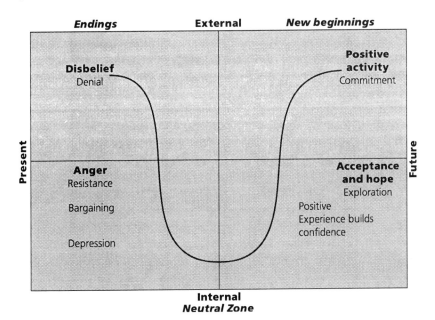

When leading a change programme it is important that everyone realises that these stages are both inevitable and natural. It is not possible to bypass a phase, although sound leadership does speed up the transition. We must not confuse the various stages and we must look for signs to identify the progress made, thus to see signs of resistance is positive; disbelief has been overcome and we can now move to bargaining. Figure 19.3 shows the overlap of the grieving cycle on the four stages often associated with change.

Individual responses to organisational change vary according to situation, position, and the amount of personal involvement. It is far easier for the person leading change to be happy about it because he or she is overseeing it and has some level of control. Those not in such a position of influence or control are less likely to be as excited, interested, or committed, about changing what they do, irrespective of any benefits they may experience from a different way of working. To gain their support their needs have to be taken into account.

Organisational leaders need to be mindful of the differing perspectives within the organisations. They must accept that people differ and that such differences are reflected in the way change is viewed. The uniform approach to decision making that can exist at board level is unlikely to occur further down. Despite sound planning, change will fail if leaders do not take into account the team and individual needs. Thus, we return to the functional leadership check-list of Chapter 5.

CHANGE AND TRANSITION

William Bridges identifies that there is a difference between change and transition.[2] Change is the external imposed event, often involving structural changes in an organisation. Change is a planned and logical process with a defined aim or objective. Transition is the sequence of emotions that employees experiencing the change feel inside and it can take time and has three phases: endings, neutral zone, and new beginnings (see Figure 19.3). The difference between change and transition can be illustrated by starting a new job. The change involves finishing projects, writing handover notes, packing up your desk, and so on. The transition involves all the confusion, distress, and excitement that you experience.

Each change occurs in a unique situation or set of circumstances, yet transitions are often very similar to each other. Transition always starts with an ending. Despite the fact that change can be initiated by a new technology or process, the psychological process inside us that accompanies the change always starts with an ending, of us letting go of something familiar.

Before there is a new beginning people through an in-between state when the old reality and identity are gone, but the new ones are not yet established in 'the hearts and minds' of everyone. This is the 'neutral zone', the state in-between the old and the new.

The ending separates people from the old 'norms' and the neutral zone both allows a mental release of the old and a birth of new possibilities. It is from the neutral zone that the third phase of the transition, the new beginning, emerges. This beginning is not to be confused with the 'official start' of the new situation that may have happened on day one of the change, working in a new organisational structure, for instance. The beginning is when people not only accept, but commit to, the new.

In making appreciations and plans (review Chapters 7 and 8), apart from considering the task-focussed factors of change, that is, why and how structurally and with what processes or systems and in what time scale, a **transition management plan** should address how to manage the endings, how to identify where people are in the process, how to enable people to move from the neutral zone and profit from the new beginning.

In planning a major strategic change Carnall[3] identifies three conditions that are necessary:

- **Stakeholder awareness.** Everyone who has an interest in the change needs to understand and believe in division, strategy and detail plans.
- **Capability.** Everyone involved needs to have confidence in their ability to not only manage the change, but to take advantage of opportunities presented.
- **Inclusion.** All the stakeholders must value their newly defined role and choose to adopt new ways of doing things.

Just as with any new initiative, for any major change to work it is crucial that every senior executive and all major shareholders and investors understand the necessity for it, and are committed to supporting whatever activity is necessary to achieve it, no matter that it may take months or years for tangible benefits on the bottom line to be observed. In large organisations major change may take five years to be seen and it is possible that senior executives leave or join the senior team in this time. Whatever their previous experience, newcomers must adhere to the plan that is being implemented and not be tempted to 'tinker' with it—as there is the risk of derailment once more.

Until effective leadership has been developed at every level in an organisation most attempts at change will, at best, take more time and will induce more stress than is necessary and, at worst, will fail. To succeed in any change, but especially rapid and major change, organisations will need to implement leadership and teamwork training programmes, and the congruent performance appraisal and remuneration systems necessary to support the intended and desired 'new culture'.

Carnall further suggests that organisations will face many dilemmas in the choices they present. The major choices they will be faced with are:

- Centralisation versus decentralisation.
- Efficiency versus effectiveness.
- Control versus commitment.
- Change versus stability.

Centralisation versus Decentralisation

The attraction of centralisation is the assumption that senior executives have a broader view of the issues facing the organisation. The assumption continues: centralised control of resources can provide greater use of assets to support functional groupings, rationalisation can avoid duplication of activities and strong leadership can be displayed in crisis situations.

Such centralisation may work in organisations to a certain point, but when organisations become too large the stresses induced by centralisation cause the system to break down. Additionally the lack of delegation and opportunities to use initiative and discretion do nothing to promote subordinates leaders' motivation or to assist in the personal development of individuals. The principles of organisation outlined in Chapter 9 should assist in decisions about this dilemma.

Efficiency versus Effectiveness

Efficiency conveys a narrow impression of achieving precisely defined objectives. Effectiveness is used in the sense of a combination of efficiency and flexibility to meet future requirements. For an organisation to maintain its flexibility requires the capacity for individuals to innovate and this means that they need some time to think and to plan ahead and escape what has become the norm of daily crisis management.

What may be seen as an 'efficient' organisation could actually be too lean to enable individual or organisational anticipation and adaptability. In the current climate of restructuring and down-sizing, few people have the luxury of taking time out to sit, to think and to plan ahead.

'Effectiveness' in people is developed through re-defining the work flow system and the scope of individual roles, training and personal development, and the organisational culture that promotes leadership and teamwork.

Control versus Commitment

Control, as discussed earlier, is often inconsistent with effective leadership. It is leadership that produces the teamwork that generates commitment. Reconsider the concept of control in Chapter 11.

Change versus Stability

It is often much simpler to leave things as they are and easier than to change. Any change initially induces a change in organisational stability, and fine judgement is needed by leaders on the scope and pace of change that is introduced and the effects it initiates.

In some situations in which a major change is being introduced it may be better to introduce every other desired change at the same time since there is a finite level of confusion that can be induced in people. In other situations minor change may need to be introduced at first, and as momentum builds the scope and rate of change can be increased. It is a fact that with effective leadership that incorporates all the ideas and principles described within this book, even the most resistant employee can be led effectively through change with minimum disruption.

Innovation

Competitive advantage can be gained by perceiving new markets and opportunities, learning from success and failure, producing more of the same, better and more cheaply; and by introducing new products or services and their delivery methods. Innovation, the introduction of innovative ideas, is thus essential to keeping the competitive edge. Companies like 3M-exist purely by innovation—30% of annual sales come from new products and people are expected to spend 15% of their time innovating. It is a fact that effective leadership promotes a tendency to action, rather than inertia, an understanding of stakeholder needs, delegation of authority and encouragement of initiative, simplicity and clarity in plans and structures and the minimisation of 'red tape'. All these are characteristics of an innovative organisation.

So what is innovation? Innovation stems from business (customer) needs and creates change.

Innovation involves:

- Doing, or creating, something new—new methods, processes, products.
- Modifying an existing process or product.
- Re-defining existing concepts, thoughts and ideas.
- Setting new standards.
- Risk-taking.

INNOVATION AND CREATIVITY

Innovation here is 'an integrated organisational process dependent on the corporate culture, organisational structure, understanding of customer and consumer needs, networking with people (both internal and external contacts), rewards and recognition that all depend on leadership at all levels within the organisation'. Thus leadership is what will make you the preferred choice of supplier, rather than just another supplier. Creativity is thought of as 'an individual process that originates ideas and concepts that may be used by an organisation to innovate'.

3M's founder William McKnight stated the following to drive the company forward in a manner that would not make it dependent upon him personally:

> Listen to anyone with an idea.
> Hire good people and leave them alone.
> Encourage and don't nitpick. Let people run with an idea.
> Mistakes will be made. . .individuals' mistakes are not as serious as the mistake management makes if it is destructively critical and kills initiative.

To foster the culture of innovation 3M focuses on:

- **Demanding objectives.** People commit to challenging and risk-taking objectives.
- **Commitment to corporate culture.** 3M is a good employer for employees who blend in. The others may leave.
- **Continuous experimentation and trials.** These ensure retention of good ideas and rejection of the bad. High levels of activity produces constant evolution. 3M encourages this with its 11th Commandment 'Thou shalt not kill ideas.'

- **Management development.** A reliance on internally sourced recruitment and selection ensures a supply of senior executives who understand the culture and organisational 'consistency'.
- **Continuous improvement.** The relentless pursuit of excellence ensures that complacency is avoided.

Is this not the application of leadership already discussed?

The essence of any corporate culture, and especially an innovative one, is the translation of the corporate values that encourage change, teamwork, and leadership into the very fabric of the organisation, its policies, systems, procedures, and aims and objectives. Leaders have to support the originators of ideas, to encourage more ideas to flow and to ensure that ideas are considered, followed through, and implemented or discarded. If they are discarded an explanation must be given. Such a culture needs a climate of trust, confidence, and open communication to stimulate the flow and facilitate the adoption of ideas. Does this not reflect the diagram at Figure 1.2 in Chapter 1?

The focus has to be on the customer since it is the customer that keeps you in business. If you consider yourself as a customer, you would want your suppliers to give you:

- Timely delivery and follow-up that meets or exceeds expectations.
- Experienced, trained people able to make decisions, to ensure a flow of communication, able to anticipate your needs, and who are accessible, responsive, and pleasant to deal with.
- Added value in their products and services.

These are all factors that are affected by employees and we respond to inspired leadership. Staff's loyalty to their employer is reflected in their customer service levels, innovation and thus, the loyalty of the customer. If staff's ideas are to flourish then the old 'head down, backside up' work attitude has to be replaced by one which continues to ask 'why are we here, what are we trying to achieve, how can we do it better?'

References

1. John Harvey-Jones, 1993, *Managing To Survive*, London: William Heinemann Ltd.
2. William Bridges, 1993, *Managing Transitions*, Reading, Mass.: Addison-Wesley.
3. Colin Carnall, 1995, *Managing Change In Organizations* (2nd edn), Hemel Hempstead: Prentice Hall International (UK) Limited.
4. John Harvey-Jones, 1988, *Making It Happen: Reflections on Leadership*, London: Collins.

CHAPTER 20

STRATEGIC DIRECTION AND PLANNING

Business and military history shows that organisations that see themselves as invincible become arrogant, inflexible, and complacent.

If your strategy is daily changing, there is confusion, and staff and customers loyalty is uncertain.

The author

It is unfortunate in business that there is so much short-term thinking and this is largely related to the performance of one's superannuation (pension) funds which are very short-term oriented. The time horizon of decision making is the big difference between us and Asia and is why they will be so powerful in the future, they have long-term vision and seek long-term sustainable performance.

John Quinn, Managing Director, Thorn Lighting Pty Ltd

In Chapter 1, Figure 1.1 illustrates the three components that lead to corporate effectiveness: the physical component, the conceptual component, and the moral component. So far the focus here is on the moral component and the leadership that will ensure its provision. This chapter provides the conceptual framework upon which all strategy can be based.

Here we consider the fundamental principles of business, strategic planning, and the link between the conceptual component and the 'fundamentals' of leadership so far described. The conceptual component of commercial effectiveness (see Figure 1.1) is a formal expression of the concepts and knowledge that an enterprise accepts as being relevant at a given time. It is the doctrine that considers the nature of current and likely future business and provides the basis on which all plans and operations are based. Be careful to distinguish between what constitutes the fundamental doctrine that leads to strategy development and what is simply 'management by technique'. As has been pointed out recently by the Australian authors Hilmer and Donaldson,[1] these techniques can be dangerous. Operating with 'zero inventory' or 'just-in-time' processes make companies in developing areas highly vulnerable to the vagaries of logistic supply. The drive for continuous improvement and operational efficiency has replaced strategy in some companies and this has resulted in declining or static prices and pressures on costs. This is leading to 'competitive convergence', rather than differentiation and sustainable profitability. Thus, these techniques must be viewed as techniques only, to be used where the situation warrants and not as a quick fix or universal panacea. They must not be confused with the fundamental principles that underpin strategy development.

BUSINESS DOCTRINE

There are certain characteristics of business that will endure no matter what the industry or the market that the operations are being conducted in. These are:

Friction. Friction is the force that resists all activity and adds to inertia in an organisation. It makes the simple difficult and the difficult appear to be impossible. Friction may be self-imposed by indecision on the part of leaders; it may be created by the physical constraints of logistics, communication systems or geography. It may be externally imposed by market perceptions or the actions of your competitors. Determination and persistence is needed to overcome friction that inevitably causes setbacks and, therefore, high morale is essential if temporary setbacks are not to dispirit those involved.

Uncertainty, chance and chaos. All business is uncertain and when major change is introduced chaos, however temporary, usually follows. Business can only be conducted against a background of probabilities, not certainties. It is a cardinal error to assume that competitors will do what is expected of them. Uncertainty and chaos are assessed by judgement and a careful balancing of risk. No matter how well any activity has been planned, chance can either create adverse effects, or opportunities. Simple, robust plans with sound planning and preparation are the best defence to bad luck. Opportunities should always be exploited and initiative, decentralised control, innovation, and improvisation, are the keys to this. Good luck is merely planning, preparation, initiative, and leadership, meeting opportunity.

Human stress. Much of business is being conducted by fewer people than in recent years, working longer hours and with more variables to consider. Technology provides efficiencies in some areas of business, but adds a stress of its own particularly with data overload. All organisations need to be acutely aware of stress and to do their utmost not to add to it by poor planning or 'bad leadership' and must remember that the foundation of corporate effectiveness is sound leadership displayed at every level.

Human emotions. Despite our best efforts to remain objective in decision making, our emotions often conflict with logic, resulting in flawed decisions and the inevitable consequences. Stress adds to the negative effects of emotional decision making.

Unlike armies, businesses do not measure victory in absolute terms, but rather measure it by degree. However, any organisation is in business to succeed and success is definable, given an understanding of the general approach to business.

Competition in business is tougher in the late 1990s than at any time in the past and the successful company is one that takes the initiative and operates aggressively, but within both ethical and moral constraints. While business is focussed on satisfying customer needs, large commercial organisations still need to focus on the way in which they are actually competing with others.

In addition to considering all the factors affecting the satisfaction of a customer's needs it may also be appropriate, therefore, to consider how to outwit competing companies in the planning process.

There are three approaches to undermining your competitors' ability to seize the initiative and, therefore, your customers.

Pre-emption. To pre-empt a competitor is to seize an opportunity before it does in order to deny it an advantageous cause of action. The purpose of pre-emption is initially negative since it seeks to frustrate the courses of action open to a competitor and in doing that it prevents your competitor from seizing the initiative.

Dislocation. To dislocate a competitor is to deny it the ability to bring its strengths to bear on a particular situation by forcing it to react elsewhere. Unlike pre-emption that is opportunistic, dislocation is a deliberate action and critically depends upon sound market research and intelligence. The purpose of dislocation is more far-reaching than pre-emption in that it is designed to reduce your competitor's effectiveness or corporate power severely. In this way you are not forced to compete on your competitor's terms.

Disruption. 'To disrupt' is 'to selectively throw into confusion operating units and plans that are essential to the coherence of your competitor's own strategy. Like dislocation this is a deliberate action that requires sound information and it is designed to reduce your competitor's effectiveness to less than the sum of its constituent parts. It is creating the inverse of synergy.

Your competitor may well be employing any, or all, of the above against you and the best defence is cohesion. Cohesion is unity; it is that which holds together the constituent parts of an organisation and, therefore, produces resilience to dislocation and disruption. It minimises a company's vulnerability and the adverse effects of missed opportunities.

The bedrock of cohesion is leadership and adherence to the fundamental principles of business that are described below. These principles are not merely a theory to adhere to, nor are they simply a model to follow. These principles are a philosophy to be understood, embraced, and applied, whenever possible, as best you can in any situation at any level of work.

THE PRINCIPLES OF BUSINESS

Before we consider how to formulate strategy we look at some fundamental operating principles. A study of both military and commercial history reveals that these principles are valid and timeless. Indeed Richard Luecke has devoted an entire book to drawing on the lessons of history of change, technology, innovation, planning and uncertainty, and global management, and applying them to the present.[2]

That these principles were first written by leaders of armies and nations, rather than by business executives, is merely an indication that the science and history of war is considerably older and better understood than the history of business. The principles employed by Gideon and the 300 Israelites in the successful repulse of the Midianites, who were '—as innumerable as the sands of the sea shore' make for interesting study. The actions of Alexander, Xenophon, Hannibal, Gustavus Adolphus, Frederick the Great, Prince Eugène, Napoleon, Wellington, Nelson, Montgomery, Patton, and Slim show that they all adhere to some common enduring and universal principles—like the laws of physics. Indeed, the most successful and prominent leaders in history have all studied their predecessors and the lessons that they have taught. As the historian John Laffin demonstrates, Patton and Sultan Mahomet (15th century) both studied Alexander, Napoleon studied Cromwell who studied Gustavus Adolphus who studied Hannibal, Alexander, and Julius Caesar.[3]

The principles of business that forms part of the conceptual component of commercial power are described below. With the exception of the prime principle that is placed first, do not place undue emphasis on the order in which the others appear.

Selection and Maintenance of the Aim

It is essential in the conduct of all activity to select and to define aims clearly and precisely. Within a CEO's strategic directive he or she might have several courses of action open, each of which would fulfil the aim. The selection of the best course leads to the mission and outlines plan being issued, the mission being a statement of the aim and its purpose. The aim and specific objectives passed on to subordinate leaders must be unambiguous and attainable with the resources. Once decided the aim must be communicated as widely and repeatedly as possible so that all can direct their efforts towards achieving the it.

Maintenance of Morale

Morale is an essential element of corporate power. High morale fosters the competitive spirit and the will to win and engenders energy, enthusiasm, and determination. It inspires organisations from the highest to the lowest levels. Although primarily a moral aspect that depends on leadership it can be affected by material conditions and leaders should do their best to ensure that the best conditions possible are provided.

Offensive Action

Offensive or aggressive action is the chief means open to leaders to influence the outcome of campaigns. It confirms the initiative on the 'attacker', granting the freedom of action necessary to secure a decisive result. When forced on the defensive this must be followed as soon as possible by offensive action. Offensive action embodies a competitive state of mind that breeds the determination to gain and to hold the initiative; it is essential for the creation of confidence and to establish a moral ascendancy over competitors and, thus, has an effect on morale.

Surprise

The potency of surprise as a psychological weapon and a tactic should not be under-estimated. It causes confusion and paralysis in competitors' senior levels and can erode the cohesion and morale of competing organisations. It may be achieved through the use of intelligence and information, technology, new doctrine, timing, audacity, simplicity, speed of action, originality, secrecy or concealment and deception about intentions.

Concentration of Force

Success normally results from the concentration of force—superior resources—in the market at the decisive time and place. This does not preclude 'dispersion' that may be valuable for the purposes of deception and for avoiding discovery.

Economy of Effort

The corollary of concentration of force is economy of effort. It is impossible to be strong everywhere and if decisive strength is to be concentrated at the critical time and place there must be no wasteful expenditure of effort where it cannot significantly affect the issue. In order to gain substantial advantage leaders have to take calculated risks in less vital areas.

Flexibility

'No plan of operations can look with any certainty beyond the first meeting with the major forces of the enemy. The commander is compelled. . .to reach decisions on the basis of situations which cannot be predicted' (Von Moltke).

Although the aims might not alter, leaders need to exercise judgement and flexibility in modifying their plans to meet changed circumstances, taking advantage of opportunities or shifting points of emphasis. Flexibility depends upon the mental component of openness of mind on the one hand, and simple plans that can easily be modified on the other. A balanced reserve of resources is a prerequisite for flexibility at any level.

Flexibility also requires common systems, processes, and terminology, in organisations as well as requisite structures.

Cooperation

Cooperation is based on team spirit, goodwill, and communication, and it entails the coordination of the activities of all departments and branches for the optimum combined effort. Goodwill, a common aim, a clear division of responsibilities, and understanding of the capabilities and limitations of others, are essential for cooperation. Unity of leadership is a means of achieving cooperation.

Administration

Sound administration is a prerequisite for the success of any operation and foresight is its key. A clear appreciation of logistic, human and other constraints is as important to leaders as their ability to make sound appreciations of situations. No plan can succeed without administrative support commensurate with the aim of the 'exercise': it follows that leaders must have a degree of control over the administrative plans proportionate to the degree of their responsibility for the 'exercise'. Scarce resources must be controlled at a high level: the administrative organisations must be flexible enough to react to changes in situations with the most economic use of the available resources.

Integrity and Ethics

A business perceived to lack integrity or to operate in an unethical, immoral, or irresponsible, manner soon loses the support of customers, suppliers, and the community at large. It is understood that superiors, leaders, and subordinates, in an organisation that prides itself on its integrity and ethical beliefs need to have those qualities.

THE LEVELS OF BUSINESS

> Our problem is that some of the Board are trying to run the business in detail while others are doing what we should all be doing on the Board; that is, working out what business we are really in and where we are heading.
>
> *A director*

Before looking further refer to 'Campaign' in the Glossary. Business occurs at three levels: strategic, operational, and tactical.

The Strategic Level

'Corporate strategy' is 'the application of corporate resources to achieve corporate policy objectives.' These broad responsibilities flow at this level:

- To lay down the policy objectives for the activities to be instituted.
- To make the limitations imposed upon those activities clear.
- To make the necessary resources available.
- To decide what operational level 'campaigns' need to be implemented to achieve strategic objectives appropriate for current circumstances.
- To identify the corporate strategic objectives and campaign objectives that constitute success.
- To allocate resources to each operational region.
- To agree operational objectives with the leader at the operational level.

The Operational Level

Joint campaigns and major operations are planned and directed at the operational level to achieve the aim of a strategic directive. It is the level that provides the gearing between corporate strategic objectives and all tactical activity within a geographical area of operations. Commonly this could be a large regional area such as that covered by the EC or the Asia–Pacific region. The operational-level leader is responsible for:

- Deciding what tactical objectives are necessary to achieve the campaign aim.
- Deciding in what sequence these objectives should be achieved.
- Allocating resources as necessary for subordinate leaders to be able to achieve their tactical objectives.
- Establishing priorities for the provision of logistic and other support.

It is often unclear how to differentiate between the tactical and operational level. The answers should help to establish which level of operation is undertaken:

- Is there a geopolitical or socioeconomic dimension?
- Does the activity materially alter the situation?
- Does the activity directly contribute to achieving a strategic objective?

The Tactical Level

Activities within a sequence of major operations are planned and executed at a tactical level in order to achieve the operational objectives of a campaign. This level is characterised by the application of integrated and coordinated units and by people at the point of main effort securing an objective. It is at the tactical level that most people are directly employed in business.

Factors to be considered in operational planning

In planning campaigns at the operational level in pursuit of strategic objectives, the operational-level leader should design campaigns around a number of 'building blocks' so people can visualise how the campaign will develop. Refer to the Glossary for a definition of these 'building blocks'.

- Operational objectives
- Centre of gravity
- Decisive points
- Sequencing
- Contingency planning
- Manoeuvre
- Tempo
- Operational pause
- Culminating point.

A campaign plan is, therefore, the practical expression of operational-level leadership and answers the questions:

- What conditions constitute success in relation to the strategic objective?
- What sequence of events is most likely to produce the desired conclusion?
- How should the resources be applied?

STRATEGIC PLANNING

An airline I travelled on had decided to do away with first class. After speaking to a flight attendant who was of the opinion that it would never work, three months later I saw that the idea was abandoned. This was an example of one of those head office solutions where a decision was made and driven through regardless of the opinions of those who are best placed to offer valuable insights. What time, credibility and resources did this experiment waste?

Malcolm Jones, CEO, NRMA Limited

> At the subsidiary that I worked for we wrote a strategic plan every year—since all the strategy came from the USA, it was really a tactical plan called strategy to justify our titles and pay packets!
>
> *A senior executive*

With barriers to trade being removed, the global market opening up, and the advance of technology continuing to affect industry, more than ever before senior executives need to plan strategically to guarantee organisational survival and growth to satisfy the stakeholders who are:

- The employees who want security of employment.
- The suppliers who want a reasonably predictable market.
- The shareholders who want some safety and return on their investment.
- The community as a whole that probably has a great interest in the continuing prosperity and local employment provided by the company (and increasingly an interest in environmental issues).
- The market that needs value for money, with services and products that meet its requirements.

Strategic plans are those plans and decisions made by leaders that relate to the achievement of desired long-term goals. From the strategic plan, all lower level tactical plans evolve. The following section provides you with the foundation for the development of a strategic plan, and we consider its tactical implementation.

STRATEGIC PLANNING MODEL

We start by using a strategic success model illustrated at Figure 20.1. Its original form was designed by Karl Albrecht.[4] Having considered organisational vision (level 1), and mission and values (level 2), in Chapter 18; and level 2, doctrine, in this chapter, we now look at other factors affecting this model. These 'factors' can be considered in the appreciation to determine the possible courses of action and to arrive at a concept of operations, that is, the outline plan. We will progress down the model.

Figure 20.1 Strategic Planning Model adapted with permission[4]

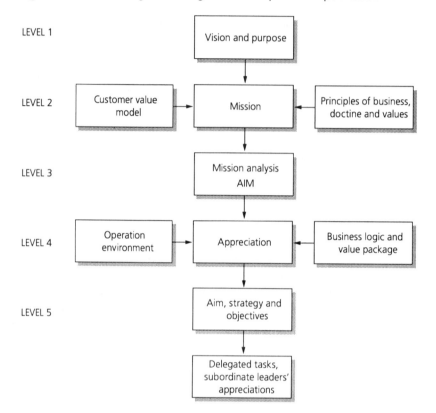

STRATEGIC PLANNING LEVEL 2

CUSTOMER VALUE MODEL

The customer value model is a set of the critical elements that define the value that an organisation provides from a customer's point of view, that is, what an organisation needs to provide to win and maintain customer accounts. This is derived from thorough, disciplined, and careful customer research.

There may be one for each major customer. The value may not be inherently in the product itself or what is delivered, but rather what it can do for the customer by assisting it to achieve a desired outcome. For example, in our homes we want electricity, not for its own sake, but for what it can do in creating light and power to operate appliances. Therefore, it is the total perception of value, the mind-set of the customer that is important.

THE HIERARCHY OF CUSTOMER VALUE

Karl Albrecht proposed a hierarchy of customer value (Figure 20.2) that is analogous to Abraham Maslow's famous hierarchy of needs. This hierarchy of customer value has four levels. In ascending order these are:

Basic: the fundamental components of your customer value package required just to be in business.

Expected: what your customers consider 'normal' for you and your competitors.

Desired: added-value features that the customers know about and would like to have, but do not necessarily expect because of the current level of performance of your competitors. This is the first level of possible differentiation and superiority over your competitors.

Figure 20.2   The Hierarchy of Customer Value

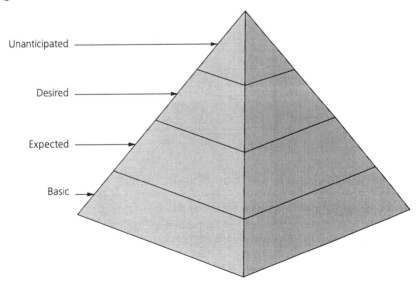

Unanticipated: added-value features that go well beyond the learned expectations and desires the customers bring to the experience of doing business with you. It may be unusually fast turnaround, an unusually confidence-inspiring guarantee, unusual expertise on the part of your employees, advanced merchandise features, or many other possibilities. These are 'surprise' features that can set you apart from your competitors and win you the loyalty of customers—if, of course, they really do add significant value in the eyes of your customers.

Customer value models can change over time. What may have been considered a desirable feature may now be considered expected. Increasing competitive performance by suppliers re-conditions customers' thinking.

STRATEGIC PLANNING LEVEL 3

MISSION ANALYSIS

This is discussed in Chapter 7, but since it is of vital importance it is repeated here. Mission analysis is designed to ensure that leaders, and through them everyone else, understands with absolute clarity what is to be achieved and why. This is the crux of the appreciation because unless the mission analysis is correct the whole appreciation may be worthless. Mission analysis helps CEOs to clarify precisely what must be achieved, so that any actions taken support 'their main efforts'.

1. **Analysis of the superior's intention.** It is essential to know and understand exactly what your superior, if you have one, intends to achieve and what your part is in his or her plan. Knowing what is wanted you can carry out the intent and are in a position to act in a positive and constructive manner.
2. **Identification of essential tasks.** The tasks given by the superior or evident from the intention must be analysed in order that the essential tasks can be identified. Some tasks may be specified by the superior; some tasks may be implied.
3. **Constraints/freedom of action/risk.** It is often difficult to decide what should be set down as constraints. The rule is that constraints are those imposed upon you. They are not those things that you decide should limit your actions as a result of considering the factors—this would be 'situating the appreciation'.

4. **Changes in the situation.** Has the situation changed since the start of the mission analysis? While you are carrying out your appreciation something could have changed. The result will be one of three cases:

    I. Yes, the situation has changed, but the plan is still good.

    II. The situation has changed, the original mission is still possible, but the plan needs to be amended.

    III. Yes, the situation has changed, the original mission is no longer valid. The plan no longer holds.

You can now write your own aim.

STRATEGIC PLANNING LEVEL 4

In Level 4, an appreciation is made of the situation with the aim that results from the mission analysis at the forefront of all thought. In addition to the factors and method I discuss in Chapter 7, the following also needs to be considered at the strategic level.

THE OPERATING ENVIRONMENT

Many people may be familiar with a PEST analysis (political, economic, sociological, and technical). Karl Albrecht identifies four additional factors: legal, customers, competitors, and the physical environment, shown in Figure 20.3.

The customer environment. The identity, wants, needs, behaviours, values, and so on, of those who do business with you. This includes not only the demographic/psychographic truths about customers, but recognises that customers can include diverse groups or organisations such as government departments, companies, or individual people.

Competitor environment. The identity, current state, likely intentions, motives, strengths, weaknesses, and so on, of those that you compete with. Competition may also be indirect. Other organisations may do things that induce customers to do less business with you. This is often a result of technological change.

Economic environment. The dynamics of markets, capital, inflation, interest rates, currency values, state of national economies, and so on, that affect demand for your product or service. Do you depend on a few major accounts, are you as recession-proof as possible, what 'shock waves' are on the way? This environment is complex and it may help

Figure 20.3 After Albrecht[4]

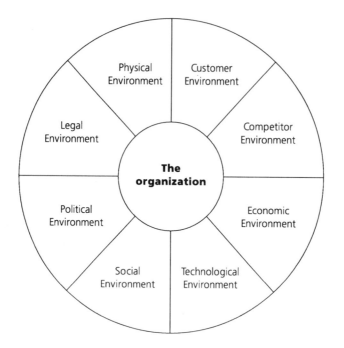

categorising the components into those that give primary and secondary effects.

Technological environment. Here I am talking of those events, trends and solutions available that can improve your capability to deliver and to add value. Technology may well assist your competitors, and may even make your product obsolete. Breakthroughs may lead to restructuring. Are you aware of the effect that emerging, or developing, technology might have on your business?

Social environment. The cultural patterns, values, beliefs, and preferences that dictate people's behaviour and attitudes. What broad social changes or issues may affect your product's attractiveness?

Political environment. National or local government policy, the interests of major 'power groups', and so on, can affect the rules of conducting business. The instability of a government, and the presence of corruption, can affect an organisation's very viability.

Legal environment. The pattern of law-making activity, existing laws and litigation all affect an organisation's success. Consider patents, intellectual property, liability, trade marks, employment law, and so on.

Physical environment. The physical surroundings of an organisation—its facilities, logistics, availability of resources, proximity to population centres, and effects of local geography, and like matters.

BUSINESS LOGIC

A modification of Albrecht's model of business logic in Figure 20.4 has five main categories: Strategic Drive, Customer Logics, Product Logic, Economic Logic, Structural Logic.

1. **Strategic drive.** What style of thinking dominates your organisation?
2. **The customer logic.** How will you define and access customers?
3. **The product logic.** What will you offer to the market to meet needs and represent some value to the customer?
4. **The economic logic.** How will you achieve profit and growth, or assess financial performance?
5. **The structural logic.** How will you structure the organisation to make the other three logics work together?

Strategic Drive

Michael Robert[5],[†] identifies that there are 10 possible elements that can be called an organisation's 'strategic drive'. Only one of these usually dominates, although customer, product, economic and structural logic still need to be considered in detail.

Products or services. This type of business is driven by the products or services it sells. Products stay much the same in terms of function. Any innovation is likely to be a case of refining the product or service.

Customers. Here it is a focus on a particular group of customers that drives strategic thinking. Market research and building customer loyalty should be high priorities.

Market type. This is a variation on the customer-driven company with the business anchored to a particular market category segment.

Production capacity. These companies focus on maximising the use of their facilities. Customers and market categories vary widely as the

---

[†] Michael Robert, *Strategy, Pure and Simple* © 1993. Reproduced with permission of The McGraw-Hill Companies.

Figure 20.4 Business Logic Model—adapted from Albrecht

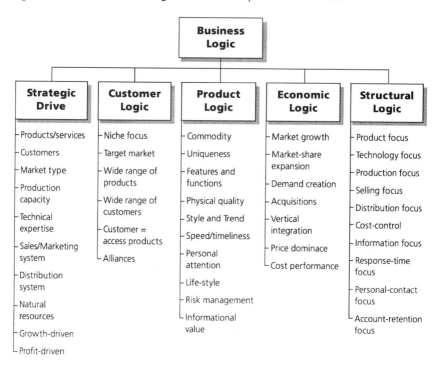

company seeks to operate at maximum capacity. Manufacturing or plant efficiency is a major concern.

Technical expertise. Technology-based companies grow by developing new applications for their technical developments. These kinds of companies may create a market segment where none existed—and often provide a diverse range of products or services. Such enterprises need to excel both in research and marketing the applications for their products.

Sales or marketing system. Here a particular method of selling is the key driver and this may exclude products and services not suitable to the methods used. There should be an emphasis on recruitment and training within a sales-driven business.

Distribution system. In these enterprises it is the method of distribution that drives corporate strategy. Whatever products or services can be sold through this form of distribution is of interest.

Natural resources. The structure of this kind of business is essentially driven by natural resources, as in the case of oil and mining companies. Exploration should be a major priority.

Growth-driven. These companies are motivated primarily by the desire to become bigger or to secure economies of scale. To succeed, this type of company should excel in financial management and must have an efficient internal data system to monitor the performance of all its divisions.

Profit-driven. Conglomerates that buy and sell subsidiaries that have little in common are prime examples of businesses steered by the desire to secure new or greater profits. All companies certainly need profits to survive, the difference here is that profit is the primary strategic drive. As for the growth-driven company, sound financial management and highly efficient data systems are essential.

Customer Logic

There are several ways to develop customer access and the avenue or combination of avenues you choose must make sense for your line of business and the potential customers that might be interested. Here are some of the main choices for customer logic.

Niche focus: a narrowly defined product or service (value package) that people buy only under specific circumstances. A concentrated marketing effort directed at a niche precludes developing a wider customer base.

Target customer base: a narrowly defined customer category, identified by a common feature or features. Existing channels can reduce the cost of reaching the customer base.

Wide product range: a range of products that enables a supplier to maximise the amount of business done with a single customer by exploiting the account and satisfying many different needs.

Wide customer range: the mass-market approach in which everything is offered that any customer might need. Geographic proximity to customers and a means of differentiation are important.

Customer-access products: a way of doing business that keeps the supplier in contact with the customer so that the supplier can make future sales without having to pay the costs of sales again.

Alliances: Partnering with other suppliers, so increased access to customers benefits all the allies. Alliances work best when the partners are not in competition and when each benefits directly from something that the other partner only has.

Product Logic

The product logic categorises the appeal that your product has to a customer. The value offered and means of differentiation are stressed.

Commodity item: as these are not easily differentiated as everyone can sell them they must form part of a package and be 'wrapped' in some attractive 'cover' to distinguish them from your competitors' items.

Uniqueness: a product with very few, if any, direct competitors is easily distinguished, but its applications or the needs that it satisfies have to be emphasised.

Features and functions: an item distinguished by its usefulness or functional appeal. But how does it differ specifically from similar products?

Physical quality: the materials or detail involved give the product a particular appeal.

Style and trend: products that follow fashionable trends tend to have a short life cycle and, therefore, a constant launch of new products is inevitable.

Speed or timeliness: the actual rapidity of delivering of the service or product is what differentiates the supplier.

Personal attention: dedication to the customer, an account manager or expert who appears to serve only the one customer is the supplier's appeal to his or her customers.

Lifestyle or self-identification: items used by the customer to express to others his or her life values, social status, prestige, or membership, in an admired social group.

Risk management: items that create trust, confidence, a feeling of security, or freedom from fear.

Informational value: information or advice sold solely for its usefulness.

Some products do fall into several categories, but the skill is in recognising which ones the customer associates with your product or 'value package' and in focussing on them.

The Product Value Package

The delivery system, or infrastructure, that provides the customer's experience with a supplier and creates the value recognised by the customer is illustrated at Figure 20.5 The complete 'value package' has to be right if the customer is to get an impression of quality and value for money.

Environmental: the physical setting in which the customer experiences the product. It includes the decor and ambience of a location.

Sensory: the direct sensory experiences, if any, that the customer encounters. This component includes sights, sounds, flavours, physical sensations, pain or discomfort, emotional reactions, aesthetic features of an item of merchandise, and the psychological ambience of the customer environment.

Figure 20.5

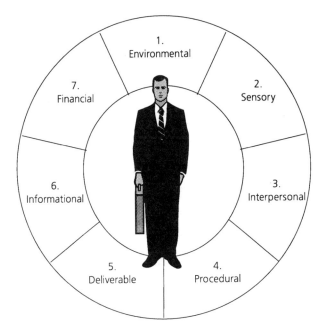

Interpersonal: the interaction the customer has with employees or, in some cases, with other customers, as part of the total experience. This dimension includes friendliness, courtesy, helpfulness, physical appearance, and apparent competence in handling important tasks.

Procedural: the procedures that the customer experiences in doing business with you. Examples include waiting, explaining needs, completing forms, providing information, going to various locations.

Deliverable: anything the customer physically takes custody of during the service experience, even if only temporarily. Examples include goods purchased, booklets or forms that are read, retained or returned.

Informational: receiving the information needed to function as a customer. Examples include signage indicating the nature of the product or service offered, instructions accompanying goods, comprehensible and unambiguous information in brochures and catalogues.

Financial: what is actually paid for the whole experience or value package.

Every enterprise should subject its customer value package to continual and critical scrutiny with the objective of constantly improving it. Using the seven components just described, enterprises can conduct a 'value audit' of the customer interface to see how well it performs. It is also important to get the direct input of customers in this audit in order to discover defects or opportunities not obvious to the leaders themselves.

Economic Logic

To achieve growth and profit the options below need to be considered. As particular objectives change, so may the approach taken to achieve the objectives.

Market growth: as customers multiply or natural demand increases, there is more total demand available to capitalise on, a rising tide from which every supplier profits.

Market-share expansion: gaining market share at the expense of other players.

Demand creation: communicating the benefits to people so well that they become customers.

Acquisitions: increasing sales volume or market share by acquiring or by merging with other companies already doing business in that category.

Vertical integration: operating at more than one step along the supply chain from raw material to finished product.

Price dominance: the right to charge a higher price than your competitors because of some added-value or quality advantage; or the ability to charge lower prices than a competitor because of a more effective cost structure and/or economies of scale.

Cost performance: having a specially advantageous cost structure that improves your profit, generates capital needed for growth, or enables you to withstand 'price wars'.

Again, it makes sense to consider more than one of these avenues for economic logic, and to look for compatible combinations. Together with your customer logic and your product logic, your economic logic drives many of your strategic choices.

Structural Logic

Your structural logic assists you to define your method of organisation, that is, the infrastructure for your enterprise. It should enable you to implement and to support the combination of strategic drive, customer logic, product logic, and economic logic that you have chosen.

Product focus: using a key product as the defining element of the operation.

Technology focus: investment in research and development directly affects the products or services provided.

Production focus: concentrating on managing the production process so skilfully that it creates a competitive advantage through product quality or cost advantages.

Selling focus: concentrating all energies on helping the customer decide to buy.

Distribution focus: getting things where they need to be when they need to be there. The 'just-in-time' concept may aid efficiencies in developed and sophisticated countries, but it is a concept fraught with danger in areas in which supplies cannot be guaranteed as reserves have to be held.

Cost-control focus: an unwavering commitment to being the lowest cost producer.

Information focus: organising around the creation, manipulation, and movement of information.

Response-time focus: gearing the whole operation to rapid response on demand.

Personal-contact focus: the customer-facing employees add value to the basic product offered by the skill or expertise.

Account-retention focus: keeping the business of the key customers, rather than having to compete for accounts repeatedly.

. . .If he gets involved in details. . .he will lose sight of the essentials that really matter. . .No Commander whose daily life is spent in the consideration of details, and who has not the time for quiet thought and reflection, can make a sound plan of battle on a high level or conduct large scale operations efficiently. . .The plan of operations must always be made by the Commander and must not be forced on him by his staff, or by circumstances, or by the enemy. He has got to relate what is strategically desirable with that which is tactically possible with the forces at his disposal.

Field Marshal Montgomery[6]

The appreciation remains the process by which a strategic leader can identify his or her courses of action and outline plan (see Chapter 7). In most organisations only the leader at a particular level has the perspective, experience, and knowledge, to make the appreciation of a situation and to develop the concept of operations or outline plan. Others may assist and contribute, but they will lack the time horizon and capability (in a correctly structured 'requisite' organisation') and, therefore, any plan will be deficient. The outline plan must be the leader's, this concept can then be passed on to the leader's staff to have the necessary detail added. In considering your own business logic think about the various combinations of the five sub-logics and see which ones combine synergistically and which are not complementary to each other.

With change in all its aspects continuing at such an unprecedented rate it is questionable whether the effort put into writing grandiose *and inflexible* strategic plans supported by detailed, time-tabled tactical plans is really worth it. The history of technology tells us that many advances that shape our lives were unpredicted. Rather than plan in minute detail, organisations may be better served by formulating a strategic concept of operations that can be exploited by flexible tactical plans. Such a concept of operation allows organisations to:

- lead change
- exploit trends and opportunities
- lead events, rather than be driven by them
- monitor business indicators

without predetermining, in detail, actions to be taken and resources to be committed.

Subordinate leaders can then seize the initiative and formulate their own plans which support the business' strategic objectives.

THE APPRECIATION AND THE SWOT ANALYSIS

Many people will be familiar with the SWOT analysis. It helps in the analysis of problems but does not identify a preferred course of action. If the appreciation process is used with *strengths, weaknesses, opportunities* and *threats* considered as factors, you will have a far more powerful model that can be used at any stage of the organisation's life, or at any level and applied to any problem. It creates a discipline of continuous self-analysis, and analysis of all the environmental factors influencing the market the organisation is in. SWOT can be linked to the following key questions—which is not an exhaustive list—to which the 'So what?' and 'Therefore' test (see Chapter 7) should be applied.

Strengths

- Does your client base consist of strong, stable accounts?
- Is your market share strong?
- Is the market stable?
- Is your product range strong?
- Are your financial resources and reserves strong?
- Is your organisation agile and responsive and the people well trained, motivated, and led well?

Weaknesses

- Are your management and employee skills and attitudes poor?
- Is your equipment obsolete?
- Do you have a narrow product range?
- Is your market share small?
- Is your company bureaucratic, rigid and inflexible—structural problems?

Opportunities

- Increased market penetration with little design change.
- Alliances, partnerships, or voluntary mergers, to leverage key organisational strengths.
- New product development.
- Access other markets or market segments.

Threats

- Reduction in market share or profitability.
- Approaching obsolescence of product range.
- Departure of key staff and loss of 'knowledge' from the company.
- Government and legal restrictions.
- Technological changes.
- Changes in customer expectations and needs.

Just as we considered with the personal qualities of leadership, a leader should capitalise on the company's strengths and minimise the effects of its weaknesses.

Weaknesses should not just be left as taboo subjects, recognised and not discussed. The root causes have to be traced back and the necessary changes have to be made.

Weaknesses may be a result of a shortage of space or insufficient capacity to meet demand, failure to meet market expectations of value and quality, untrained managers and unskilled poorly motivated front-line employees, a mature market with a product life cycle in decline, high operating costs and cash flow problems, and ultimately poor leadership.

Benchmarking is a useful process of performance comparison, part of the evaluation function of a leader. Comparison may be made to the past, numerical objectives, competitors, non-competing organisations and between internal business units.

STRATEGIC PLANNING LEVEL 5

At this point remember that an 'aim' is 'a general statement of what is to be done and its purpose'. 'Objectives' are 'statements of discrete, measurable goals that have to be attained in order to achieve the aim'. Once you have made your appreciation(s) on the various aspects of your business you could find it helpful to tabulate your results as follows:

Aim	Objectives	Strategy	Evaluation
Intent and purpose expressed in words	Concrete goals expressed in numbers and dates	Concept of operations expressed in words	Measures of success expressed in numbers and dates

IMPLEMENTING STRATEGY

The next point. . .is the selection of commanders. Probably a third of my waking hours were spent in the consideration of person-alities. . .Merit, leadership and the ability to do the job were the sole criteria; I made it my business to know all commanders and to insist on a high standard. . .Good senior commanders, once chosen, must be trusted and backed to the limit. . .Every officer has his ceiling in rank above which he should not be allowed to rise. . .The judging of a man's ceiling. . .is one of the great problems which a commander must solve and it occupied much of my time.

Field Marshal Montgomery[6]

. . .An army is a most sensitive instrument and can easily become damaged; its basic ingredient is men and, to handle an army well, it is essential to understand human nature. Bottled up in men are great emotional forces which have got to be given an outlet in a way which is positive and constructive, and which warms the heart and excites the imagination. If the approach is cold and impersonal, then you achieve nothing. But if you can gain the trust and confidence of your men, and they feel their best interests are safe in your hands, then you have in your possession a priceless asset and the greatest achievements become possible. . .Every single soldier must know before he goes into battle, how the little battle he is to fight fits into the larger picture, and how the success of *his* fighting will influence the battle as a whole. . .The whole Army then goes into battle knowing what is wanted and how it is to be achieved. And when the troops see that the battle has gone exactly as they were told it would go, the increase in morale and the confidence in higher command is immense—and this is a most important factor for the battles still to come.

Field Marshal Montgomery[6]

In developing strategy you require an incisive mind, intellectual capacity, a relevant time horizon (see Chapter 9), and analytical skills. As important, if not more so, are the skills and personal qualities of leadership to make things happen. The point is not one of minimising the crucial importance of strategy development, but of highlighting the effort and leadership necessary for implementation. *Many organisations have sound strategies but they lack the leadership at every level to implement it successfully.* The implementation of strategy is vital to organisational survival, so it is crucial that leadership filtering down from the boardroom harnesses energy and engenders commitment from the whole company.

The implementation of strategy comes down to junior and mid-level managers displaying their own leadership qualities and example (Chapter 6) while adhering to the key functions of a leader (see Chapter 5). This is why the selection of managers and their leadership training is critical for all organisations. Re-read the earlier sections on 'the nuts and bolts' of leadership before proceeding to Chapter 21.

References

1. Fred G. Hilmer and Lex Donaldson, 1996, *Management Redeemed: Debunking the Fads that Undermine Corporate Performance*, Sydney: Free Press Australia (a Division of Simon & Schuster Inc. New York).
2. Richard Luecke, 1994, *Scuttle Your Ships Before Advancing And Other Lessons from History on Leadership and Change*, New York: Oxford University Press.
3. John Laffin, 1966, *Links Of Leadership Thirty Centuries of Command*, London: George C. Harrap & Co. Ltd.
4. Karl Albrecht, 1994, *The Northbound Train: Finding the Purpose Setting the Direction Shaping the Destiny of Your Organization*, New York: AMACOM (a division of the American Management Association).
5. Michael Robert, 1993, *Strategy Pure and Simple*, New York: McGraw-Hill.
6. *The Memoirs of Field-Marshal Montgomery of Alamein, K.G.*, 1958, London: Collins.

CHAPTER 21

TRAINING FOR AND DEVELOPING LEADERSHIP

> The rocks in my path today are the building blocks of tomorrow.
>
> *Anonymous*

So far everything discussed is about what a leader needs to do or to be in order to exercise effective leadership. If the highly desirable situation is to be developed in which leadership and teamwork (as described so far) become a way of life and, therefore, continuous improvement, change and innovation become the norm, a number of steps must be taken.

Developing a culture of leadership and teamwork is based on training, education and development (both formal courses and on the job training); on environmental factors—example, mentoring, coaching, opportunity and on the 'requisite' systems—recruitment and selection systems to identify the potential to be trained, recognition and remuneration to encourage the display of what is desired, and the performance management systems to assess what has been achieved and to identify any gaps for training to close.

If the philosophy underpinning recruitment and selection, training and development, recognition and remuneration, and performance management are not congruent mixed messages are sent throughout the organisation and a state of confusion follows. It is imperative that

Figure 21.1 Factors Affecting Organisational Culture

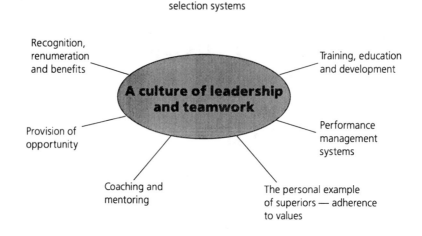

all the above-mentioned systems and processes are integrated and, as mentioned in Chapter 1, they can, and should, all be derived from the definition of leadership and a leader (on which this book is based) and the template for leadership training (Figure 1.3).

> Leadership: the capacity and will to rally people to a common purpose willingly, and the character that inspires confidence and trust.
> Leader: a person responsible for achieving objectives through the work of others and for building and maintaining the team that he or she is part of.

In this chapter we only consider training and development as it is so relevant to the rest of this book; the other 'requisite' systems deserve a book of their own.

The purpose of training is to develop in individuals and groups, the knowledge, skills, behaviour and attitudes that are required for successful performance in their employment—competence.

As with everything else, unless we are clear about our aim and the objectives that have to be attained in order to achieve it, we will never know whether we have achieved the aim or not. Therefore, the following aim is suggested.

AIM

The aim of leadership training is to develop participants' awareness of the nature and practice of leadership, so that they can apply leadership skills and knowledge and display leadership qualities with confidence and understanding to increase team effectiveness, performance, and profitability.

TRAINING OBJECTIVES

Leadership training should be designed to achieve the following training objectives, the order of which does not indicate priority:

1. To extend participants' perspectives and understanding of the relationship between leadership and management.
2. To understand and apply the theory of the functional approach to leadership.
3. To develop the personal qualities of leadership and to display the will to lead.
4. To develop clarity of thought and purpose and to understand the problem-solving, decision-making and planning process (mission analysis and the appreciation).
5. To understand the importance of communication in the leadership process and to develop the ability to communicate.
6. To understand the factors that influence morale.
7. To develop an understanding of the role, dynamics, characteristics, building, and maintenance of teams in business.
8. To understand the leadership of change and its effects on people.
9. To understand the role of leader as coach.
10. To understand the nature of motivation and the relationship to delegation.
11. To understand the meaning and nature of, and necessity for, integrity, trust, loyalty, confidence, and moral courage.
12. To understand the necessity for, and inter-relationship of, loyalty and discipline.
13. To understand the meaning of vision, mission and values, and their part in organisational leadership.
14. To assist individual career development and motivation.

APPROACHES TO LEADERSHIP TRAINING

While capable trainers, with credibility and expertise in the subject they are teaching, are vital to the success of any training so much hinges upon developing effective leadership, the salient features of sound instruction are highlighted here.

The key to successful training and instruction lies in the imaginative and common sense application of three fundamental principles that are:

- To make good preparation and planning.
- To promote and maintain the desire to learn.
- To confirm that training has been assimilated.

Preparation and Planning

Planning takes time if it is done properly and it is completed more quickly and efficiently if it is done in a logical sequence. The trainer or instructor must have a clear aim at the start as this affects the design of the lesson or programme, the equipment used, and the method by which evaluation of assimilation is made at the end. The aim must be clear to both trainer and student alike. In achieving the aim, a number of objectives will probably have to be attained along the way—both for a programme and for an individual section or lesson.

The lesson plan. Any trainer should write out a lesson plan for every lesson. In outline every lesson needs a beginning, a middle, and an end.

    1. The beginning breaks naturally into three parts.

    (a) Preliminaries are preparations that cannot be made until the class assembles such as a safety brief, issuing specific books or equipment, and so on.

    (b) Revision to check relevant learning from earlier lessons and to also gets the students thinking.

    (c) Introduction in which the instructor should state the AIM of the lesson, explain why it is important, and then give any incentive to generate students' attention.

    2. The middle is the main teaching part of the lesson. It should be arranged in a logical sequence of stages with some sort of check or test at the end of each stage to establish whether or not the students are learning. When teaching skills, as opposed to knowledge, the sequence 'explanation, demonstration, imitation, practice' should apply.

    3. The end is a well-established procedure to close a lesson and to ensure also that the desired aim has been achieved. This is the sequence:

    (a) Take questions from the class to enable them to clear up any doubts.

    (b) Test for confirmation to see whether the instructional objectives have been achieved.

    (c) Pack up the training venue so that the lesson may end precisely on time.

    (d) Give a summary to emphasis the main points.

    (e) 'Look forward' to interest the group in the next lesson in the programme.

Rehearsal. Every trainer should, wherever possible, rehearse the lesson to ensure that timings are realistic and to clear up any difficulties that may occur. It is best to use two or three colleagues as an audience, and to listen to their advice.

Confirmation that Training has been Assimilated

Confirmation at several stages in a lesson is designed to ensure that the training objectives are achieved by its completion. When it is done well, confirmation checks that at each stage of a lesson learning has taken place. It also allows a pause so that students may clear up any doubts they have by asking questions, and the knowledge that some form of check will take place acts as an incentive to students to pay attention.

Confirmation may take place at any time during a lesson to see if the class is still 'with' the trainer and alert. There are, however, times when it should be done:

- At the start of the lesson to confirm assimilation of the previous lesson or, for example, to confirm that preparatory reading has been done.

- At the end of each stage to ensure that learning is taking place.
- At the end of the lesson to ensure that the training aim and objectives have been achieved.

Confirmation need not be stereotyped. There are many ways in which it can be done that give variety and generate interest, such as revision periods, quizzes, discussions, exercises, competitions, students 'teaching' and 'supervising' each other.

Generally speaking you are testing and confirming three aspects of learning.

Knowledge This is usually confirmed by asking questions and obtaining answers orally or in writing.

Skills giving a presentation or making an appreciation is one example. These are best tested by asking students to perform the skill in question.

Attitudes and behaviour such as accepting the importance of a concept as the value of loyalty. Attitudes are measured in two ways.

- By asking questions about situations and requiring the student to give an opinion or explanation. This is best done orally, unless the written ability of the student is very high.
- By watching the students' behaviour. Do they treat people with respect and insist that their peers do the same.

Attitudes and behaviour are usually measured over a sustained period because they tend to change rather slowly.

Promotion and Maintenance of the Desire to Learn

Trainers could be teaching individuals who are not particularly interested in learning. The onus is then firmly upon the trainer to arouse their interest and make them want to learn. Having gained their interest, the trainer must do his or her best to maintain it. There are a number of definite steps that do help in this rather complex process of motivation.

Promotion of the Desire to Learn

Before the lesson you can create interest in the training before the class assembles by:

- A look forward from a previous period.
- An interesting programme designed to attract attention and to keep students fully informed.
- Advertisement by using any display that arouses curiosity and promotes interest in the subject.

At the beginning of the lesson develop the interest of the class during the introduction to the period by giving:

- The aim in a clear statement of what is to be learnt.
- Give a realistic reason why it is important that the class learn it.
- An incentive if there is any reward to be gained, material or otherwise, from learning the subject.

Maintenance of the Desire to Learn

Keeping every member of the class wanting to learn and, therefore, interested throughout the lesson is your responsibility. To this purpose the main factors are:

- Variety. The good trainer always is experimenting in new ways of making his or her training more varied, interesting, and imaginative. Good aids, different ways of presentation, and competitions are means of achieving this.
- Activity. Strive for maximum activity in, and involvement by, your class. This normally takes the forms of:
  - Questions when teaching facts.
  - Practice when teaching skills.
- Looking your class in the eye, particularly when asking questions. This makes individuals feel they are committed and involved.
- Use of the senses. Students absorb teaching more quickly and effectively if training is designed to take maximum advantage of the senses through which they learn, that is, SIGHT, TOUCH, HEARING, SMELL, TASTE. Remember that about 80% of all information that we absorb comes to us through the sense of sight, so make the maximum use of visual material.
- Realism. Training must be realistic. The following will assist you:
  - Simulation of conditions and effects.
  - Realistic aids. 'Painting the Picture.' A convincing story.
  - Relation of the training to everyday life. The practical application of the training must be understood.
- Simplicity. Training must be simple. Little will be learnt unless it is understood. Pitch training at the level of the particular group being taught.
- Avoidance of distractions. Distractions must be avoided whenever possible. They may be caused by poor conditions of work, or by the trainer's own mannerisms, for example, constant repetition of the same word, rattling keys in pockets, and so on.
- Be enthusiastic. There is nothing like trainer's enthusiasm for motivating a group.

Finally, remember if the group has worked well, give it a 'pat on the back'. This encourages the students and give them an added incentive to learn.

In any activity there is no substitute for experience. Leadership training must provide opportunities for the practice of skills, reflection on experiences and development of personal qualities in a realistic, challenging and stimulating manner if any real progress is to be made. There are a number of approaches that are well known if not currently popular and I give a few words here about each of the more commonly encountered approaches.

THE QUALITIES APPROACH

A study of great leaders reveals their personal qualities. However, such a combined list, even if based only on a few leaders, would be lengthy and could include some abstract attributes. In Chapter 6 I stated that no two leaders, if asked for a list of essential qualities for leadership, would give the same answer. The study of leaders and their leadership goes a long way to explaining the need for the qualities of leadership. This study must be constantly encouraged; it should include the setting of essays and holding study periods with invited speakers.

There are two problems with this approach to leadership training. Firstly, not every great leader had all the qualities, even if you accept the list of 16 given in Chapter 6; and second, it is impossible to teach qualities merely by study. Remember that some leadership qualities are innate in each selected leader in different degrees; but some have to be learnt; and most can be developed by thought, feedback, and practice. Qualities can only be developed over time, although exposure to stress and pressure that makes demands on the trainee to display such qualities can accelerate the process.

This leads to the personal growth programmes that can vary from 'touchy feely' through to the rigorous adventurous training approach. The latter is based upon the concept 'not training of the body but training of the mind through the body'. Widespread evidence is available of permanent and deep changes (for the better) resulting from this latter approach that is considered in more detail below.

Generally participants learn to take responsibility for their actions and to develop their self-confidence, self-esteem and understanding of themselves. This is a vital foundation to effective leadership, but stops short of addressing a leader's role, necessary skills, and responsibilities.

THE SITUATIONAL APPROACH

The national situation in Germany in the 1930s produced Adolf Hitler and the situation in Great Britain in 1940 produced Winston Churchill. By the end of 1945 both situations had changed and both leaders had been superseded. The leaders evolved out of the situations. This approach to leadership is impractical in any organisation as leaders are selected or imposed on a particular situation, and the aim must be to train them to cope with as wide a range of problems as possible. No organisation can wait for leaders at any level to evolve.

THE TASK/PEOPLE RELATIONSHIP APPROACH

Many American behavioural psychologists have concentrated on the relationship between task and people. Notably Hersey and Blanchard espouse their theory of Situational Leadership® examined briefly in Chapter 14. In this theory leaders vary their style to suit the level of maturity or development of their followers. Often this type of approach involves proposing a model and using a diagnostic tool to orient participants. This is valid, but it does not address what a leader has to consider and do to actually lead; nor does it develop the leader's character.

If you think long and hard, many bad displays of leadership have been caused by the 'leader' not actually realising the full scope of his or her role and responsibilities to, and for, the team.

THE HUMAN RELATIONS APPROACH

The human relations approach can be viewed as the politically correct approach suited to an ideal world in which everyone is well meaning, well motivated, tolerant of everyone and everything, completely democratic, and oriented to learning. Philosophically there is nothing inherently wrong with this 'principled' approach other than it overlooks human nature and the reality that not everyone is continuously well motivated, some people are self-centred or ambitious, some people really do not want to share leadership. You can see that the list is endless. Until human nature changes, this will not be an approach that many participants will either relate to, or be able to employ, at work.

THE CONCEPTUAL APPROACH

The conceptual approach may involve academic study of any, or all, of the various theories of leadership and it is traditionally the domain of business schools. While leadership theory may be learnt, without any practice or experiences from which participants really do learn why it is necessary or correct to apply the concept, it is debatable whether the participant will ever apply the learning in the future. It is impossible for most people to develop their capacity to do something merely by discussing a concept and the fundamental understanding of why it is important or the attitudes, values or motivation to use it will probably be lacking. The basics of leadership are learnt by doing it.

THE FEEDBACK APPROACH

Diagnostic tools and profiling techniques are frequently used to act as feedback processes. These can assist a leader to learn about how he or she is perceived, and what his or her strengths and weaknesses are. While they show the need to change such tools do nothing to improve a leader's capacity to be effective, and it is arguable whether it does much to develop character. There is a difference between realising that you are indecisive and actually doing something about it.

The biggest drawback of these tools are that it is possible to 'label' or 'pigeon-hole' an individual or to develop attitudes linked to well-defined stereotypes accompanying these labels and they frequently fail to alter any behaviour. We vary in every possible degree; in our personalities, perceptions, aspirations, skills, strengths and blends of qualities. We come in every possible shade and cannot be so well defined as any paper tool would have us think. Profiling alone is an easy and ineffective option.

THE SKILL-BUILDING APPROACH

The skill-building approach is commonly used and while traditional 'hard' skills can be learnt, such as planning and problem solving, it is difficult to develop skills that require cognitive or psychological skills or the display of preferred behaviour. The skills approach may, there-fore, be thought of as producing a capable 'mechanic' lacking 'the personal touch'. Chapter 5 outlines the skills required, but it takes the personality of Chapter 6 to apply them effectively.

THE FUNCTIONAL APPROACH

The functional approach is based on Adair's three circles model of task, team, and individual, needs and the core functions of planning, brief-ing, controlling and coordinating, supporting, informing, and evaluating.

The functional approach stems from a study of group dynamics and involves the skills approach above. It establishes what a leader does, what a leader's role and responsibilities are, but not what he or she is.

Professor Adair and the staff of The Royal Military Academy Sandhurst devised a simple model which clearly sets out what a leader has to do in order to achieve a task, build a team, and to develop individuals. This is a useful starting point, but it does not tell a leader how he or she exercises leadership. Leadership is closely concerned with the qualities of the individual; the art of leadership primarily has to be learnt through experience.

Given that this is the only approach that does cover the full scope of a leader's role as shown on the functional leadership check-list (if only briefly covering each 'box' on the matrix) this has much to commend it. The functional leadership check-list forms the cornerstone, the foundation of knowledge on which all further training in concepts, processes, skills, or personal development, can be based.

THE COMPOSITE APPROACH

Leadership is not an exact science that can be learnt from a book, or in a classroom, and practised in a mechanical fashion. It is an individual and personal quality that is born and is evident in some, but can be developed in others. It is an individual expression of long-established principles that have not changed as human nature has not changed over the millennia. Leadership is not a skill in itself, but a combination of skills and personal qualities that can be developed and applied with thought and common sense.

The leader and the people who follow represent one of the oldest, most natural and most effective of all human relationships. Leadership is of the spirit, compounded of personality and vision; its study a science and its practice an art. A leader must be successful, for it is only with success that high morale can be achieved and through that efficiency in the workplace.

Since none of the above approaches are complete in themselves, the Leading Initiatives (Australia) Pty Limited combines all of them in the composite approach, tailored to each group's needs and includes most, if not all, of the following components:

1. Experiential and/or adventurous training
2. The template for leadership (Figure 1.3)
3. Development centre approach
4. Leaderless and leader-appointed tasks
5. Personal challenges
6. Team events

7. Skills training
8. Feedback of behavioural evidence and debriefing
9. Conceptual theory and knowledge
10. Structured initial and continuation training
11. Strategies for transfer of training.

Experiential and Adventurous Training

A mind that is stretched by a new experience can never go back to its old dimensions.

Oliver Wendell Holmes

Experience is not what happens to you but what you make of it.

Aldous Huxley

Any activity that involves team work helps you with your work environment.

John Quinn, Managing Director, Thorn Lighting Pty Ltd

Experiential training is training that can be a simulation of a type of task encountered at work, or it can be a more practical exercise such as a team initiative task involving the practical resources of planks, ropes and oil drums, etc., combined with leadership and teamwork to cross an obstacle. These exercises reproduce the dynamics of the workplace, particularly when pressure is applied via cut-off times, standards to be achieved, or some other form of presented target. It is best conducted in groups of six to eight people to facilitate the logistics of the task itself, participation by all, and observation and debriefing at the conclusion. Whatever the nature of the exercise, fundamental interpersonal relationships are highlighted and the need for mutual trust and confidence, clear and open communication, unity of effort, participation, clarity of thought, planning and leadership (see the team-work template at Figure 4.2). They are useful exercises for team building, but for leadership training that has to focus on developing the ability of the individual to be able to lead, these exercises provide an understanding of the characteristics of groups and teams (see Chapter 4), and stimulate the desire to learn to improve the leadership effectiveness of all those participants who do have the will to lead. Such exercises are useful in assessment centres when leadership or

312

leadership potential is being assessed and evidence of the qualities and capacity to lead (Chapters 5 and 6) are demonstrated.

Such exercises can be cyclical in that the following process is applied and re-applied:

1. Theory and concepts are presented.
2. Action and experience gives an opportunity to practise the concept.
3. Observation and reflection provide greater learning.
4. Application to the workplace is discussed and commitment to it is made.

Careful and planned debriefing (using the sequence of: facts, inferences, metaphors, applications, commitment model), combined with journal-keeping is the key to ensuring learning is transferred to the workplace.

> Great things are done when men and mountains meet,
> this is not done by jostling in the street.
>
> *William Blake, English poet*

> It is wrong to coerce people into opinions, but it is our duty to impel them into experience.
> We are all better than we know, if only we can be taught to realise this then we may never again settle for anything less.
>
> *Kurt Hahn*

Let us briefly draw the distinction between experiential and adventurous training. All adventurous training is experiential, but not all experiential training is adventurous. For example, a problem-solving exercise or initiative task conducted on a tennis court outside a conference centre is experiential, but hardly adventurous. A practical task such as conducting a river crossing in a fast-flowing and swollen river is both experiential and by its nature adventurous. More rigorous, challenging and adventurous locations do much to form bonds that are difficult to break between participants (a network of peers) and build a level of self-confidence and self-esteem that is difficult to surpass.

Clipper 96 is about adventure but it is also about taking time out. The benefits of such activities are that the participants are forced to share, forced to become a member of a practical team, forced to realise that teamwork does matter and that good teamwork achieves results as well as a happier working environment. These are all simple lessons but the revision does no harm. The participants take back these relearned lessons into their normal business but far more importantly, they take a realisation of what really matters and what does not. The sea is ruthless and never tires. To survive at sea people have to learn to select and concentrate on what matters and ignore what does not. It helps people to select the right priorities in life. Reducing sail in a squall takes precedence over a mealtime—that is a very simple example.

Sir Robin Knox-Johnston

Adventurous training is frequently poorly understood as people often associate the words 'adventurous training' with the Outward Bound organisation. Outward Bound has its origins in 1941 when Kurt Hahn, with the support of Lawrence Holt and his Blue Funnel shipping line, opened the first sea school. From this, adventurous training—expeditions—on land and at sea as a means of developing the whole person, has evolved in both civilian and military institutions, initially in the UK and subsequently worldwide. For both young and old it counters the softness of character and boredom of mood that results from the unprecedented security and affluence of life and freedom of action in the welfare state, and the failure to accept responsibility for ourselves because modern life makes it the easy option to ride on the backs of others, demand our rights, but ignore our obligations.

Sailing, especially long passage races, has taught me the value of discipline. You have to stick to a disciplined regime of feeding, resting, maintaining the boat and equipment, and the way in which you sail the boat—changing sail, navigating, everything. If you don't do what you know you should when you should, you'll have a problem. It's exactly the same in business. . .Sailing has strengthened me, the demands it makes has taught me the determination and fortitude

> needed to get through some very tough times in my personal and business life. In the 1970s my whole business collapsed—the economy and its financing made it inevitable. It was the character that sailing helped develop that made me say 'I won't be beaten', and I have bounced back. . .Adventure training is good for everyone, we should all take part in it. Without question it develops character, too many of us live in a 'cotton wool' environment that prevents us becoming robust and resilient to life's challenges. . .And we need adventurers to inspire other people. . .The greatest fear is always the unknown, adventure training helps you feel comfortable with this fear, this risk—not in a cocky way but in a quietly confident, professional style.
>
> *Ian Kiernan, sailor and founder of Clean Up Australia*

The common misconception is that such training is purely physical (although there is no doubt that physical fitness assists in our ability to manage stress and sustain high energy levels, and physical training is, therefore, to be encouraged), but people generally fail to realise that its roots lie deeply in the educational philosophy of Kurt Hahn, founder of both Gordonstoun School and Outward Bound. Hahn regards the 'foremost task of education to ensure the survival of these qualities: an enterprising curiosity; an undefeatable spirit; tenacity in pursuit; readiness for sensible self-denial and above all, compassion'. Surely these objectives are all desirable in the effective leader and team member?

The Outward Bound schools were founded on the following principles:

A residential four-week course, open to all without bias, based upon a spiritual foundation, and present a set of conditions to allow self-discovery. Those conditions include self-discipline, teamwork, adventure and some risk, physical hardship, and service to the community. These are the foundations for moral and civic virtue, and a meaningful and healthy life.

Physical challenge is not an end in itself, but the instrument for training, the will to strive for self-control. Overcoming our weaknesses is far more important than developing performance in our areas of strength. Emphasis is on the concept that each participant should strive to compete with or against an external standard, and learn to cooperate and collaborate with others, not compete against them.

> What lasts from an educational experience is not the enhancement of memory, it is the enhancement of being. But it is beliefs about the nature of man, what he may become and what is his destiny, with the morality that flows from these, that enhance a man's being. . .Also the modern mind does not possess these old certainties! It is distrustful of self and so has come to distrust nearly all the beliefs that are essential to civilised thought and conduct.
>
> *Basil Fletcher*[1]

Plato's view of the purpose of education is that it is the harmonious and concurrent development of the individual in mind, body, and spirit. In modern terms 'synergy' is the word to describe the 'interaction between these elements that allow them to feed from and to nourish each other'. Will we ever have the same depth of understanding of this as the ancients had before us? The experience of more than 2 million participants in Outward Bound adventurous training programmes in 28 countries alone demonstrates that such training fosters a sense of self-control, self-confidence, and a sense of service to others. It helps people to discover their true powers and to learn true values.

Considerations

There are certain issues with adventurous training that need to be resolved in a corporate context.

1. **Time.** To achieve a lifelong lasting change in behaviour and values, a programme has to last at least seven to 10 days, in my experience. It takes at least two days before participants start to 'spark'—use their initiative and take responsibility for thinking and acting for themselves. Companies report a change in personality (for the better) after intensive four-day programmes, but the intensity of those programmes does not allow for much discussion of concept, or reflection upon experience.

2. **Group composition.** If people are to be satisfied by the achievement of overcoming real challenge that implies physical stretch as well as intellectual and emotional stretch, a group must be of similar physical ability. No one will enjoy an expedition in which a person with a medical condition is a burden to himself or herself and to others and who prevents any real adventure from being encountered. Challenge and achievement is all relative thus, what is challenging for one group is not for another. Streaming groups in

316

this way allows everyone to go beyond their perceived limits and to stretch to their maximum. Implicit in this selection is a thorough knowledge by the training team of the condition of every individual.

3. **Training team.** The training team's composition and experience are critical. There are many adventure holiday operators trying to win a piece of the corporate training market share. While they can usually conduct an event *per se*, their backgrounds frequently lack: any real understanding of corporate life and commercial issues, any real conceptual understanding of leadership and teamwork that can be imparted, and basic training and instructional ability. They, therefore, often reinforce any negative corporate perception of adventurous training—that it can offer little value to management development. Implicit in the training team's knowledge and experience is thorough safety and risk-management planning.

4. **Lack of managerial confidence.** Many 'managers' are reluctant to encourage subordinates or peers to undertake such a course because they lack an understanding of how such training works or because they lack the moral courage, self-confidence, or willpower to 'sell' the idea to their people. It all seems too far beyond the comfort zone for so many yet, paradoxically, the people who gain most from this form of training are always those most resistant to doing it. The improvement in self-confidence and 'interpersonal skills' is noticed by all, whether it is admitted by the individual or not.

We are all cripples to a greater or lesser extent, bound by habit, convention, circumstances to lower aims and achievements than lie within our potentialities. . .There is a danger in thinking that it is bad to expose deep-lying, self-inflicted wounds to the light of day. Some people believe. . .that it is better to avert one's eyes when human failings are exposed; or better still, that exposure ought to be avoided. But is not the character of a boy shielded from such experience crippled even more surely? Does the stutterer improve by being told not to talk?. . .The art of inspiring confidence in another is a delicate art, but it should not for that reason be neglected.

Adam Arnold-Brown[2]

Some people are overly concerned at the possibility of psychological damage done to those who fail a test. It is a fact that not everyone

317

succeeds despite being physically capable, they are limited by their own self-belief. Modern life is hard, especially in business with its ups and downs. We, therefore, have a duty to strive and to develop in everyone the mental robustness and resilience to learn from failure and to not be destroyed by it. I believe that the lack of character development, this lack of robustness, is a significant contributory factor to the increasing number of 'Post Traumatic Stress Disorder' cases.

The greater the challenge, the greater the sense of achievement and the learning. It is a fact that the most successful courses are all conducted in the worst weather conditions. Bad weather forces mutual dependence and brings people together very quickly.

The real value of adventurous training lies in the psychological, rather than the physical, benefits. On the mountainside or at sea, differences between people fade into the comradeship of shared adversity, allowing the attitudes and behaviours necessary for effective leadership and teamwork to develop naturally, away from normal hierarchical restrictions. In such conditions leadership, clear thinking, keeping calm under real pressure, mental flexibility, and mutual trust and confidence, are all developed by exposure to natural and uncontrollable extremes. To remain comfortable in inhospitable conditions requires real leadership and teamwork: teams form and the benefits of teamwork and leadership are rapidly assimilated.

As a head-hunter it was always apparent that those people who currently or had previously engaged themselves regularly in demanding activities, especially those that incurred some degree of risk such as offshore sailing were always more comfortable with themselves, less prone to suffering from stress and less prone to inducing panic in others than their peers who had lacked such life experiences. The solo climbers, sailors and parachutists had the strength of self-reliance and self-confidence, (although one or two had too much individualism to fit into close teams), the hockey and Rugby team players and fully crewed sailors had confidence and a more natural affinity for close working relationships and the value of teamwork. Those who engaged in adventurous outdoor pursuits also seemed to able to transfer the vital awareness of the natural environment and weather to an awareness of people and the market generally at work.

The author

Adventurous training thus provides:

- Growth of self-esteem and self-confidence by overcoming a challenge thought unattainable (see the need for these qualities in Chapters 2 and 6).
- Development of mental robustness and resilience to stress and pressure.
- An exploration of, and a true understanding of, self, personality, strengths, and weaknesses.
- Growth of initiative and acceptance of responsibility for your actions.
- More incisive judgement of character, understanding of perception and understanding of and empathy towards others.

Most importantly, adventurous training sows the seeds of character from which effective leadership will develop. Few people realise that concurrent with adventurous training in 'wild country', the assimilation of knowledge and the practice of skills and use of concepts already presented in this book is entirely possible.

> Without the instinct of adventure in young men, any nation, however enlightened, any state, however well ordered, must wilt and whither.
>
> *Trevelyan*

Template for Leadership

I first proposed the template for leadership in Chapter 1 at Figure 1.3, and everything connected with the development of leadership should fall into one of its component parts. It assists in focussing attention and ensuring a logical order of progression. By referring to it, the trainee leader can track his or her own progression.

Development Centre Approach

The whole of life and work should be one big development centre in which the developing leader is constantly faced with leadership situations to resolve, and then has his or her performance objectively debriefed and discussed, based upon the observed display of his or her personal qualities, behaviours and demonstrated skills—behavioural evidence that cannot be denied. The development centre approach generally uses a language of behaviours (that are the outward manifestation of values, beliefs, and personal qualities) and such centres are based upon the theory that:

319

Competence = Skills + Knowledge + Behaviour Attitudes

Compare this with the template for leadership. There is a remarkable similarity with the skills and knowledge in the definition of 'competence' giving the capacity, to be applied with the necessary behaviours being the demonstration of the personal qualities of leadership. The competency profile at Appendix A to this chapter, describes the desired demonstration of leadership for each 'phase' of the functional check-list and links the action to the required personal qualities from the blueprint in Chapter 6.

Leaderless and Leader-appointed Team Initiative Tasks

The conduct of leaderless experiential teamwork and initiative tasks is an interesting exercise. Company directors, junior managers and supervisors alike invariably create the same confusion and demonstrate the same problems and learn the same lessons. When properly debriefed such exercises give an understanding of team dynamics (Chapter 4) and an understanding of the relevance of and necessity for the functional leadership check-list.

Having effectively generated the desire to learn, the individual's leadership can be developed using training exercises in which only the nominated leader receives the brief. The appointed leader then makes things happen from start to finish. Among other things such exercises with an individual in the spotlight clearly show those who do not have the will to lead.

Exercise debriefs should follow the model sequence:

Figure 21.2

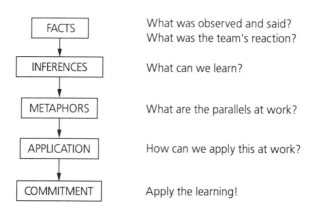

This should be linked to the demonstrated application of the functional check-list and the display of the qualities required, that is, a development centre approach.

Personal Challenges

I have discussed in depth self-confidence and the ability to stretch. To balance perceived versus actual risk and make a calculated decision is essential to effective leadership, therefore, confidence training is vital. Climbing and abseiling, high ropes challenge courses, and most aspects of adventurous training, contribute to this. There should be no reluctance to use such methods, although inevitably there will be those people who think that such tasks are beyond them and who baulk at the idea. This is where the experience of the training team directing staff is critical to the success of such activities. In addition to the self-confidence aspect, these challenges promote self-awareness, and can teach the need for mutual trust and confidence in the team if the activities are so designed to require the whole team's active participation.

Team Events

Activities in which a team task revolves around a specific process that, after debriefing and reflection, is repeated several times will show what is possible by continuous improvement and learning. Such exercises usually involve the stripping, use of components, and reassembly of a purpose-built 'object'. When several teams concurrently work on the same task in close proximity it is possible to teach lessons that centre around the notion of competition versus cooperation (see Chapters 4 and 10). These exercises, when repeated, can show a dramatic improvement in 'performance' that leads to the release and experience of considerable team spirit—a feeling that the trainee leaders should then strive to reproduce in their own work teams.

Skills Training

'Skills training' is 'the assimilation and practice of processes and techniques that lead to an increase in a person's "mechanical efficiency".' When teaching skills the mnemonic EDIP—explanation, demonstration, imitation, practice—practice—practice is a useful tool. Skills training might be limited in scope, such as learning and applying the appreciation process, or it might be wider ranging as in applying the functional check-list, appreciation process, communication skills and coaching, and the like, during a leader-appointed initiative task.

Feedback and Debriefing

When used correctly, debriefing of all activities and feedback (ideally from superior, peers, and subordinates) will develop self-awareness, assist in promoting the need and desire to learn, and assist with the ongoing tailoring of the course and allocation of leadership appointments for the various activities. The feedback can also take the form of self, superior, peer, subordinate assessments, that can be conducted both pre-course and at intervals post-course.

Instant feedback during the practical exercises by fellow participants and, afterwards, by both participants and the training team turns every exercise into a development centre.

Individual post-course interviews with the training team is very useful for the participants. For some people it will have been the first time in their lives that they have had an honest and objective assessment of their strengths and weaknesses given to them.

It is usual for those who show little confidence and no will to lead and who often have been promoted out of technical roles into leadership roles with little consideration given to their selection and training, and who are clearly uncomfortable in such jobs, to make career changes. This lack of will to lead and lack of confidence will certainly have been recognised by their subordinates and also the superior, even if the superior has only the slightest grasp of the quality of leadership provided by subordinate leaders. If the struggling would-be leaders have not already realised it after such practical training, they will usually discuss it, for deep in their heart of hearts, they know it to be true, despite whatever rationalising that may overtly take place as blame is passed onto their 'subordinates'.

This sort of practical training allows an assessment of people, even if it is not officially planned. Everyone can see whether their fellow participants are making progress or not and that this may to lead to such 'casualties' changing roles or employers. In the long term those people making transitions will be happier in a job that they can be good at, and their teams and companies will benefit from the departure of a capable technical expert or 'specialist' who is a poor line manager and who is replaced by a capable leader. Experience has shown that this is a very positive aspect of leadership training.

Conceptual Theory and Knowledge

> In developing leadership, military and historical examples make an interesting and stimulating change from reviewing the performance of a well-known company in decline or in continued growth. The analogies are obvious and the decisions and their outcomes very clear cut.
>
> *Kathy Rozmeta, Learning & Development Manager,*
> *Coca-Cola Amatil Limited*

Throughout this book I have laid out the conceptual framework on which leadership can be based. Concepts and theories provide principles that should guide actions, but they should not enslave leaders to their dogmatic application. Any philosophy of leadership has to be embraced and understood and not treated as a model for application in every situation.

Experiential exercises can teach much about the need for certain qualities, behaviours or skills to be applied. When combined with the application of tools such as the functional leadership check-list, mission analysis, and the appreciation, they become far more powerful.

It is my firm belief that aspiring leaders must have a fundamental understanding of what makes themselves 'tick', and how they are perceived by others, and what morale, discipline, moral courage and teamwork, and so on, really are, and why they are important. Otherwise learning knowledge is rather like pouring water into a bucket with a hole in the bottom. The knowledge will not remain—but if it does, it probably will not be used.

This is why adventurous training (incorporating some basic tools, processes, and concepts) is so beneficial as the starting point in leadership development. Ideally, all aspiring leaders and existing managers will have had the experiences early in life that teach the basic understanding of self and others, the need to stretch, the value of morale and determination. Sadly, many people have not had such experiences and, therefore, to some degree, this training is giving them, relatively late in life, the lessons that should have been learnt in earlier years.

Structured Initial and Continuation Training

The initial training package has to set the context for all follow-on training and needs to focus on the fundamental qualities, behaviours,

323

and skills, necessary to fulfil the demands of the basic leadership role. The initial package should be conducted in groups of six to eight participants each with their own dedicated member of the training team who should guide and nurture them throughout the programme, including all pre- and post-training assessments, interviews, and so on. As many groups should be trained concurrently as can be freed from the line since the nature of the training will have a team-building effect among participants.

Participants should be of a peer level in the hierarchy. This prevents the embarrassment of failing in front of subordinates or superiors. Since all learning is done from analysing mistakes and little is learnt from success, exercises should be 'testing'. If adventurous training is planned, participants need to be of similar ability levels. That way there is no 'struggling' or 'cruising' by anyone. A mix of cross-functional peers, or peers from major suppliers and customers ('supply chain training') bring additional benefits of networking and a greater understanding of business in general.

The environment in which programmes are conducted needs careful thought. It is possible for a group of a high physical ability level to learn the initial course as part of an adventurous programme that covers large distances in 'wild country'. Meanwhile a group of a lower ability level can have the same learning experiences of living together in the bush (in which the whole of daily life of cooking, pitching tents, and so on, becomes the domain of natural leadership and teamwork), but with the exercises sited only minutes' walk away. At the other extreme is a programme based at a conference centre and using only experiential not adventurous training. Any conference centre should be away from distractions. The availability of bars and jacuzzis does nothing to help trainees focus on what really is important and what really does matter. If there is no stress or pressure or real unfamiliarity (and the outdoor environment provides that), life is too comfortable and the mask that is worn to work each day remains. To break bad habits and strip away the veneer to reveal the real character beneath needs an environment in which a sustained and determined effort is required from every participant for their every waking moment. True personal qualities and character are only revealed and developed under conditions of stress.

The initial programme should cover personality (Chapter 2), perception (Chapter 3) group and team dynamics (Chapter 4), functional leadership (Chapter 5) and mission analysis, the appreciation, and briefing (Chapters 7 and 8), the underlying philosophy of leadership (Chapter 1) and leadership qualities (Chapter 6). That comprises a self-contained package that will make a definite improvement to leadership on the job.

If sufficient experiences have been created to develop a trainee's character, fundamental understanding of his or her responsibilities and role as a leader, and to create the desire to further learn and to develop his or her own leadership ability, then a combination of collective and self-taught individual continuation training can cover the remainder of the subject areas forming chapters within this book. A particular emphasis should be paid to morale, motivation, and organisation (Chapters 12, 13 and 9).

Invited speakers, individual and group business-related projects, presentations to colleagues, and training of subordinates, and so on, should all be used to assist in the assimilation of skills and knowledge, and the transfer of training to the workplace.

Strategies for Transfer of Training

Strategies for transfer of training can, and should, be employed at all stages of training to maximise the effect of the training dollar and this is where the value of so much training is still lost.

Before training the following guidelines assist in tailoring programmes and promoting the desire to learn.

Assessments. Superior, peer, subordinate and self-assessments of participants' leadership, using the profile at Appendix A as a base. These are often overgraded no matter the source since many people are unaware of the meaning of so many of the attributes that they are assessing.

Participant interviews and pre-course questionnaire. These should be conducted individually and in confidence to gain commitment to the programme, customise the course as far as possible, and also to build trust between the training team and the participant.

Offer reward or recognition for course performance. When properly presented by the employer, reward and/or recognition can act as a powerful incentive to committing 100% of energy and concentration to the course.

Identify opportunities to use new skills after training. Many new skills or knowledge are lost because they are not applied after training on return to work. A plan has to be worked out in advance.

During training these guidelines need to be observed.

Provide opportunities for practice. This ensures the assimilation of new skills and concepts.

Systematic and progressive training. A logical progression to increasingly higher levels of expected performance. Some easy tasks or exercises to build confidence followed by harder and harder exercises to stretch participants even further.

Develop peer coaching. This ensures peer contact, support, and encouragement. It normally will develop naturally but may need to be stimulated by the training team.

Role models. The training team has to 'walk the talk' and by its actions set the example to follow. This is particularly valuable in adventurous training when morale fluctuates and can be influenced by the training team to act as a reference point and lesson. The training team has to follow the functional leadership check-list and, in particular, recognise good performance.

Provide regular feedback. The training team should provide constant individual feedback and counselling in addition to the post-exercise group debriefs and peer feedback.

Relate lessons learnt to workplace application. All debriefs must link lessons learnt to past experience and future application in the workplace.

'Ideas and applications' notebook. Participants should keep a journal of their own key learning for each part of a programme. This aids reflection and may be used for discussion or kept private.

<u>After training.</u>

Develop an 'action plan'. This is a personal and group action plan developed after the course and it encourages participants to apply new skills in the workplace and to continue to learn.

Reports and feedback. Oral or written assessments of progress and performance assist in developing individual development programmes. They are useful as part of a performance management system, but participants must be told if this is going to be the case.

Re-entry interview. An interview conducted by the participants' superiors can assist in the transfer of training and give recognition or additional counselling as required.

Provide support and opportunities to practise. The culture and participants' superiors (ambient leadership) will largely determine the support given. Every trainee must be given the opportunity to practise and develop leadership. This can be done in several ways:

- Routine duties.
- Delegated duties.
- Extra-mural appointments, for example, organising social and sporting events that also contribute to team-building.

- Provide individual coaching. This could overcome specific people's blocks to the use of new skills.

Post-training assessments. Post-training assessments after an initial course provide a measure of the individual's progress. It is usual after a well-run course for the grading of self and peer participants to be significantly lower than the grading pre-course. This is because of the move from 'unconscious incompetence' to 'conscious incompetence'. People will become aware of just how much there is to learn about leadership.

Conduct evaluation survey. This procedure is relatively standard, but to have any meaning should be done three weeks after the event when the immediate 'high' has dissipated.

Provide refresher and continuation training. The appetite, once whetted, must be continually stimulated.

Review performance management system. If the performance management system does not assess the lessons that managers are expected to transfer from training into daily work then the training function loses its effectiveness and credibility.

References

1. Basil Fletcher, 1971, *The Challenge Of Outward Bound*, London: William Heinemann Ltd.
2. Adam Arnold-Brown, 1962, *Unfolding Character: The Impact of Gordonstoun*, London: Routledge & Kegan Paul.

APPENDIX A

THE IDEAL LEADERSHIP COMPETENCY PROFILE

This profile is based on the key leadership qualities (Chapter 6) and the functional leadership check-list (Chapter 5).

Serial	Function	Related Qualities	Competency and Characteristics
1	Planning	Initiative, Intellect, Communication, Judgement	Anticipates events, takes the strategic view and can articulate a vision.
2	Planning	Decisiveness, Flexibility, Loyalty, Judgement, Self-discipline, Common Sense	Uses analysis, wisdom, experience and judgement to make decisions in a timely manner. Asks for advice and participation from others.
3	Planning	Intellect, Judgement	Takes a broad view of problems and 'thinks big', has a wide perspective, customer-focussed.
4	Planning	Judgement, Flexibility, Initiative	Has new ideas or adopts others' ideas—gives credit. Can appreciate good ideas, and can lead change and innovation. If ideas or plans do not work, can readily evaluate and re-plan.

Serial	Function	Related Qualities	Competency and Characteristics
5	Planning	Initiative, Intellect, Judgement, Self-discipline	Uses 'mission analysis' and the 'appreciation' process to produce effective solutions. Makes valid deductions and does not overlook hidden factors.
6	Planning	Initiative, Intellect, Flexibility	Plans effective processes and can organise time, people, and resources effectively, can build synergy and capitalise on success. Can maximise efficiency and simplify processes.
7	Planning	Decisiveness, Intellect, Judgement	Sets aims and objectives, and orders work by priority.
8	Planning	Judgement, Humanity, Knowledge	Allocates work fairly and equitably, deals evenly with all classes, races, cultures, and so on, of employee.
9	Briefing	Knowledge (of subordinates), Humanity, Judgement, Self-discipline	Is able to delegate and refrains from interfering. Trusts people to perform, stretches and develops subordinates to meet their career needs, and gives clear direction. Knows what motivates individuals.
10	Briefing	Communication, Enthusiasm, Self-confidence	Clearly explains to individuals their tasks in a simple, succinct, and logical manner. Keeps the team informed of the 'bigger picture'.
11	Briefing	Communication, Enthusiasm, Loyalty, Knowledge, Self-confidence, Humanity, Pride, Willpower	Can motivate and inspire individuals and build and sustain morale and *esprit de corps* in teams.

Serial	Function	Related Qualities	Competency and Characteristics
12	Briefing	Communication, Moral Courage, Enthusiasm, Self-confidence, Flexibility	Is effective in formal and informal presentations to a variety of types/sizes of audience, can quickly change style as necessary. Presents true, but unpalatable, information.
13	Briefing	Communication, Intellect, Knowledge	Writes clear, concise, succinct, and unambiguous, documents.
14	Controlling and Coordinating	Willpower, Moral Courage, Self-discipline, Self-confidence	Takes charge in a crisis and overcomes resistance. Is tenacious and determined.
15	Controlling and Coordinating	Knowledge, Willpower, Communication	Understands how the organisation (and informal internal groups) work. Knows where decisions/policies originate and how to ensure support.
16	Controlling and Coordinating	Knowledge, Integrity, Moral Courage	Can step in and resolve conflict firmly in a timely and effective manner. Is not afraid to say and do the right thing.
17	Controlling and Coordinating	Knowledge, Integrity, Moral Courage, Consistency	Trusts people to get on with the job and make decisions.
18	Supporting	Knowledge, Pride, Communication, Enthusiasm, Integrity, Humanity, Loyalty	Can inspire, motivate, and thank the team/individuals, recognising success/effort.
19	Supporting	Judgement, Self-discipline, Knowledge	Ensures good administration and that supporting systems work efficiently.
20	Supporting	Humanity, Consistency, Loyalty	Is genuinely interested in, and cares about, people. Listens actively and acts where, and how, necessary.
21	Informing	Intellect, Knowledge	Stays aware of the 'big picture' and progress.

Serial	Function	Related Qualities	Competency and Characteristics
22	Informing	Communication, Enthusiasm, Consistency, Self-confidence	Briefs everyone on progress/the situation. Ensures information flows in the team. Denies opportunities for rumours to start.
23	Evaluating	Intellect, Knowledge, Judgement	Monitors/measures progress in task, compares with benchmark and changes plans as necessary.
24	Evaluating	Courage, Self-confidence, Initiative, Loyalty, Flexibility	Can learn from failures/mistakes and not blame others.
25	Evaluating	Judgement, Flexibility, Knowledge, Initiative	Identify team/individual training needs—Coaches and creates a learning environment.
26	Evaluating	Communication, Intellect, Initiative, Knowledge, Humanity	Listens to feedback and acts where appropriate.

Other Characteristics of a Leader:

Will to lead	The leader must actually want to lead. If he or she does not actively seek leadership of a team then the 'leader' will never succeed because the determination and motivation is lacking.
Willing acceptance of responsibility	This is linked to the desire to lead. The leader must seek responsibility for the well-being, training, career planning and actions of his or her team. Team members' successes are the leader's successes, as are failures. The leader must accept total responsibility for the team and never abdicate or attempt to delegate that responsibility.
Balances paradox	Can be forceful or humble as the situation requires. Can be a leader or supportive team member. Can be both tough and compassionate. Can maintain 'traditional values' and can be highly adaptable to new operating techniques.
Customer focus	Dedicated to understanding customer needs and exceeding expectations. Demonstrates the relentless pursuit of excellence. Has the trust of customers.
Company values	Sets an impeccable example and adheres to organisational values.
Recruitment and selection	Selects the best people available and is not frightened that hiring experts diminishes the leader's role or status.
Business acumen	Aware of market trends and able to recognise opportunities—'street-wise'.
Self-awareness	Knows own strengths, weaknesses, habits, and tendencies—always trying to develop self. Can balance personal life and work.

CHAPTER 22

CONCLUSION

If you have arrived at this point without skipping through any of the chapters, you should have started to develop a more complete understanding of the true nature and practice of leadership—both its scientific study and artistic application.

I have provided you with the conceptual framework on which you can base your leadership. Remember that concepts and theories provide principles that should guide all actions, but they should not enslave leaders by their dogmatic application. Any philosophy of leadership has to be embraced and to be understood, and not treated as a model for continuous application, if it is to work.

Most of what you have read has been understood and practised in some quarters for centuries. The history of management studies does not go back more than 70 years or so, yet much of what has been presented here has evolved from the history of the profession of arms and that is considerably older.

Revolution is simply evolution happening in a compressed time frame. Business is going through revolutionary times and is suffering from an inability to change easily, yet most armies have been able to evolve a structure and systems that enable this to happen with minimum pain. As Dr Elliott Jaques pointed out in a letter to me in 1997, the British Army is a perfect match to this theory of the requisite organisation. However, it did not follow a theory and implement it overnight—the British Army as we know it today, evolved over 350 years of bloody experience—with many lessons going back much further in history.

So what of the future? I suspect that the management pendulum will continue to swing from excessively layered structures to overly flat, indecisive ones, from over-controlled teams to direction-less self-satisfying leaderless teams, and so on. Eventually the pendulum will come to rest with a requisite structure, a defined concept of leadership and teamwork that endures, and integrated supportive HR systems.

Change is affecting everyone and the most noticeable aspect is the speed at which business now operates. Time frames for action in the 1990s are very compressed in comparison to past years. The speed at which things have to happen is approaching the time compression of events and their observed consequences in war.

War requires not only effective leadership and teamwork, but a greater degree of authoritative direction, clarity and subordination than business has done to date. There is a little time for debate when effective enemy fire is a real and present fact of life—something has to be done right away!

Could it be that as data processing speeds up the flow of work in business, that business complexity not only requires teamwork to resolve problems, but that a greater degree of timely decisiveness by leaders (and, therefore, less time for participation and debate in teams) has to be developed and accepted by everyone? If this is the case then business has no option but to accept the military model of leadership and command based upon competence, mutual trust and confidence, and requisite structure.

The question is: will companies continue to follow fads, or to stick with something that is proven to work, no matter that it may take some investment before the benefits are seen? Will you be both a good leader and a leader for good, and make something happen?

INDEX

Adair, Professor John
  functions of leadership 59
  three circles 59, 223
Adler, Nancy 225, 231
adventurous training 312–317
Albrecht, Karl 17, 251, 252,
  284–288, 290
Allport,— 26
appraisals 162, 163
appreciation 296–298
  format of 98, 100
  review of 104
  pitfalls 104, 105
Aristotle 68, 88
Arnold-Brown, Adam 317
authority and
  appointment 22, 133
  delegation 22, 135–136
  leadership 213–215
  responsibility 22, 132

Belbin, Dr Meredith 47, 148
Bennis, Professor Warren 4
Blake, William 313
Bonaparte, Napoleon
  on morale 188
British Army ix, 1, 228, 333
business
  doctrine 275–277

levels of 280–282
logic 289–292
principles of 277–280
procedure 115–116

Carnall, Colin 269, 270
centralisation 270
change
  behavioural 263
  grief cycle and 266–267
  resistance to 263–267
  stages in 262
  transition and 268–269
charisma 88–90
Churchill, Winston 68
coaching 160, 161
commercial effectiveness 15, 16
communication
  ability 81, 82
  and inspiration 287–288
  in teams 158, 159
competence 320, 328–332
Confucius 23
control 172, 173
  influence and 174
  timing of 174–175
coordination 171–172
culture
  communication across 229–231

decision making 231–232
defined 224
values in 224
variations in 225–229
de Gaulle, General Charles 24
de la Billière, General Sir Peter on
morale 194, 200
respect 219
responsibility 135
success 200
teams 52
decisiveness 84
determination 78
direction
orders and 170
verbal requests and 171
discipline
collective 234
imposed 234
reasons for 237–239
self- 85, 234
duty, sense of 236

efficiency and effectiveness 270
Eisenhower, Dwight D. 11
enthusiasm 81
evaluation 175
and failure to meet objectives
176

Fitzroy, Robyn 89, 189
Fletcher, Basil 316
flexibility 83
Fortescue, Sir John 236
functional leadership check-list 62, 63

gentlemen 67

Hackett, General Sir John 22–23,
216–219
Hahn, Kurt 313–315
Harvey-Jones, John 9, 10, 70, 77,
80, 125, 253, 259, 260
Henderson, Colonel G.F.R. 24
Herzberg, F., 2 factor theory
182–183, 213
Holmes, Oliver Wendell 312

humanity 83
Huxley, Aldous 312

individualists 31
initiative 76–77
innovation
change and 271–272
creativity and 272–273
3M 271–272
values and 254
inspiration
components of 86, 87
communication as a part of 87,
88, 122
integrity 72–76

Jaques, Dr Elliott 13, 132, 133,
137–142, 151, 333
Jones, Malcolm 17, 88, 189, 241,
282
judgement 82

Kiernan, Ian 113, 216, 314–315
knowledge of
job 79
self 80
subordinates 79
Knox-Johnston, Sir Robin 68, 69,
86, 191, 215, 233, 314

Lao Tze 11
leader–follower relationship 167,
215–219
leadership
Adair three circles 59–61
ambient 205
defined 8, 9, 10, 11
episodic 47, 205, 206
functional check-list 63, 268
functions of 123
levels of 205
organisational 205, 249
situational 210–212
strategic 280
styles of 207–213
template for 19–20
teams 46

X&Y style 207–209
Lonergan, Karen 8, 68, 89, 126, 131, 189
loyalty
    customer 245
    effect 242
    innovation and 244
    integrity and 72, 74–76, 241
    staff 245–246
    value of 247
Luecke, Richard 103, 223, 277

Machiavelli 20
Maslow, Abraham
    hierarchy of needs 17, 179–183, 208, 213, 236, 263
McGregor, Douglas 84, 207–209
McLean, Robert 8, 45, 90, 188, 235
Matchan, Chris ix
mentoring 162
mission 252–253
mission analysis 99, 101–102, 286
Montgomery, Field Marshal Viscount 6, 8, 11, 12, 66, 77, 121–122, 195–201, 235, 295, 298–299
moral courage 68–72
morale
    administration and 201
    components of 192
    comradeship and 198–199
    discipline and 197
    factors affecting 195–201
    foundations of 191–194
    leadership and 196
    Montgomery and 195–201
    self-respect and 199
    Slim and 191–194
    success and 200
Moran, Lord 68
Morton, Garry 184
motivation
    behaviour 183–184
    communication 184–185
    delegation 129–131, 186–187
    Herzberg 182–183
    in practice 185–186
    Maslow 179–182
    Morton 184

objectives 173, 174, 176
officers 1, 67
operational level 281
organisation
    defined duties 131–132
    delegation of tasks 129–131
    grouping of tasks 129
    principles of 127
    requisite of 137–142
    span of control 128–129
    standardisation 137
    unity of leadership 126, 127
Outward Bound 314–315

paradox 256, 257
perception
    attitudes 43
    controlling 42–43
    distractions 41
    how it works 37
    influences on 39–40
    of problems 95
    reasons for 36
personality
    brain 28
    emotions 30
    genetics 27
    learned experiences 27
    values 29
plan
    briefing 116–119
    cascading 119–120
    outline 104
    sequence 113
Plato 316
pride 83
problems
    decision making 96–105
    perception of 95
    solving 96–105
    types of 95

Quinn, John 58, 177, 190, 216, 260, 264, 274, 312

Reichheld, Frederick F. 242, 243
Robert, Michael 289–291
Royal Military Academy
  Sandhurst, The
  functional leadership 59
  serve to lead 19
  template for leadership 21
Royce, Josiah 242
Rozmeta, Kathy 131–132, 190,
  222, 323

Sandhurst *see* Royal Military
  Academy Sandhurst (The)
Schopenhauer, — 222
self-confidence 80, 133, 263
self-discipline *see* discipline
self-esteem 33, 263
Selye, Hans 248
service leadership 17, 19, 22
Situational Leadership® 210–212
Slim, Field Marshal Sir William
  11, 50, 70, 80, 84, 85, 191–194,
  223, 233, 259
Special Air Service (SAS)
  team size 47
  values 255
standardisation 137
strategic
  level 280
  plan 282–300
strategic leadership *see* leadership
Strong, James 13, 44, 91–92, 250
structure 124, 125, 137–140,
  140–145
styles of leadership 207–212
Sun Tzu 9

tactical level 281–282
teams
  characteristics 45–46, 49
  coaching 160–161
  cohesion 56
  competition 147
  composition 155–156
  conflict 166
  development of 53, 164
  discipline 49

empowerment 47
forming 54, 146–148
leadership–follower relations 167
maintenance 165–168
mission 46
norming 55, 150–154
performing 55, 155–159
roles and tasks 148, 157
self-directed 46
storming 55, 148–150
3M 271–273
training
  adventurous 312–317
  aim 303
  approaches 308–311
  conceptual 323
  debriefing 320, 322
  development centre 319
  experiential 312–317
  feedback 322
  objectives 303
  personal challenges 321
  principles of 304–308
  skills 321
  template for 19, 20, 302, 319
  transfer of 325–326
Trevelyan,— 319
trust 13, 44, 90–92
Turner, E.S. 67

values 206, 224, 253, 254
vision 250–252
Vroom, V.H. 209

Walsh, Chris 46, 69, 90
Wareham, John 29–30
warning brief 114–115
Watson, Thomas, Jr 256
Wavell, Field Marshal Earl 235
Wellington, Duke of 10, 124
Whiteley, Alma 254
willpower 78

X&Y theory of leadership style
  207–209